Character, Choices & Community: The Three Faces of Christian Ethics

Russell B. Connors, Jr.
and
Patrick T. McCormick

PAULIST PRESS
New York/Mahwah, N.J.

Cover design by Cynthia Dunne

Interior design by Joseph E. Petta

Library of Congress Cataloging-in-Publication Data

Connors, Russell B., 1948-
    Character, choices & community : the three faces of Christian ethics / Russell B. Connors, Jr. and Patrick T. McCormick.
        p.   cm.
    Includes bibliographical references.
    ISBN 0-8091-3805-0 (alk. paper)
    1. Christian ethics. 2. Christian ethics—Catholic authors. I. McCormick, Patrick T. II. Title.
BJ1241.C67   1998
241—dc21   98-23867
                                                                        CIP

Published by Paulist Press
997 Macarthur Boulevard
Mahwah, New Jersey 07430

Printed and bound in the
United States of America

Table of Contents

Dedication

For
Patty and Elizabeth
For
Guay and Riley

Preface.

Why write (or read) this book? After all, as one can see from even a cursory glance at our own endnotes, there are already a number of fine introductions to Christian ethics available. For along with some excellent seminary or graduate school texts, there are also quite a few very good anthologies of historical and/or contemporary essays and several wonderful books on Christian conscience or moral decision making, as well as a couple of terrific issues-oriented texts relying on either a question-and-answer or a case-methods approach. So what makes this text distinctive? There is only one way to answer that question, and that is to talk about the goals, methods and audience we had in mind as we set out to write it.

Goals

We wrote this book with three goals in mind. First, we have tried to uncover and name what we saw as the essential elements of moral experience—*person, action* and *community*. And so, after the general introduction in chapter 1, we devote a chapter to each of these critically important dimensions of morality (chapters 2, 3 and 4), exploring their identity and examining their *dynamic* and *interdependent* relationships with each other. And indeed, not just in the these introductory chapters, but throughout the whole book we continue to invite our readers to explore and reflect on the importance and interplay of these three fundamental dimensions of moral experience.

Second, because this is a book about *Christian* ethics, we have made an effort to identify some of the central commitments and themes of the Gospel, or the Christian *story*, and to examine their implications for Christian living and Christian ethics. This is especially evident in chapters 5 and 6, which examine the narrative dimension of moral experience and, more specifically, the ways in which the Christian narrative impacts morality. But it is also evident in our discussion of sin and Christian moral conversion in chapters 11 and 12, where we attempt to describe moral decline and moral growth from a specifically Christian perspective. Still, as we hope will be clear to our readers, it is not just in these chapters, but throughout the whole book that we have tried to point out the connections between our Christian faith and moral experience.

Third, this is a book about *moral decision making,* so we identify and examine the resources and processes we rely on when making moral judgments. Hence the chapters on conscience and conscience formation (chapters 7 and 8), as well as those on moral norms and modes of moral reasoning (chapters 9 and 10). And because of our focus on *person, action* and *community,* these chapters on moral decision making examine not only the choices we make (personally and together), but also how those decisions express who we are, form who we are becoming, and affect the communities of which we are a part.

Method

Three presuppositions inform the method of this text. First, as we discuss at some length in chapter 1, we assume that moral experience is at the very heart of our experience of being human, and that morality is about our call to human flourishing. Therefore, if we want to know where we need to be going as persons and communities we need to pay close attention to what is going on in our lives and the lives of those around us. This presupposition about the centrality of moral experience is the reason why we continually invite our readers to identify and critically analyze concrete moral experiences, their own and others'. For we believe that Christian ethics is a process of critically engaging our moral experience(s) in the light of our Christian faith. This may often seem risky and unsettling, but it is also the way to foster our flourishing as human beings and as followers of Christ.

A second presupposition evident throughout the text is that moral experience and ethical reflection are not only personal in nature, but communal as well. Indeed, we believe that the communal dimension of moral experience is one of the most important points in this book, and we attempt to show its significance again and again. For as we elaborate in chapter 2, to be a person entails, among other things, being in relationship with others. The moral life is not lived alone, and ethics is not engaged in privately. And so, concerned, as others are, about the tendency toward individualism and moral privatism in our culture, we invite our readers to pay attention not simply to the *particularity* of moral experience, but to its *commonality* as well.

Still, to call attention to the communal nature of moral experience is to do more than merely acknowledge that personal moral experience has a communal frame of reference. Throughout the book we call attention to the fact that communities themselves are moral actors. This leads us to examine the moral significance of social structures and institutions. For good or for ill, these structures and institutions are both expressive and formative of who we are as communities and persons. This dimension of the communal nature of moral experience is consistent throughout the text. It has influenced not only how we describe the dynamics of moral experience, but also how moral decisions are made and how moral norms are formulated. In the final chapters the realities of sin and conversion are described in this communal manner. And so we give an account not only of the dynamics of *personal* Christian living, but describe the call of Christian *communities* to respond to the grace to turn from sin and be converted to Christ.

A third presupposition of our work concerns the narrative dimension of moral experience, both personal and communal. We highlight the fact that human experience is primarily narrative in character. The same can be said of moral experience. This is why we use the moral stories of persons and communities to understand and contextualize the ethical evaluation of human action. We rely on the trajectory of story to reveal moral character, and we discover the moral context of persons by referring to the communal stories of the "tribes" of which they are a part.

What is said of stories generally is true also of our Christian stories. So when this text seeks to unpack our moral and Christian moral experience, it does so by focusing on the stories which give direction to and help us make sense of our lives as Christian believers.

Audience

We have written with two audiences in mind. First and foremost, we have set out to provide a readable, "user friendly" text for undergraduate introductions to Christian ethics. In our experience, many of the textbooks currently available do not have such students in mind, but seem to have been written either for seminary or graduate students, or for undergraduates majoring in theology or religious studies. Those are not the students who occupy most of the desks in our classes at Gonzaga University or the College of St. Catherine. Generally, we have bright practical-minded students majoring in other disciplines who take our courses to fulfill an undergraduate requirement and who, we hope, have some interest in morality and perhaps even in Christian morality. Those are the students for whom we wrote.

During the 1996–97 school year we used a draft of this text in our courses. The response of the students was very encouraging. They found the text readable (even interesting!) and especially appreciated three things: the abundant use of stories and cases, the questions for reflection and discussion interspersed throughout the book, and the conclusions at the end of each chapter.

The second group of people for whom we have written are serious-minded adults interested in ongoing religious formation. Our text provides an overview of the fundamental elements and themes of the moral life generally and of Christian morality specifically. Used in structured adult religious education settings or simply on one's own, this book could be a vehicle for helping adults (who are not ethicists or theologians) to identify, name and analyze their moral experience and to connect it with the core of their Christian faith. If even a little bit of that happens, our efforts will have been well worth it.

It is important for us to identify the Catholic nature of ourselves and of this text. We are both Catholic theologians teaching in Catholic universities. Obviously, our work is an expression of who we are and where we are located. At the same time, as another glance at our endnotes will indicate, our work is not sectarian in nature. We have drawn heavily from the contributions of Christian ethicists from many denominations. Gratefully, that is the way Christian ethics is done these days.

Moreover, for both of us, a large percentage of our undergraduate students—approximately 50 percent—come from traditions (Christian and non-Christian) beyond Roman Catholicism. And of course, some of our students have no religious background, or freely acknowledge their alienation from the religious tradition of their upbringing. Those are our students. We have written for them, attempting to do so in an inclusive, straightforward, nontechnical, practical-minded way. We have tried to describe what we think are the exciting and fundamental dynamics of moral experience itself, and then to "flesh out" what they might look like in the light of the Christian story. Our students—from a variety of religious backgrounds—have reported that the book helped them identify and name their own moral experience and to make connections with their religious faith. We hope that happens for you as well.

Before we proceed, some words of thanks are important. This book has been several years in the making. Along the way we have been blessed with the love and encouragement of many people. We are who we are, and we do what we do, because of the support of others. Life is like that, and we are grateful. George Smiga and Pat Griffin are friends whose patience and support have been constant. Tim O'Connell, Tom Shannon, Rich Gula, Anne Patrick and Mike Place are colleagues whose work has both nourished and inspired us. Members of the theology departments at The College of St. Catherine and Gonzaga University have encouraged us. Students at both of these schools have challenged us and, we like to think, brought out the best in what we have done. And finally there is Dick Sparks. It was Dick who first suggested that we undertake this project, and at various stages along the way he read our manuscript and offered a host of valuable comments and suggestions. The book is ours; its imperfections are particularly ours. But what you will read is better for Dick's contribution. Our thanks to you all.

Chapter One.
Experience: Morality's Starting Point

Introduction: Three Cases

1. Your mother, an elderly widow living alone in a third-floor apartment in the declining Chicago neighborhood where you grew up, suffers from cataracts and arthritis, making it increasingly more difficult for her to get around or take care of herself. Over the past two decades most of her friends and acquaintances from the parish and neighborhood have died or moved away, leaving her with fewer and fewer human contacts and supports, while the buying power of her Social Security pension has dwindled significantly. Indeed, her mailbox has been broken into twice in the last three years, and she was accosted last October coming home from the A&P.

This morning, your only sibling Ray telephoned from Chicago to say that after thirteen months on unemployment he has finally been able to find a decent job, but needs to move to St. Paul within a week to start work. Mom, as you suspected, is completely unwilling to go with him.

What do you feel in response to this story? Do you sense a need to respond? Do you feel a tug to do something? Does the word "should" or "ought" come to mind? Along with a desire to help, do you also feel an "obligation" or "duty"? Can you say why?

You hang up the phone. Ray's news is upsetting, and you would like to do something about the situation. But you know how stubborn she can be about the old neighborhood, and about her independence. You also know that it took you and your spouse six years to find jobs in the same town, and that your children have finally found a school and neighborhood where they feel safe and comfortable. Chicago is a thousand miles away, and your mother is losing the only real support system she's had for the last three years. But you don't see how you can go and rescue her.

Now what do you feel in response to this story? How would you describe how this situation is affecting you? Do you still feel a need to respond to Ray's call?

2. You are reading a magazine article that documents that the United States, one of the wealthiest and most powerful nations on the planet, spends *less* on health care for its poor or foreign aid to needy countries than many less wealthy nations, and has an infant mortality rate in its inner cities rivaling the poorest third world nations. The article's author suggests that the new upper class in America is growing increasingly distant from and indifferent to the plight of the poor both here and abroad, and that recent social policy has restructured taxes in a way that, in the author's view, allows the well-to-do to abandon their duties to support public transportation, education, housing and health. As a result, America is increasingly becoming a divided land, where the rich and poor live in two separate and unequal countries, and where more and more of our children are born into chronic poverty.

What is your initial response to this article? What is your response to the idea that social structures are increasingly separating America's rich and poor and undermining our common commitment to public education, health and housing? What is your response to the assertion that one of the wealthiest nations on the planet spends so little taking care of its children? Is that response different from what you might feel upon hearing that some children in one of the nation's cities were harmed in a hurricane?

3. You are driving home late one night from a party, just the slightest bit "tight" from a drink or two more than your usual, and a little annoyed at your spouse's suggestion that she drive. You continue driving on the narrow country road, but you have slowed down at her insistence. And it is just then that you come upon an African American man in his mid-twenties who is trying to wave you down to stop. His car has veered off the road, and as you pass by you can see someone

slumped over in the driver's seat. Uneasy of what might be going on, and unsure of your ability to help, you continue on your way. You and your wife are silent for some minutes. Eventually, she turns on the radio. You're quite certain that probably you couldn't have been of much help anyway.

What do you feel in response to what has happened? What is your response to your choices, your own behavior, in this case?

Feeling the Moral Dimension of Life

In all three of the cases listed above, what we are feeling—though in different ways—is our encounter with the *moral* dimension of our humanity, a dimension that continues to surface again and again as we move through and reflect on life's various experiences. In the midst of our daily routines at home, school or work or in those critical moments when we find ourselves facing tough decisions about personal or public issues, we often sense what the Irish theologian Enda McDonagh refers to as the "tug" of the moral in our lives. Sometimes we experience that tug as a call to act or behave in a certain way, while at other times we feel it as a weight or judgment resulting from something already done.[1]

In the first case described above many of us might feel the moral tug as a *should* or *ought* calling us to *do something* for our ailing mother, or to *be a good* son or daughter to her. We might describe the experience of getting Ray's phone call as one that reminds us of a "duty" we have as children, or as something evoking a sense of "obligation" in us to be of assistance to our mother. The second part of the case might well cause us to feel some confusion or consternation as we try to sort out what seem like competing or conflicting *shoulds* or duties. Indeed the moral dimension of experience sometimes makes us feel like we are stuck on the horns of a dilemma. In the second case our awareness of the moral dimension of experience might well be felt as a judgment—perhaps an angry one—at the wrongness of social policies that facilitate inadequate care for, even the abandonment of, our poorest children. And finally, most sane and healthy persons would experience

3

some guilt about having refused to stop at the scene of accident simply because the victims were of a different color.

These differing feelings—the sense of a *should* or *ought,* the judgment that something is wrong, and the guilt for shameful and cowardly behavior—signal that we are encountering the moral dimension of life. They let us know that within the tapestry of our lived experiences we are coming into contact with the demands of morality, and they challenge us to deal with those demands. These tugs remind us that we need to make moral choices about the sorts of persons we are to become, about the actions we are to perform or avoid and about the kinds of communities we are to construct.

Take a moment to reflect on some experiences in which you felt the "tug" of the moral dimension of life. Identify experiences in which you sensed the "should" or "ought" of a duty, the weight of judgment, or the burden of guilt. What was it about the experience that made you aware of an obligation, and what role did experience play in helping you sort out what you needed to do?

Beginning with Experience

Because the moral dimension of life first shows up not in ethical theories or moral principles but in lived *experience,* because this *experience* shapes and forms our moral obligations and because it is ultimately this *experience* that we need to return to and deal with in morality, it seems eminently reasonable that we should begin our reflections on morality with experience itself, and that we should continue to test our moral theories and principles against our lived experiences. Indeed, when we try to live morally without attending to and staying in close contact with our experience we end up with abstract principles having little to do with our lives and offering little or no moral guidance.

Unfortunately, it has often happened that Christian morality was seen as something handed down to us from on high by people who wrote and taught theories and rules from books alone, paying little or no attention to what was actually going on in people's lives. Or if experience was used at all, it was the experience of a very small group of persons and not that of the bulk of humanity. Exclusion of lived experience, or at least the lived experience of most people, does not generate a genuine morality. The norms and rules of such a morality are likely to be experienced as only the imposed will of distant "experts," instead of genuine moral wisdom and guidance for living our lives. In recent years feminist and liberation theologians—theologians whose work and writing starts from the experience of women and/or the poor and oppressed—have shown how experience must be a source for morality, and they have reminded us of the dangers and injustice of excluding or forgetting the experiences of *any* groups or persons.[2]

Experience, then—our starting point for morality—is what is actually going on in our lives. It's in our experience as persons and communities that we confront moral choices and issues, that we feel the tug of the moral *ought* and the weight of past deeds. To be sure, we *trust* our experience because it is real, and from it we can learn things about ourselves and about what morality calls us to be and to do. But at the same time, we need to be able to examine, understand and *reflect critically* upon our experience.

Social reformers of the nineteenth century, for example, experienced the grave sufferings and injustices experienced by children working in mines and sweat shops. They saw and heard about unhealthy working conditions, met with unsavory and avaricious employers and visited the filthy shanties and unsanitary tenements into which large immigrant families were crowded. They also went to churches and government halls where they heard of the dignity and worth of all persons and the rights and equality of every human being. From these experiences *and* from their critical reflections on them they came to see the awful wrongness (immorality) of the child labor practices of the day, and they pressed for social reforms. Morality, then, begins with experience, reflects critically upon that experience, makes a moral judgment, and calls for a moral response.

But it is not enough to say simply that morality begins with, reflects upon, and draws lessons from experience. After all, nearly every wrong opinion or judgment is based on an anecdotal account of some experience that taught the storyteller a very foolish lesson. (What about all the folks who claim that smoking is not dangerous to their health because they had an Uncle Willie who smoked two packs of Camels a day and lived to be ninety-seven?) Morality challenges us to reflect deeply and critically upon our experiences and to be thorough

5

in the experiences to which we pay attention. As the ethicist Daniel Maguire notes, we need to bring "sensitivity, reflection and method" to the moral examination of our experiences. Otherwise we are dealing with opinions and biases that are simply undigested experiences.[3]

In the process of attempting to unpack the moral dimension of our lives—to discover who we ought to be and what we ought to do—it is essential that we not just pay attention to and reflect upon individual experiences, isolated parts of these experiences, or even a single interpretation of these events. Instead, we must look to the *whole* of our experience, and we must be willing to ask any and all questions about it. To really understand what is actually going on we can't just take a snapshot of one single incident, or accept one person's report. We have to examine patterns and relationships thoroughly, look deeply into the essence of things, and investigate all relevant circumstances and consequences. And to understand the moral implications of our experiences we need to attend to a variety of perspectives.

Thus we need to look at the breadth and depth of our experiences, to examine them from a number of points of view and to look at the experiences of others as well. Usually this sort of thorough examination must be a shared enterprise, one engaged in with other persons. In this way, hopefully, we can overcome the narrow biases of our own perspectives and benefit from the differing experiences and insights of many. By looking at the experience of others we attempt to understand the larger shape, implications and consequences of our choices and actions. In particular we do well to pay attention to the experiences and insights of those who are adversely affected by our choices and policies. We need to stand in their shoes and "walk around in their world" for a while.

It would be good to ask, for example, what the practice of slavery might look like not just to the plantation owner or to the accountant, but what it would look like to the woman or man in chains, or how it squares with the insights of the Gospel or the Bill of Rights? What does an international trade arrangement look like to all the parties affected, or how does it measure up to what we believe about social justice? How does the American invasion of Panama look to the Panamanian people, or French nuclear tests look to the people of the South Pacific?

In particular, to make adequate moral judgments we need to examine the experiences of persons whose voices we hardly ever attend to, of persons who are too small, weak or frail to get our attention. Could laws establishing segregation in our schools or outlawing strikes have been tolerated if the experience of Blacks and laborers had been seriously considered? We also need to listen to the experiences of those whose voices are harsh and critical, who show us the sordid underbelly of our actions and choices, whose contact with the effects of our decisions gives them an important—if somewhat challenging—perspective. Think of the moral insights the Israelites gained from listening to the critical voices of prophets like Amos, Hosea and Jeremiah, or what America learned about its own injustices from social critics like Martin Luther King, Jr. or Dorothy Day.

Indeed, if we are truly wise we will pay attention to the experience of the generations of people who have gone before us, giving special attention to the moral and religious insights from the past. In Christian morality, therefore, we pay special attention to the thoughts of saints and scholars like Thomas Aquinas and the teachings of church councils like Trent and Vatican II. For part of our experience is that we live in a world where others have gone before us and left advice and guidelines to help us sort out dilemmas and make good choices. As Sir Isaac Newton said of his own discoveries, "If I have seen further it is by standing on the shoulders of giants." So too we benefit from those on whose shoulders we stand, for encoded into the stories and parables, rules and laws handed on by our predecessors are a wealth of experiences which have been examined, reflected upon and ultimately distilled into moral wisdom.

Morality, then, begins with experience. We must take experience very seriously, so seriously that we examine it thoroughly and carefully, most often with trusted others.

A legislator is proposing a state law forbidding single persons from becoming foster parents. Believing that experience is the place to begin our moral evaluation of this proposal, what kinds of experiences do you think need to be investigated? To whose experiences should we pay attention? What sorts of questions should be asked about these experiences?

7

The Moral Dimension of Life

We human beings are complex creatures, and our experience as human beings has numerous dimensions: emotional, rational, religious, artistic, political, athletic, et cetera. In our laughter, tears and anger, for example, we discover the *emotional* side of our experience as persons. In our study, planning and problem solving we encounter the *rational* dimension of our lives. Our songs, dances and paintings point to the *artistic* aspect of our nature, while our running, jumping and throwing remind us that we can have *athletic* experiences as well. Our prayers, hymns and churches—as well as our attempts to grapple with questions of the ultimate meaning of life itself, with birth and death, love and loss—illustrate that our experience as humans also has a *religious* dimension. And, very importantly, our organizations, communities and structures keep us from forgetting the *political* side of our lives. All of these dimensions, and more, are part and parcel of the integral or holistic experience of being human. Moreover, these dimensions of our experience regularly overlap with one another. Remember, for example, how Mozart's artistic genius created music for religious worship which often moved people to deep emotional expressions, and how Jefferson the politician used his tremendous intellect to help forge a new kind of political reality.

The dimension of our experience as humans that is the focus of our attention here is, of course, our call to be *moral*. In numerous settings we experience not only a capacity to be *political, rational, emotional, artistic* or *athletic,* but also the presence of the *moral* dimension of our lives. This *moral* dimension of our experience is extremely important. Indeed, some would argue that it is the most important dimension of being human. For morality is concerned with our struggle to become and be *fully human persons and communities*. Morality is not just about our attempt to be fast, strong or coordinated athletes, or even gifted artists capable of creating beauty, symmetry and harmony. It is about our struggle—like Pinocchio—to become authentic human beings. Of course, it might also be argued that the other dimensions of human experience also concern our attempt to become fully human. Religion, for example, is concerned with developing our relationship with God, who made us and who calls us to full humanity. In our view,

8

all of the above dimensions of human experience are important for becoming fully flourishing persons and communities.

As the ethicist and psychiatrist Willard Gaylin has noted, one of the things that makes humans different from other animals is that we are not completely governed by instincts, but have the freedom to make choices. Indeed, although we have certain predetermined potentials as persons, we do not come with all the instructions for becoming adults or civilized beings hard-wired into our brain or DNA. Instead, we humans have a threefold freedom to make choices about the kinds of persons we will become, the kinds of things we will do, and the kinds of communities we will fashion for ourselves and our children. To borrow an idea from Mary Catherine Bateson's book, *Composing A Life: Life as a Work in Progress,* we have the capacity, to some degree at least, to compose our lives, that is, to determine the kinds of persons we will be, the kinds of actions we will or will not perform and the kinds of communities we will construct.[4] No enterprise is more important

It is because of this freedom that humans—alone among all the creatures on this planet—have a moral dimension to their experience. And it is because of the object of these choices that this moral dimension is so important. For morality is about our attempt to make free and intelligent choices that will build up our humanity, that will make us and our world more fully human. Morality is about our struggle to achieve the full humanity which we are *invited* but not *forced* to embrace. As beings with a moral dimension we feel a threefold "tug" towards full humanity, a tug calling us: (1) to become "good" persons, (2) to do the "right" thing and (3) to build "just" communities. But we also have the freedom to say no to that tug. So morality is about our attempt to sort out what we ought to do with this freedom in the areas of our character, actions and communities.

Morality's Three Concerns

As implied above, morality is concerned with answering three questions: "Who ought we be?" "What ought we do?" and "What sort of community ought we construct?" As a result, much of the conversation in morality is about: (1) Our **CHARACTER**—the kinds of persons (good or bad) we are now or are becoming, (2) Our **CHOICES FOR**

ACTION—the (right and wrong) decisions, judgments and behavior that make up our lives, and (3) Our **COMMUNITIES**—the moral fabric and nature of the (just and unjust) systems, structures and groups which we form and live in.[5]

Character and Goodness. In the moral dimension of our experience we feel a call to become "good" persons, and so morality is concerned with the sorts of persons we are and the sorts of persons we are becoming, which means it is concerned with our *character*. For in moral experience it is our character that hears the call of the *ought* and feels the tug of the *should*. So too, when we make moral choices about what we will do or become, it is our character that is at stake. For in the moral dimension of our experience our choices both *express* and *shape* our character as persons.

And what is our character? Briefly, our character might be described as our own *unique moral identity*—the sort of human being (good, bad, indifferent) we really are in the core of our being, in the inner sanctum of our true selves. Character is that specific and very particular configuration of good and bad habits, affections, attitudes and beliefs that makes up a person. It is who we really are in our hearts. This character is not set in stone, but—like us—grows and changes as we make choices that *either* deepen the already existing habits and tendencies (good or not so good) that are part of us already, *or* that contribute to the creation of new habits and tendencies (again, good or not so good). Character, then, is the very specific kind of person we are and are becoming as a result of the choices we make in the context of the communities of which we are a part.

Although everyone's character is a bit of a mystery, and can be known only imperfectly and indirectly—still we do gain some insights into our own or others' character by looking to our/their deeds, habits, affections, attitudes and beliefs. We get an idea of who someone really is by examining the things they do, the ways they respond, think and feel about their world. These insights may lead us to describe one's character as basically good or bad. We make such judgments (especially about ourselves) by looking not simply to individual deeds and behaviors, but especially to patterns of behaviors which indicate a person's virtues or vices. We want to emphasize, however, that judgments about character always involve a bit of guesswork (a person's actions never completely "capture" the depth of a person's character). Even more importantly, such judgments ought to be made provisionally—we are all a work in progress; no one is finished.

Jot down the names of three historical or fictional persons you would judge to be of good moral character. After each name list three or four virtues you would associate with these persons. Do the same with three historical or fictional persons you would judge to be of bad moral character.

Actions and Rightness. In the moral dimension of experience we also feel a "tug" or call to do the "right" thing, often so that we can help others and become "good" persons. So morality is also concerned with our actions, which we describe as RIGHT and WRONG. Our actions include all the things we choose to do, say, think and feel, as well as the things we choose *not* to do, say, think or feel. Our actions are an important part of moral experience for three reasons: (1) Actions *express* our character, giving us a window into the kinds of persons (good or bad) we are. (2) Actions also help to *form* that same character, impacting upon the kinds of persons (good or bad) we are becoming. (3) Actions *impact* the world around us (helping or harming ourselves, our neighbors, our world) for good or ill.

Normally, actions are considered to be morally *right* if they express good character, or help to form one, *and* if they produce a good or beneficial effect in our world. Actions are seen to be morally *wrong* if they express or help to form *bad* character, or if they produce a bad effect in the world. Thus, they are right if they help us become more human. But actions are also important to moral experience because they remind us that morality is not just about good intentions or self-improvement. Morality is also about our duty to be good to other persons. So actions are right if they help build up the humanity of others as well.

Community and Justice. Finally, in the moral dimension of experience we are also concerned with the sorts of communities we come from, live in and construct with other persons. Communities are organized and structured associations of persons which have established ways of behaving (known as structures, systems and institutions). In moral experience we pay attention to the ways in which the communities or groups of persons help or harm other persons or groups.

It is important to look at the moral dimension of communities for

11

four reasons: (1) Human persons are social by nature. We are born into, live in and constantly form communities, and we need these communities not only to survive, but in order to become fully human. We cannot become truly human in complete isolation from other persons. (2) Human persons are profoundly affected by the character of the communities they live in, support or construct. Persons can be harmed or helped by these communities. Morally they can be nurtured or malformed by them. (3) The communities we live in and form have their own sort of moral atmosphere or character, shaped by their social structures, systems and institutions, and seen in their social customs, expected roles and rules of action. This character can be good or bad, depending upon how it impacts the people of the community and upon whether it builds up or tears down their humanity. Many people would say that while democracies have great potential to be good communities, tyrannies do not. (4) Often the greatest and most pervasive impact we can have on our neighbors is through the communal actions we take in our social structures, systems and institutions.

Normally, the morally good community is seen as just, while the morally bad community is viewed as unjust.

The Dynamic Relation among Character, Choices and Community

The three concerns of morality are not unrelated. Instead, in moral experience there is a dynamic and interdependent relation among character, actions and communities, with each influencing and being influenced by the other two. Thus:

1. The character of persons is affected by the communities they live in and the actions they perform; and that character in turn shapes future actions and impacts the evolving shape of the community.

2. The actions we choose flow from our character and are influenced by our community. At the same time these actions modify our character and impact the evolving shape of the community.

3. The communities we live in are the fruit of our past deeds and character, while their structures and systems in turn influence our developing character and the actions we may perform.

Much of what is being said here concerns the nature of justice. We will discuss this at greater length in a future chapter, but for now we can say simply that justice is both a virtue of persons and a quality of communities that foster right relationships among people. Let Mrs. Baker, a high school math teacher, be an example. Mrs. Baker is known as a just teacher because of the fair and respectful way she treats *all* of her students. The virtue of justice is part of her character. As important as that is, however, it is incomplete without the wider notion that justice is also a quality that needs to characterize communities and social structures. And so Mrs. Baker's classroom is known as a fair and just place, where the principles, procedures, and practices (the social structures) that characterize what happens there are fair and respectful of all. Notice that although there is a distinction between the justice of a person (the virtue of Mrs. Baker) and the just social structures of a community (a quality of her classroom) there is a connection as well: the justice of the classroom has a whole lot to do with the justice of the teacher![6]

Thus, character, choices and community are part of the dynamic and interdependent cycle of moral experience.

Morality and Ethics: Some Differences

Morality is concerned with persons becoming good, doing the right thing and building just communities. But how are we to know just "who is the good person?" or "what is the right thing?" or indeed "what is the just community?" We need a critical way to study and think about morality.

Ethics, which is the systematic and communal reflection on and analysis of moral experience, asks what "the good," "the right" and "the just" are. Ethics tries to show—based on reasoned reflection— why this character (and not that one) is good, why this action (and not that one) is right, and why this community (and not that one) is just. Thus ethics is a sort of grammar of morality, offering reasons or arguments to support or critique different moral practices or rules. If we assert that killing innocent persons is wrong or immoral, that is morality. If we try to explain and/or justify that judgment, that is ethics.

Another distinction is between "descriptive" and "normative" ethics. Descriptive ethics attempts to describe or explain moral behaviors or the moral customs of groups without trying to evaluate them morally. Normative ethics (in which we will be engaged) examines moral actions and practices in an effort to make judgments about their rightness or wrongness. Thus normative ethics argues that some actions and practices are better than others and offers reasons why.

It should also be noted that although ethics can be done by individuals—anyone and everyone—a large group or community often develops its own ethics, one that reflects that community's experiences, convictions, values, norms and goals. And so there exists Jewish ethics, Buddhist ethics, feminist ethics, Christian ethics and so forth, each with many different varieties and subsets. This is a book about Christian ethics, written especially in light of the Catholic Christian tradition.

Moral Experience—Some Conclusions

1. Morality begins with the recognition of a sort of "tug," pointing to a call persons experience to become fully human beings (good) and to create authentic (just) communities by recognizing, respecting and responding to other persons (doing what is right).

2. This moral tug comes to us in and gets its shape from our lived experience. To understand what sort of persons we should become, what sort of actions we should perform or avoid, or what sort of communities we should construct, we need to reflect upon our experience critically, thoroughly and with the help of others.

3. Morality is concerned with answering three questions: "Who ought we become?" "What ought we do?" and "What sort of communities ought we construct?" Thus, morality is concerned with character, choices and community, which have a dynamic and interdependent relationship with one another.

Discussion Questions

1. Take a relatively long *Op Ed* piece from last Sunday's edition of a major paper. In the author's analysis of a situation, what importance is given to people's experience? Whose experience is paid attention to

in his/her argument? How would you critique the author's use and analysis of experience? Is it thorough or broad enough? Is there sufficient critical reflection on experience? How would you improve on his/her use of experience?

2. Imagine that you need to resolve the situation described in the first case at the start of the chapter (involving Mom's declining health). Which and whose experiences would you need to investigate before making a judgment? Who would you speak with in gathering information about differing experiences? How would you describe the moral duties generated by these experiences?

3. As a newly elected representative you need to decide whether or not to support "affirmative action" legislation on behalf of minorities and women. What sorts of experiences (whose and what kind) should you pay attention to in making this choice? What kinds of questions do you need to ask of the experience we have had with this issue, and how would you find the answers to those questions?

Chapter Two.
Character: On Becoming Good Persons

Introduction: Glimpses of Character

1. "A bishop, therefore, must be above reproach, husband of one wife, sober, temperate, courteous, hospitable, and a good teacher; he must not be given to drink or brawling, but be of a forbearing disposition, avoiding quarrels, and not avaricious. He must be one who manages his own household well and controls his children without losing his dignity, for if a man does not know how to manage his own family, how can he take charge of the congregation of God's people?...He must moreover have a good reputation with the outside world, so that he may not be exposed to scandal and caught in the devil's snare." (1 Timothy 3:2–7)

What sort of character is the author of 1 Timothy looking for in a bishop? Why would the moral character of a bishop be of such importance to the early Christian community? Why is the "character issue" so important to many people when choosing an elected official?

2. "I'm sorry to have to ask you this at such an awful moment, Mrs. and Ms. Ramirez," the young ER resident noted diffidently, "But Raul's organs could save a life, perhaps a number of lives if we can act swiftly."

"What are you saying?" Alicia cried. "You come in this waiting room—where we were harassed for an hour and a half about an insurance card—and tell my mother and me that we have just lost a son and a brother, that our Raul is never coming home from this place. And *then* you want us to sign a piece of paper that says you can cut him up and give his organs to patients in this hospital of yours, to people who probably wouldn't have given us the time of day? What do you expect of this family?"

Looking uneasily at Mrs. Ramirez's hands, and at the religious medal wrapped around her fingers, the young doctor turned to Alicia and answered, "I'm not expecting anything, Ms. Ramirez. And I am sorrier than I can say for what must be the worst loss any mother and sister could experience. But for the sake of a number of other mothers and sisters who I don't know and haven't seen, I'm hoping to God that yours is a family of extraordinary compassion, grace and courage."

Can it be that sometimes groups of people—families and even whole societies—can be described as having a certain kind of moral character? Try to describe the character of some groups: your family, our country. How is the character of a group formed?

3. "It is necessary to single out the moral causes [of economic injustice] which, with respect to the behavior of *individuals* considered as *responsible persons,* interfere in such a way as to slow down the course of development and hinder its full achievement...it is not out of place [here] to speak of *structures of sin,*...rooted in *personal sin* and thus always linked to the *concrete acts of individuals* who introduce these structures, consolidate them, and make them difficult to remove. And thus they become stronger, spread, and become the source of other sins, and so influence people's behavior.... Among the attitudes [behind these structures]...two are very typical: the *all consuming desire for profit,* and *the thirst for power.*" (Pope John Paul II, *The Social Concerns of the Church,* #36–37)

How is the moral character of individual persons related to the structures of society, structures that may be just or unjust ("structures of sin," as the pope calls them)? Why does overcoming social injustice depend not only on structural reform, but on "a conversion of the hearts"? (Pope Paul VI, Evangelization in the Modern World #36;18)

We have said that the three key elements of morality are character, choices and community. In this chapter the focus is on character— what it is, and how it is formed. More precisely, we will address three questions: (1) What is character? (2) Why is character so important for morality? (3) What might good character "look like"? As part of the answer to that last question we will propose that to be good at being moral (to have good moral character) requires being good at being human, and to be good at being human requires the development of six important human capacities.

What Is Character?

Christian ethicist Stanley Hauerwas says that to speak of character "...is to recognize that our actions are also acts of self-determination; in them we not only reaffirm what we have been but also determine what we will be in the future. By our actions we not only shape a particular situation, we also form ourselves to meet future situations in a particular way."[1]

For Hauerwas—and for us—character refers to the moral identity of persons, an identity found in the depths of their being, an identity which is both unique and self-chosen. Character holds persons together as coherent and integral beings. By means of this central identity persons are able to pilot the course of their lives and to fashion their ongoing formation as human beings. So we suggest that *character is the core, unique, self-chosen and integral moral identity of a person.* Let us examine the elements of that definition.

CORE MORAL IDENTITY

Character is who we are in the core of our being; it is the moral shape of our true or inner selves. It is not just who we pretend to be, or even who we might aspire to be. It is who we really are, and who we are in the process of becoming through all our choices.

Imagine for a moment that persons are three-layered creatures. On the surface or first level one encounters our observable behavior, all of those routine or not-so-routine choices we make about the kinds of actions we will or will not perform, the kinds of things we will or will not say. People observing one or more of these deeds or choices get a glimpse of us, and from that encounter they may get a clue as to who we are. But it would be a mistake to conclude too much from such a snapshot. First impressions can be very misleading. To be sure, they are incomplete. Would we really "know" Gandhi or Stalin—or anyone for that matter—from having met them only once, or heard one story about them?

On a person's second and deeper level we find those attitudes, affections and habits which, like underground springs, feed the stream of actions and words that flow from us. Here are the deeper choices we have made as persons, choices about how we will see the world and how we will behave over the long haul. Here are our virtues and our vices. If someone knew us for a long time, if they observed how we behaved in good times and bad, if they heard what we thought of ourselves, our neighbors, the world, and even God, they would get a much better understanding of who we are. They would begin to have a much more accurate grasp of our character.

Still, even these character traits, my particular virtues or vices, don't capture the whole person; they don't reveal the full mystery of the *me* at the core or center of my being. Think, for example, of all the work historians and biographers have done trying to find out just who Joan of Arc, Abraham Lincoln, Harriet Beecher Stowe or John F. Kennedy really were, and how the complete character of these persons still eludes our grasp. Or consider how people we thought we knew better than anyone else are still capable of surprising us, making unexpected choices, even changing the direction of their lives. Looking at their early lives, could anyone have predicted that St. Paul would become Christianity's greatest apostle, that Dorothy Day would give her life to the Catholic Worker movement, or that Otto Schindler would risk everything to save eleven hundred Jews from the Holocaust?

Our character is at the very center of us. It is the *mystery* of the *me* who is behind all of my actions and words, and even behind all of my virtues and vices. Certainly our character is not separate from our deeds or habits, but neither does it consist simply of the sum of these parts. Character is the personal center which can never be completely defined, but is always forming and unfolding. It is the *me* I am and the *me* I am becoming.

UNIQUE MORAL IDENTITY

Character might also be referred to as our "moral fingerprint," for each of us has a unique character, a unique moral identity. The uniqueness of our character flows in part from the fact that we have different talents or skills, and also in part from the things that have happened to each of us that have not happened to anyone else. We might be able to imagine how we'd be different people if life hadn't been so hard (or perhaps so easy), or if we'd had different parents or lived in another time. Our character is uniquely our own not only because of the way we have shaped and formed it through the *choices* we have made, but also by our *responses* to what has happened to us on our life's journey.[2]

Our character is the ongoing work of art of our moral lives, the living sculpture of all our options and choices, and the fullest expression of the kind of person we are making of ourselves. There is an old saying that we are not responsible for the face God gave us, but that we *are* for the one we have by the time we are fifty, for we have shaped it with the tracks of our smiles, frowns or scowls. So too, our character is the distinctive stance we are taking to face the world, the place where we have decided to make our last stand. No enterprise is more important.

SELF-CHOSEN MORAL IDENTITY

It should be clear from what we've said already that our character is not like our DNA structure; it is not given to us at conception, nor is it something we can attribute exclusively to our environment. Rather, character for persons is something we choose and shape through our judgments and decisions, as well as by the way we respond to the people we meet and to what happens to us in the stories of our lives.

For the truth of the matter is that in every one of our moral choices, particularly in our most important and habitual ones, we are not just choosing what we want to **do**, we are also deciding what sort of person we want to **be**.[3] In the story about the Ramirez family at the beginning of this chapter, the decision about organ donation is not only a choice about what they are going to do, but more profoundly, it represents a commitment about the kinds of persons they are striving to be. In contrast, in the second book of Samuel, chapters 11 and 12, King David thinks he can commit adultery and murder and not be a different sort of person. The prophet Nathan shows him how badly he is mistaken by revealing to him the sort of person he has already become. So too in Shakespeare's *Macbeth,* the Scotsman and his wife think they can murder and betray and not be affected by it; Lady Macbeth's waking dream reveals what a haunted monster she has become through her villainy.

To say, however, that our character is formed through the choices we make does not mean that it is fashioned in a vacuum. We don't build our character like a model plane—in our basement. Instead, our character takes its shape in the conversation between us and our world. All of our choices are made in *response* to differing opportunities, challenges and invitations. We become brave by choosing to do what is difficult in the face of danger, or loving by choosing to be generous in response to another's need. Our character is shaped by the dialogue of invitation and response. As Enda McDonagh argues, moral situations are those in which we find ourselves called to become moral; we shape our character by our responses in those situations.

To connect this with religious faith, character is formed by the choices we make *in response to the call of God and our neighbor.* Character is who we are choosing to be in response to the offer of friendship and the call to love that we receive from God and through our neighbor. Taking a cue from Matthew 25:31–46 ("…for I was hungry and you gave me food…."), Christians do not choose to be good in some abstract or theoretical sense, but in response to the needs of the people around them. Our lives are continuing encounters with God and neighbor; our character is the person we become in and through such encounters.

INTEGRAL MORAL IDENTITY

Finally, character refers to the fact that as persons we are capable of pulling ourselves *together,* of forming a solid and firm center that holds to its purpose and behaves consistently in all different sorts of settings. Again, as Hauerwas suggests, "we often speak of *integrity* of character, thereby closely identifying integrity and consistency with the meaning of character. We talk of strength or weakness of character as a way of indicating whether someone may be relied upon and trusted even under duress."[4]

Character, then, refers to the *integration* of our choices and habits into a consistent and coherent *me,* so that I can face the world with a steady, unifying vision and determination. In building character we are forming a strong central identity that can pilot the course of our lives,

21

"in good times and bad, in sickness and health, et cetera." Although this enterprise always remains a kind of "work in progress" for us all, young and not-so-young, hopefully a more mature person will have a richer and more well-defined character than an adolescent or child. Rudyard Kipling's poem "If" describes nicely the challenges of a boy taking on the character of a man, and Alice Walker's *The Color Purple* allows us to chart the young Celie's efforts at finding her own voice as an adult woman, thereby discovering her own true center. In both of these works we see that a person of character is able not merely to respond to isolated events, but to set a course through life, piloting one's own life and making a mark in the world. Character implies that we are self-determining in the most important way—that we can shape not only our choices, but our very selves.

History, literature and movies offer endless examples of persons whose character was formed around a "yes" to God and neighbor, as well as those whose character was, to borrow a line from George Lucas's Star Wars, *"given over to the dark side of the force." Take three of each and show why you think these six persons had character that was a core, unique, self-chosen and integral moral identity.*

Why Is Character Important?

The second question for us to address regarding character is simply, *why* is it so important? *Why* is it so important to stress that morality is concerned not just with right actions and just societies, but also with the character of persons? We suggest three reasons.

First, **only persons can—in the fullest sense—be morally good or bad,** and it is in the character of persons that moral goodness and badness are disclosed. Actions can be right or wrong, helpful or harmful, and societies can be just or unjust; but since only human persons have free will and a self-conscious intellect, it is ultimately persons who are the bearers of moral goodness or badness.

Indeed, while it makes some sense to use the word *moral* to describe actions and societies, that word is best used in reference to persons, and, in particular, in reference to character. While it may sometimes be relatively simple to determine if an act was right or wrong, we cannot really know its *full moral meaning* unless we know something about the person or persons from whom it flowed. The same may be said about a society. This is not to suggest that good intentions alone can render every act or society moral, but simply to insist that the primary carrier of moral meaning is the human person.

Second, **only persons can be moral agents,** and this agency flows from and shapes their character. Only persons can be the source of actions that are not merely accidents or the expression of instincts, but freely and consciously chosen words, deeds and habits which express and form moral identity.

Only persons can do morally right or wrong actions, for only persons can obey or refuse the tug of moral experience. Only they can freely and consciously choose to respect or reject the invitation to recognize and respond to their neighbors. Only they can choose deeds and habits that draw them closer to or further away from their goodness as persons.

So, even if guns and nuclear weapons are very dangerous, the NRA bumper sticker is at least correct in asserting that it's *people* and not guns who commit *murder,* for only persons are capable of such moral immoral choices. By the same token, only persons can be heroic or compassionate in the full sense of these terms, for only persons can self-consciously decide to do what is morally right or wrong.

Third, **only persons can construct moral or just communities,** and for this they need moral character. While ants may build complex and highly organized colonies, and wolves form effective packs for hunting and survival, only human beings are capable of freely and intentionally constructing either the just and humane societies to which morality calls us, or the tyrannical and oppressive regimes which morality condemns. And, to a large degree, it is our character as persons that shapes and forms the communities we construct, maintain and support. In many ways these communities are our character writ large.

That is why, in one of the introductory paragraphs to this chapter, Popes John Paul II and Paul VI are so concerned about reforming the moral character of persons as a means of constructing a just society. As the theologian Avery Dulles has noted, classical thinkers like Plato and Aristotle, as well as Christian writers like St. Augustine, have argued

23

that it is not possible to construct a just society with laws alone; there must also be moral integrity in the hearts of its citizens.[5]

Therefore, morality pays attention not just to actions and communities, but also to the moral character of persons because the tug of morality is experienced by persons—in their moral center—and this tug challenges them to develop good moral character by doing right things and building just communities. Good character is required for right actions and just communities; it is a central aim of our moral call.

Earlier we asked you to reflect on the character of people you know through history, literature or movies. A more difficult—and personally risky—assignment might be this: try to describe the kind of person you would like to be at the end of your life. What kind of moral character do you hope will be yours? How is your work-in-progress coming?

"Good" Moral Character: What Does It "Look Like"?

Having identified character, and having considered why it is important, it is time to ask *"What would good moral character 'look like'"?* There are a number of ways to answer that question, but we will focus on three possible answers, answers that may seem to be quite different from one another, but which complement and reinforce one another.

TO BE GOOD IS TO BE LOVING

One possible and popular answer to our question about good character is to suggest that a good person is one who *loves*. Enda McDonagh argues that moral goodness is about answering the call or tug to recognize, respect and respond to our neighbor (by "neighbor" McDonagh means all other persons). That would mean that a person of good character would be someone whose interests do not end with his or her own ego boundaries. Instead, good character enables one to care about others, to enter into loving relationships with others, to reach out to strangers and even enemies with compassion and empathy.

Certainly it would be difficult to think of someone whom we genuinely admire as good who was *not* capable of loving others, who was

24

not capable of reaching beyond himself or herself.[6] And while we could find countless admirable qualities among the hundreds of saints the church holds up for us as models of goodness, clearly every one of these persons sought to love God and neighbor. Thus, at the heart of being good is a loving response to others, a response that reaches beyond self and seeks to do good for those around us.

TO BE GOOD IS TO BE VIRTUOUS

A second way of describing persons of good character is to say that they are, or are becoming, VIRTUOUS. And what are virtues? In keeping with much of classical Western thought, we suggest that *virtues are those good moral habits, affections, attitudes and beliefs that lead to genuine human fulfillment, even perfection, on both personal and social levels.* By contrast, vices are poor moral habits, affections, attitudes and beliefs which hinder human fulfillment or perfection, both personally and socially.

Virtues, then, are not simply good moral habits of action, but they include those attitudes, affections and beliefs from which actions flow, and which are themselves deepened through consistent effort and choice. Whether we are talking about justice, prudence, temperance and fortitude (four virtues that have received great emphasis in Western thought), the three Christian virtues of faith, hope and charity, or other important virtues such as openness, hospitality, compassion and generosity, all virtues entail not only repeated acts of behavior, but also include sustained commitments to be a certain kind of person. Justice, for example, is not simply a matter of acting justly, it includes all those attitudes, affections and beliefs that help sustain a person's or a community's commitment to *be* just. Understood in this way, virtues are not garments to be worn, but the stuff of one's soul.[7] In Aristotle's words, "virtue is that which makes the one who has it good, and the work that he or she does good."[8]

Note that virtues not only work together to create an inner peaceful harmony for individual persons; they also help produce right actions and just communities. In this way, virtues always have a communal dimension to them. Furthermore, we believe it is appropriate to use the word *virtue* (or *vice*) to describe not only the character qualities of individuals, but of whole groups and societies. For example, has not

South Africa taken steps in recent years to become a more just nation? We think so. Admittedly, the virtues of large groups are harder to pin-point and name, for what is generally true of a group of people may be more or less true of individuals within that group. Even so, virtues concern not only what I do and who I become; they also concern what we do and who we are becoming.

A brief word about two kinds of virtues is important. As noted above, the virtues of justice, prudence, temperance and fortitude have received great attention in Western thought. They have been called *cardinal virtues*. The word *cardinal* comes from a Latin word that means "hinge," and so these cardinal virtues have been thought to be essential for human living, virtues upon human flourishing "hinges." Moreover, they are virtues which all of us need to strive for if we are to become truly good and if our communities are to become just.

For all their importance, however, Christian writers like St. Augustine and St. Thomas Aquinas have argued that the cardinal virtues alone offered an incomplete picture of human goodness. According to Christian faith, all persons are made in the image and likeness of God and are destined for salvation in Christ, and so the call to goodness also demands response to God's creative and saving actions toward us. In this perspective, full human goodness requires faith and hope in, as well as love for God. In addition to the four cardinal virtues, then, the fully virtuous person would be shaped by the three *theological virtues* of faith, hope and love. Augustine and Aquinas both emphasize that what is distinctive about these virtues is that in large measure they are gifts from God. They are *received* more than *acquired*. To be sure, God is generous in offering them to all, so our charge is to be open and to receive these special gifts that help us to believe in, to hope in and indeed to love the God who has first loved us. Most often Christian theologians have maintained that it is love— love of God and love of neighbor—that is "the mother and root of all virtues."[9] So in the end, the virtuous person turns about to be the loving person.

To Be Good Is To Be Fully Human

A third way of describing persons of good moral character is to say that they are, or are becoming *fully human persons*. By this we mean

26

that they are well along the way to achieving their full potential as moral human beings.

This "full humanity" may at first be a hard notion to grasp, but without putting too fine an edge on it, most of us would probably agree that Clara Barton, the founder of the Red Cross, was better at being a fully flourishing human being than Adolph Hitler. In some way this full humanity is what Pinocchio was looking for when he wished to become "a real boy," or what the tin woodsman, the scarecrow and the cowardly lion were all looking for when they came to Oz in search of a heart, a brain and some courage. Notice, in fact, how we often describe persons whose character seems (as far as we can tell) to be something far less than good as "inhuman," perhaps even "monstrous." And notice how we often describe genuinely good persons as particularly "humane," indicating that the degree to which they are moral is the degree to which they have developed their potential to be fully human.

In this sense morality is concerned with the task of becoming more genuinely human. Note that none of this is to imply that persons of bad character are not still persons in the sense of not having moral rights and claims. The point, rather, is that our humanity is not simply a treasure to be received and tucked away in a safe place, but instead, it is a gift that must be nurtured and developed.

What Does It Mean to Be Fully Human?

So, then, what does it mean to be FULLY HUMAN (or GOOD) PERSONS, and how is it that responding to the moral call to love others and to develop virtue can make us more truly human? One way to answer that question is to try to identify the specific characteristics of being a human person. If we can name some of the essential characteristics and capacities of what it means to be a human person, then we may get a sense of what we must be and do to become better at being human.

Numerous authors have tried to identify the basic shape of our humanity. The Jesuit theologian Karl Rahner argued that a list of the basic characteristics of our humanity would include our embodiment, spirituality, sociability, uniqueness, freedom and a capacity for relationship with God. The psychiatrist and ethicist Willard Gaylin has suggested that love, conscience, work, emotions, freedom, dependency, sexuality and our capacity for symbolic language are what make us uniquely human.[10] Although these and other lists may differ in places from one another, a survey of such efforts reveals that a handful of characteristics surface again and again in attempts to describe the truly human. We suggest that human persons are characterized by (at least) six basic traits. *Human persons are FREE, INTELLIGENT, RESPONSIBLE, UNFOLDING, SOCIAL AND SPIRITUAL.*

To be a person of good character—to be a fully flourishing human person—involves not only being loving and not only being a person of virtue, but it entails "being about the business" of developing these fundamental human capacities. Let us look at each of them.

First, human persons have a capacity to be FREE. This capacity relates to our deeds, our virtues and our character.

Deeds: The Freedom to Choose. First, we human beings have the power of choice, the freedom to chose the things we will do or not do. Unsheathed from the power of instinct, we can choose our words and deeds, our hobbies, jobs, spouses and elected officials. But notice that this is both a power and a burden, for while we are free to make choices, we also MUST make choices. And *sometimes,* of course, they are difficult; *often* they require courage; *always* we must take responsibility for their consequences.

Notice too that when choices are complex or difficult, we must do the moral homework of preparation and investigation, so that our choices are made with intelligence and integrity, reflecting not only the wisdom of others, but the integrity of our convictions and consciences. Vices like sloth, cowardice and imprudence can weaken our ability to make choices well. So at our worst, we "jump to conclusions" that are not warranted, we vote without preparation or intelligence (or perhaps we don't vote at all), or we skirt our responsibility altogether, hoping that some difficult matter will go away or that someone else will take care of it. The point should be clear: the freedom to choose is a great blessing, but it carries with it serious responsibilities.

Habits: The Freedom to Change. Not only do we have the capacity to choose what we will do, we also have the power to form habits, the power to shape our own character, to grow and become different.

28

We can choose not only "to pick up" a hobby or sport, but to stay with it, to dedicate ourselves to it, and make it a part of who we are. So we can "take up" painting casually, or we can choose to *become* a painter. We can "have a child," or we can dedicate ourselves to learning to *become* the best parent we can be. As any of us know who have tried to lose a few pounds, learn to play the piano or take up a new language, serious change requires commitment, and usually involves hard work, patience and humility. Such virtues are a part of exercising our freedom to change ourselves, to become more fully human.

Character: The Freedom to be Good. Finally, we humans beings have the capacity for freedom, not only in regard to isolated actions or habits, but also in regard to our very identity, our character. We have the liberty to hand our whole lives over to God and neighbor, to reform or change the very direction of our lives. We have the freedom to fashion our own character, to shape our deeds, attitudes and habits onto one single course, to pull ourselves into a person whom Hauerwas would describe as "having character." This is the "fundamental stance" and "basic freedom" that Karl Rahner and Josef Fuchs wrote about. It is the freedom to say yes to God and goodness from the very core of our being. This type of freedom manifests itself in the choices we make about deeds and habits. It is the deepest (although most elusive) type of human freedom, the freedom to become fully human.[11]

Note that this type of freedom—freedom of character—is usually not exercised all at once. Rather, most often it is in and through the specific choices we make about the deeds we will perform and about the habits to which we will commit our energy that we fashion our moral character. Sometimes an immensely important choice about an action, one made with a high degree of awareness and freedom, may be so significant that it may either radically reaffirm or reverse one's fundamental stance in life, from goodness to badness or from badness to goodness. But most often the freedom we have to fashion our character is exercised less dramatically. The way we exercise our freedom in regard to action and in regard to virtue is the day-by-day way we "compose our lives" and fashion our character.

Second, persons have the capacity to be INTELLIGENT, a capacity that can be exercised in at least two ways:

Our intelligence concerns mental skills. Like the canny or calculative intellects of Sherlock Holmes, Madame Curie or Albert Einstein, we human beings have an amazing capacity "to find out." While this intelligence is partly given at birth, this raw talent can be developed through good habits of health, disciplined study and integral research. Thus, we can become "smarter" through study and learning. At times new information—such as about persons who suffer from mental disorders—may have significant impact on us morally, enabling us to respond to others not with disdain or condemnation, but with solidarity and compassion. At the same time our intelligence can be weakened by prejudice, sloth or dishonesty. Indeed, not only can these vices harm the intelligence of individual persons, they can pollute the intelligence of communities. Bias and laziness, for example, can find their way into a community's policies and social structures. Racism and sexism are good examples.

Our intelligence concerns wisdom. Our capacity to be intelligent, however, concerns more than the ability to seek information. It also includes understanding, consciousness, wonder and even that passionate hunger for goodness, truth and meaning which we refer to as wisdom. The wise person is often quite different from the merely smart or clever one, and it seems clear that virtues like prudence, compassion, humility and even courage are part of that wisdom, while vices like greed, apathy, cruelty and foolhardiness undercut real wisdom. The Nazi physicians who performed monstrous "medical experiments" on prisoners of war without their consent might have been clever, but they were certainly not wise. The capacity for wisdom requires that our intelligence be placed at the service of goodness.

Third, persons have the capacity to be RESPONSIBLE, a capacity that can be understood in two ways:

Responsibility means Accountability. We human persons have the capacity not just to choose between different options before us, but to give an answer *for ourselves* in these choices, to decide who we will be and how we will stand in response to the world. Thus, our choices are not just our *choices,* but also *our* choices, choices for which we take ownership. This means that we can and must take responsibility for, be held accountable for, not only our deeds and our habits, but also our very selves.

Responsibility means Integrity. The capacity we have for responsibility is at the same time a capacity for INTEGRITY. By this we mean the capacity to live and act out of a consistent, coherent vision, one that enables us to do what we promise, and be who we say we are. We have already seen that a variety of virtues are necessary for us to be genuinely free and intelligent. So too, in order to achieve full responsibility for our deeds—and especially for ourselves—we need integrity, and integrity requires virtues like honesty, discipline, self-sacrifice and a host of others. Integrity is the ability to give our lives direction, commanding it as a captain does a ship. Without virtues like honesty and discipline our character will be chaotic, and there will be neither integrity nor responsibility.

Fourth, persons have the capacity to be UNFOLDING.

Human persons have the amazing capacity to unfold, to grow through various stages and crises into persons who are increasingly more complex and yet coherent. This power to unfold is more than a freedom to choose. It is a talent to expand, freely and intentionally, beyond present boundaries and limits. We have this capacity for growth not only as individuals, but also as communities. So we move from infants to adolescents to real adults, and our societies move from tyrannies to democracies, from oligarchies to just communities.

Very often we seem to grow by facing crises and challenges, and by responding to fresh opportunities in each moment. In the early stages of development much of this growth is aided and supported by our environment. But if we are ever to grow beyond the minimal stages of development, to unfold into our true potential as persons, we will need to choose to take greater and greater risks and face deeper and deeper challenges. Developing the ability to risk, to change, to face new challenges, to be open to new ways of thinking, and to suffer the loss of old habits—all of this requires virtues like courage, prudence, love, faith, hope and a commitment to higher goods and goals. Such virtues help us to grow, to unfold, and in this way to move toward a greater degree of our full human potential. What is true of plants may be true of human persons: the moment we cease to grow is the moment we begin to die.

Fifth, persons have the capacity to be SOCIAL.

Persons are social by experience, need and nature. For persons live with, depend upon and are made for other persons. Indeed, our capac-

31

ities for language, friendship, politics and sexuality point to the human orientation to community. Although we may enjoy solitude, we require community in order to discover and achieve our fullest selves as persons. Indeed, we know that children who are deprived of the rich associations of a healthy community find it hard if not impossible to become healthy adults. Is it not the case that some of our deepest joys as persons happen in the context of friendship, love and community; while many of the depths to which we are capable of sinking involve cutting ourselves off from one another?

Sixth, persons have the capacity to be SPIRITUAL.

Finally, there is a spiritual dimension of human existence. There is a hunger and thirst in us that is not satisfied simply with having or accomplishing, but which moves us to look beyond the horizons of our here-and-now existence to seek answers to ultimate questions.

And so we wonder why we are here in the first place, what the origin of all that exists might be, why it is that we love, suffer and die, and whether what happens in our lives and in our world is the result of chance or fate, or whether there might be some ultimate source or ground of it all. Many, of course, answer affirmatively to that last question, and many name that "ground" as God. Even more boldly, Christians believe that God is an amazingly loving God who has been and remains among us in and through the person and the Spirit of Jesus Christ. If St. Augustine was right, the hunger within us that moves us to seek answers to such ultimate questions is itself a "holy hunger": "You have made us for yourself, O God, and so our hearts are restless until they rest in you." The ultimate restlessness within the human heart, therefore, is not a sign of pathology, but of our capacity for spirituality, and of our hunger and thirst for God.

Christians and other religious persons throughout history have argued that this capacity for a spiritual life is enriched by the practice of virtues, and particularly by love. The author of the first letter of John in the New Testament said it this way: "No one has ever seen God. Yet, if we love one another, God remains in us, and God's love is brought to perfection in us" (1 John 4:12). So how is our hunger for ultimate meaning satisfied? How is our thirst for God quenched? In and through our love for one another. If being good at being a human person includes responding to and nourishing our capacity for "the holy," then love of one another is the path we must follow. The practice of the virtue of love is, thus, both the doorway to the sacred and the path that leads to human flourishing.

On Moral Character—Some Conclusions

1. We become Persons of Good Moral Character by habitually answering the CALL to recognize, respect and respond to other persons as creatures fashioned in the image and likeness of God, thus loving God and our neighbor in our actions, habits and lives.

2. In this way we develop VIRTUES, positive habits of action, affection and belief which form GOOD moral character and facilitate the development of our full humanity.

3. Response to the CALL to love God and neighbor, and the development and practice of VIRTUE is what enables us to become FULLY HUMAN PERSONS. Concretely, this means becoming more fully free, intelligent, responsible, unfolding, social and spiritual.

Discussion Questions

1. Choose six words to describe someone you admire, or pick six words you hope someone might write on your tombstone in half a century or so. What six words would you select? What would these words tell us about your own or your friend's character?

How would someone go about making these words true of himself or herself? What would you need to do to make these words true?

2. You have been visited by a magician who tells you that you can make one of three wishes for your baby. You may ask for health, wealth or virtue. Only one can be granted. What would you choose? Why?

33

Chapter Three.
Choices for Action: Right and Wrong

Introduction: Toward "Doing the Right Thing"

1. "It's an opportunity," Lisa suggested, "just an opportunity." Lisa told her husband, Bob, that she was planning to visit John, a former neighbor, who had just come home from the hospital. "An opportunity," she said, "that's all." Bob wasn't sure.

Bob and John had been friends, or at least Bob thought so. But then Bob learned that John had spread some rather nasty stories around the neighborhood about some of his business practices. He had distorted the truth badly and had damaged Bob's reputation in their circle of friends. Angry words were exchanged; they haven't spoken since.

John and his family moved to another part of town a year ago. Bob was happy about that. But yesterday Lisa received word that John had been diagnosed with cancer in both lungs. Unfortunately it is well advanced, and so simply keeping him comfortable is the plan. Lisa knows the visit will be hard, but she wants to go. For Bob, the issues are deeper. Should he leave well enough alone, or is this some sort of opportunity? He's not sure.

Is this an opportunity? If so, for what? For whom? What would this visit ask of Bob? What would it "say" or express about him if he were to do this? What might it do to Bob?

2. Anna Williams is in shock. Her two-dollar lotto ticket has just won her $3.2 million. She can hardly breathe. The single parent of three teenagers, Anna is a thirty-seven-year-old widow working two jobs, commuting three hours a day and keeping a small army of credi-

tors at bay. She has been through welfare, "workfare" and sometimes, it seemed, warfare.

$3.2 million. Perhaps it's a mistake, or some sort of sick joke. What in the name of God will she do with this sort of money? What will it do to her? Even now, even in the midst of this shock, she begins to sense that this wealth is not just an answer to her prayers. It's also a question.

What might Anna Williams do in this situation? How will what she does "say something" about who she is? How will her decision impact her? Others? Is what we do in such dramatic moments more important than what we do in ordinary moments?

3. "Something has to go." That's what the spokesman for the board's finance committee offered as an explanation at the parents' meeting. The tax levy was defeated (again) in the recent election. The money was needed for a number of things, among them the high school's athletic programs. So now some cutbacks are necessary, and as the spokesman for the board explained, cutting the funding for the girls' programs seemed logical: these programs were somewhat new to begin with, not nearly as longstanding as the boys' programs. It just seemed like the right thing to do. Some agreed; some didn't.

What does the proposed cutback "say" about the finance committee of the board? About the local community? What would it "say" to the local community? Alternatives?

The Importance of Actions

We have said that morality is about character, action and community. In this chapter the focus is on ACTIONS, our choices to do and not to do certain things. Most of us don't need to be convinced that actions are critically important for morality. Wouldn't most of us agree that what is important is not simply what we *claim* is in our hearts, or what we *intend,* but what we actually *do*? Because they express and form our developing character and impact upon the world around us, actions get a lot of attention in morality.

35

Indeed, for a long period in the history of Christian morality nearly *all* the focus was placed on actions (the "Morality of Doing"), often overlooking the importance of character (the "Morality of Being"), and underestimating the significance of communities ("Social Morality"). For centuries Catholic moral theology was designed to prepare priests to be confessors. The textbooks used sought to help future priests (and, in turn, penitents) to determine the rightness or wrongness of individual acts.[1] Was a certain act a sin or not, and if so, what kind of sin: a mortal sin? a venial sin? What were the circumstances and consequences of the act, the intent of the agent and the means used to accomplish this goal? Attention on individual human acts dominated these books, displacing any significant discussion of character or community. For this reason many criticized Catholic morality for being abstract, rigid and legalistic, looking more like a law book than a helpful guide for Christians seeking to build moral character and just communities.[2]

Recently, however, much of this imbalance has been redressed. With the rediscovery and resurgence of "virtue ethics" over the last two decades, as well as the growing importance of Catholic Social Teachings, character and community are well on their way to reasserting their rightful place within Christian morality.[3] Nonetheless, even with this rightful reemphasis on character and community, actions remain an important concern for morality.

This chapter will unfold as follows. First, we will discuss the "dynamics" of moral action. Second, we will describe the subjective and objective dimensions of actions. Third, we will focus on the three levels of the subjective dimension of actions, followed, fourth, by an analysis of three levels of the objective dimension of actions. And fifth, we will discuss several important factors in judging the rightness and wrongness of human action.

The "Dynamics" of Moral Action: Expressive, Formative and Effective

We suggest that human moral activity has a certain kind of "dynamics" about it. Our actions are **expressive, formative** and **effective.** That is, our actions (at least those actions which we freely and consciously choose) do three morally important things: (1) They *express* (though partially and incompletely) the person we are (our character); (2) they *form* (again, partially and incompletely) the person we are becoming (our unfolding character); and (3) they *effect* changes in the world around us (rendering help or harm to ourselves and others). In other words, our actions express and form our character and impact the world around us.

It is worth considering the moral significance of our actions in the light of Christian faith. Christian faith suggests that we human persons — created by God and re-created in the power of the Spirit of Jesus Christ, the Spirit of God — experience a twofold moral call from God. We feel a moral tug urging us to strive to become fully human persons by developing and growing in virtue. And at the same time we experience an equally important call from God to reach out and *love* our neighbors — including strangers, enemies and particularly those in need — and to do so in concrete human action that is effective and helpful.

In other words, God challenges us to live up to our destiny or vocation as creatures made in the image and likeness of God *and* to recognize, respect and respond to that God-like quality in our neighbors. In this way we become virtuous (and thereby move toward the fullness of our humanity) *in and through* our loving responses to others. Indeed, that is one of the great paradoxes of humanity, that it is by transcending our own concerns and reaching out to others that we become most fully human. As theologian Walter Conn has argued, it is through the process of "self-transcendence," that is, of "moving beyond ourselves" that we achieve or own self-realization and fulfillment.[4] In the words of St. Francis of Assisi, perhaps more simply but no less profoundly, "it is in giving that we receive."

Note that it is in our ***actions*** that we respond to our call to love. For it is through our actions that we struggle to become fully human by developing and growing in virtue, and it is in our actions that we reach out to our neighbors with love. Indeed, all through our lives God invites us, through the options and opportunities placed before us, to respond to this, the mysterious moral call to love God in and through loving our neighbor, and in that way to contribute to our own self-development — in essence, to love ourselves. Should we forgive this offense or carry a grudge; should we help this stranger or pass by; should we take the afternoon off to visit our elderly grandmother or attend to our own needs at home; should we support aid for the poor or demand lower taxes? Of course not all of our options have such clear moral implications, but many do. We are constantly being invited to decide not only *what we will do,* but *who we will become.*

Admittedly, our character, unfolding and mysterious as it is, is more than the mere sum of our actions, and certainly more than any one of our deeds, even a very important one. Our actions help to express and shape the mystery that is our character. But that character is always larger, richer and more mysterious than any set of deeds. Even so, our actions remain an important part of morality because in them we are answering God's twofold moral call tugging at our hearts—to become fully human by reaching out to our neighbors.

*Recall a character from a film or a novel, someone who faced and then made an important decision about what to **do**. How was that person's action expressive, formative and effective? Recall one of your own important decisions; answer the same question.*

Subjective and Objective Dimensions

Christian ethicists have often identified two distinct dimensions of our actions, the *subjective* and the *objective*.

The subjective dimension of our actions refers to the way our deeds express and form our character, how they help to affirm or refute God's call to become fully human. Do our actions reveal someone moving *towards* or *away from* God's call to full humanity? Do they help to build up or tear down our good character? What do these actions *tell us about,* or *do to* the person performing them? By examining the subjective dimension of our actions we are seeking to discover exactly what persons are trying to "say" about themselves and who they are seeking to become through their deeds. This dimension of human action pays attention to what's in our hearts, and what our deeds are doing to those hearts.

The subjective dimension of acts highlights the fact that human acts are always *personal* or *subjective,* in that they flow from and shape the persons who perform them. For since we normally perform our actions with sufficient freedom and intelligence to know what it is we are

38

doing and to consent to where these choices are leading us, our actions are usually a partial but real expression of our intent, and indeed of our developing character. To the extent that we have freely and knowingly chosen these deeds, they bear the stamp of our character, and because we consent to where they are leading us, we end up being shaped by their mark as well. They are expressive and formative.

The phrase "to the extent" in the second-to-last sentence is important. We don't always choose our acts freely, or understand what we are doing. There are, after all, accidents and honest mistakes, and we sometimes act under duress or the influence of unavoidable ignorance, uncontrolled passions or even controlled substances. Actions performed in such a condition don't usually express who we are or who we are becoming, and are—from the subjective perspective at least—of diminished importance.[5]

The point is that our genuinely human acts (i.e., those committed with sufficient freedom and intelligence) represent our personal or subjective response both to the options before us and to the deeper values they represent. They are our choices about what we will do, who we are and who we will become. So in choosing to take an extra job to help pay for her daughter's braces, Alice is not only deciding to get the braces, she is also making a choice about the kind of parent she wants to be, and indeed—at least partially—about how she wants to respond to God's call in her life. So her action partially reveals her unfolding and mysterious character and helps to shape its further development.

The *objective* dimension of human action is also important. This refers to the impact of our deeds in the real world. To inquire about the objective dimension of actions is to look beyond subjective intentions and to ask what our actions are really doing to ourselves and others—whether they are truly helping or harming ourselves or our neighbors.

Notice that it can happen that an action—more likely, a pattern of actions—may have a helpful or harmful impact upon us objectively regardless of our subjective intentions. Consider the Johnsons. They remember very well how, as children, their parents would bring (sometimes nearly drag) all four of them to Aunt Mabel's every Sunday after church. Usually they didn't enjoy those visits, to put it mildly. Aunt Mabel told the same stories over and over, and there was never anything to do (and certainly nothing to eat!) at her house. They couldn't wait to get home. But now, years later, people say things like this:

39

"How devoted those Johnsons are to their elderly parents." The value of care for and devotion to the elderly, so much a part of the Johnsons now, has a whole lot to do with those visits to Aunt Mabel. Sometimes our actions, especially patterns of actions, can have an objectively positive impact on those who perform them regardless of subjective intentions.

But consider also the Conway's kids. Like so many others, theirs was a home in which racial slurs and epithets were simply part of the family vocabulary. You wouldn't say they hated minorities or people of color or that they intended to be racist. As adults, however, the Conways have gradually had to "own" the bigotry within them. They have come to appreciate that regardless of their intentions as kids, their use of such racist terms or jokes was not at all innocent or neutral. It had an effect upon them objectively that they are now attempting to undo.

But the objective dimension of our actions is especially important because human actions are also *interpersonal* and *social:* they go out into the world and shape the lives of others. They impact others—for good or ill—and often quite differently from what we would claim our intentions to have been. To be sure, our actions are not just the things we are saying about ourselves; they are also what we are saying and doing to the world around us.

It is impossible to lead a life or perform an action that has absolutely no impact on others—even if it is the impact of *not* having chosen another act. The objective dimension of our actions points to this impact and reminds us to look beyond our intent to what we are really doing in the world, to where our acts go and what they do once we have unleashed them.

For if our actions are really meant to respond to God's moral call to love, and if that love is not just a romantic notion or a warm feeling, but is really an attempt to recognize, respect and respond to the dignity and worth of others in an effective way, then the rightness or wrongness of an act will not just be a matter of intention, it will also and always be about what this act really *does,* about its effect. We are not simply obliged to think well of others, but to live and act in ways that make the world a better place, to do those things which help, not harm. The objective dimension of our acts, then, is concerned with what we are actually doing in the world.

Given our twofold moral call from God to become fully human by loving others, it seems clear that both the subjective and objective dimensions of our actions are important, for the moral quality of an act is shaped both by the character of the acting person and by its impact on the world. We want to know how an act expresses and forms our character, as well as what its effects are on others. Although it is often helpful to be able to distinguish between these two dimensions, it is ultimately impossible to understand fully the moral meaning of a human action without paying attention to both its subjective and objective dimensions.

What seems helpful about this distinction between the subjective and objective dimensions of actions? How might this distinction be misused?

Subjective Dimension: Three Levels of Acts

Conversation about the subjective morality of actions has often focused exclusively on individual deeds, like an act of heroism, a murder or a decision to share an inheritance. But if we really want to get a fuller picture of the person acting (especially ourselves!) and of the moral meaning of actions, it is important to examine three distinct levels of human acts: individual deeds, habits and fundamental options. Put differently, to really know a person we need to see what they do each day, what they are doing over the long haul and who they are choosing to be in their core.

INDIVIDUAL DEEDS

In our day-to-day lives we make judgments and decisions about a whole host of things. Shall we watch TV again tonight or write an overdue letter to a friend; shall we apologize for a foolish remark or simply let it pass; shall we tell the truth about a car accident or "fudge" things a bit on the insurance claim?

Subjectively, the moral meaning of an action relates directly to the person's intention, freedom, understanding and commitment. By *intention* we mean what the person was trying to accomplish in and through

41

the action under consideration. If, for example, a person's intention was actually to hurt another or to deceive those who have a right to the truth, then the action performed to accomplish such an end obviously reveals something negative about the character of that person. Sometimes, however, a person might perform an action that is harmful to others or dishonest without necessarily intending to do so or perhaps not fully intending to do so. What such an action "says" about the person involved is more ambiguous. Thus the subjective moral meaning of an action depends greatly upon the intention of the actor, even though judging the intention of another is "tricky business," to say the least.

In addition to intention, it is also the case that freedom, understanding and commitment have a great bearing on the subjective moral meaning of an action. When individual actions are done with real freedom, understanding and commitment, they can express and shape character in important ways. And the more freedom, understanding and commitment one brings to a decision, the more subjectively significant such an act becomes. Often we seem to live our lives on something like "automatic pilot"; many of our actions reconfirm established habits and patterns without a great deal of thought. Such actions may well have limited moral importance.

Sometimes, however, very important or difficult choices can engage our freedom, understanding and commitment so fully that we may be saying and doing something extremely significant in them, giving a profoundly new direction to our character's development. Such acts may well be defining moments in our lives. In such choices or actions we may feel ourselves called upon not only to decide among various options, but to choose the very course of our lives. Naturally, such moments and deeds are quite rare, but it is possible to make such critical choices and to confirm or reverse what seemed like the very direction of our lives.[6]

HABITS

As important as individual actions can sometimes be, as a rule they tend to be less important than our habits. As the repeated actions or patterns of behavior that we develop over a long period of time, habits express and shape our character more deeply and permanently than isolated, individual acts.

42

Habits are important because they are deeply ingrained into our personality, and so they tend to define how we can be expected to behave over the long haul. Habits are our particular and personal character traits. As a result, they tend to give us a better picture of who we are and who we are becoming than do our individual actions. Our habits represent deeper sorts of choices than simply picking a course of action in one particular setting. To form a habit is to set a course about how we will think, feel and behave regularly. In this way habits reveal a deeper intentionality than most individual acts.

It is worth reflecting for a moment on the decision that a habit represents. Such decisions are often invisible. We may not remember stopping to reflect on the decision to develop a particular habit, but we did make such a choice, and we reaffirm it each time we repeat the habit. The truth is that habits tend to be *more* important than individual actions because they reflect a choice about how to live our lives over the long haul and because they are deeply incorporated into our personalities. Thus it is not surprising that in traditional Christian morality the seven "deadly sins" — lust, avarice, wrath, sloth, pride, envy and gluttony — were not individual acts, but habits.

FUNDAMENTAL OPTION

The most important decision of our lives, the most significant option we ever face is not a decision about an individual action or an option about a particular virtue. Rather, it is the decision, the option, regarding the persons we are striving to become. Behind all our deeds and habits there is one choice, one option, that gives shape and meaning to our lives in an ultimate sort of way. This is what theologian Karl Rahner has called our "fundamental option." This option is about the kind of person we are to be; it is about our very character. This option represents the persons we are choosing to become in response to God's two-dimensional invitation to be authentically human in and through a life of love. We may become a resounding "yes" or a deafening "no" to that invitation. That is our most fundamental option.

Such an "option" involves the total gift of oneself; it is not likely to be fully expressed or achieved in a single, individual act, or indeed in any set of habits. This option is always "a work in progress," the work of a lifetime. Even so, one does not make such a fundamental option except by means of individual acts and habits which consistently and coherently confirm the basic direction of one's life. One does not become good by wishing it, or even by simply willing it, but by choosing again and again—and yet again—to respond to God's moral call in this concrete setting and in these regular choices. Like Rome, our fundamental option is not built in a day, but day in and day out for the whole course of our lives.

This means that ultimately the real subjective moral significance of our individual acts and habits is to be found in the way(s) they affirm, weaken or reverse our fundamental option. Do our actions and habits reveal a character moving toward or away from goodness and love? Toward or away from God? Do they confirm or refute an "Amen" to God's twofold moral call? And how significantly do they contribute to that project?

Looking, first, to characters in novels or films with which you are familiar and, second, to your own life, give an example of each of the following: (1) an individual action that was morally less significant subjectively because of a diminished degree of knowledge and/or freedom; (2) how someone began to ("decided to") form a habit, but perhaps without fully realizing they were doing so; (3) how someone's action in a dramatic or decisive moment might well have been a "fundamental option."

Objective Dimension: Three Levels of Acts

Curiously enough, our understanding of the objective morality of actions has also been hampered by a certain individualism, only here the problem has been that instead of paying too much attention to individual acts, we have paid too much attention to the acts of individuals. That is, we have tended to ignore (expect in limited areas) the way or ways persons and communities cooperate in their acts, and particularly the ways in which large groups or societies act as single or interdependent organisms. As a result Christian morality has often paid a great deal of attention to private questions of morality (like sexual behavior or personal honesty and theft) while overlooking larger and pervasive issues of social morality (like unfair taxation, unjust wages or ecological harm).

Some of this failure to examine the interpersonal and social dimensions of morality can again be explained by the fact that much of Catholic morality was developed with the aim of helping individual persons examine their consciences and confess their sins, or perhaps by the fact that we are often stymied by the complexity and intractability of social injustices and intimidated by the structural reforms required to address such problems. Better, we sometimes think, to let sleeping dogs lie.

Nonetheless, the fact is that while the things which we do as individuals are very important, so too are the things we do in cooperation with others, as well as the things we do as societies or nations. Indeed, one could argue that over the long haul it is our communal and social actions which have the greatest impact for good or ill in the world. Even the heroic and radical acts of the best among us tend to produce the most good when they help to transform our larger social laws and practices.

Therefore, if we are to understand the objective dimension of our actions, we will need to look at all three levels on which persons act: the *personal,* the *interpersonal* and the *social.*

PERSONAL ACTS

These are the acts we perform *as* individuals, the ordinary and extraordinary things we do which have an impact not just on ourselves, but also on those around us. Such personal acts go out from us, and, like ripples created by a tossed stone, they produce effects for good or ill in the world. Because we "threw" these acts, they bear our mark; we are responsible for them. Usually, when we think of the morality of our acts, these are the deeds we consider.

Such acts are certainly important, for they constitute much of what we are doing in the world. Appropriately, we tend to assess the objective rightness or wrongness of our individual acts by their impact on others. So we ask, do they help or harm? Do they recognize, respect and respond to our neighbor? And indeed we argue that the wrongness of stealing, murdering or molesting stems from the fact that such actions harm someone else, or at least they harm another without sufficient reason.

INTERPERSONAL ACTS

Still, our acts are not always isolated stones we throw out into the world. Sometimes they are part of a game of catch we are playing with others. That is, our acts make up part of an ongoing conversation we are having with others, often a fairly predictable and established conversation in which we all play different parts in a larger game. Thus, our acts are important not just for what they seem to do individually, but for the way in which they contribute to a larger pattern, a pattern which can be helpful or harmful.

Long before modern psychology introduced us to "dysfunctional" families, dramatists like Tennessee Williams (*The Glass Menagerie*) and Eugene O'Neill (*Long Day's Journey into Night*) gave us haunting portraits of parents and children trapped in maddeningly destructive and exasperatingly predictable patterns of behavior, interlocking actions and reactions that invariably brought out the worst in everyone. So too, in Sartre's *No Exit,* hell is produced not by a single act but by a series of interlocking responses in which the characters seem to cooperate in the work of their own damnation.

Counselors caring for such "dysfunctional" families try to make them aware of the destructive interpersonal dynamics going on in their households, and the roles and rules by which they operate as family units. They try to help these families address and change some of their basic patterns and strategies for communicating, loving, working and living together. To escape such dysfunction, individual members will need to stop "cooperating" in interpersonal acts and habits that are ultimately unsuccessful, indeed that are quite harmful.[7]

In the same way, we need to recognize that many of our own actions are part of established patterns we have settled into at home, school or work; interlocking habits in which we trigger and react to the responses of others. Such patterns can be helpful or harmful. If we are blind to the ways in which we contribute to and sustain such interpersonal actions, we will not truly see what we are actually doing in the world.

SOCIAL ACTIONS

Finally, we also act as whole communities, societies or nations. We pass laws, establish customs and set up policies, and we continue to abide by and support such practices, or we seek to reform or abolish them, replacing them with newer and (hopefully) better ones. Although our social structures, systems and institutions may not look like the deeds of individuals, they are in fact the ways in which *we human persons* behave as members of communities. They are what *we* are doing as societies. The social structures of our societies are *ours;* they are the result of free and conscious choices made (and continuously reaffirmed) by human beings. And, like the things we do on the personal and interpersonal levels, these institutions and customs have an effect—indeed, a tremendous effect—for good or ill in the world around us.

We will examine social actions more fully in the next chapter, but for now suffice it to say that they are an essential part of what we are doing in the world, and that any attempt to judge the objective morality of our actions that ignores the social dimension would fall very short of the mark. For example, suppose that each year I give a Christmas turkey to the nearby homeless shelter, and occasionally give a dollar or two to local charities, all the while supporting zoning restrictions and tax laws that create a greater burden on the poor in our community than is right and just. In the long run, wouldn't the homeless and the hungry be better off with a fairer share of the city's services and a smaller slice of its tax burden than with an occasional turkey or handout? To know what we are really doing in the world we need to see what we are doing, not only personally and interpersonally, but socially as well.

*This past section has **distinguished** among personal, interpersonal and social actions. Give both a positive and negative example of how these three types of human actions are **related**.*

Judging the Rightness and Wrongness of Actions

As we have already seen, to understand fully the morality of an action, we need to look at its subjective and objective dimensions. We need to ask if an action expresses and helps to shape good moral character, and whether it actually expresses recognition, respect and a loving response to our neighbors. Although there is some overlap, one could say that, roughly speaking, the subjective moral meaning of an act flows from the agent's *intent* while the act's objective moral meaning is the result of its *means, circumstances, consequences* and viable *alternatives*. Still, since every real human act includes both subjective and objective dimensions, it is only by thoroughly examining all of these factors that we can discover the full moral meaning of a real human act. In taking this approach we rely largely on the work of moral theologian Daniel Maguire in his essay "Ethics: How to Do It."[8]

THE INTENT

What are we trying to accomplish or achieve in this act? What is the end or purpose of our action? Why are we doing this? These questions attempt to identify our *intent* or motive, and, assuming that we are acting with sufficient freedom, understanding and commitment, it is that intent which largely shapes the subjective moral meaning or direction of our acts. For achieving that intent is what we are really trying to do in the act, and this intent (at least partially) reveals our character as choosing good or evil.

It should be clear that for an act to be morally right our intention must be good, for we can hardly be doing the right thing while intending to do evil. So even if we perform an act that does some good (like giving money to the poor), if our intent is evil (buying votes for a political office), then the person performing such an act is doing something morally wrong.

Sometimes, of course, a good intention may require performing an action that involves significant harm, harm which would *not* be justified *except* to achieve a good end or purpose. (Thus, the end does sometimes justify the means.) So, for example, because the surgeon's intent is to heal or to save life, we say it is right for her to cut us open, something we would not allow someone else to do, such as a mugger.

Still, this doesn't mean that a good intent can justify every action or means to accomplish it. For not every particular means is capable of achieving the good intended, at least not without undoing that good in the long run. Sometimes a particular means is so fraught with harm or so disordered that we simply cannot achieve the end we seek by using it. Suppose that as a scientist I could get valuable, even potentially life-

48

saving information by performing highly dangerous and painful experiments upon healthy infants. The harm done to the dignity and health of those innocent children would not only outweigh any benefit that might come from abusing them, it would make a lie of any claim I might have that my aim was to serve humanity, for I would be systematically ignoring, even trampling upon, that very humanity through what I would actually do. Such a means could not really bring me to my supposed end. And if I were willing to perform such an action—such abuse—it may well be that my real intent is not the good of others, but my own prestige or glory.

THE MEANS

How do we accomplish our ends? What tools do we use to get the job done? What concrete steps do we take to reach our purpose? These questions point to the *means,* which helps to shape the objective moral meaning of our actions. As the previous paragraph has illustrated, the means used to accomplish our purpose is very important, for we must be capable of using the means to achieve our good end with the minimum possible harm, and without undermining the good that we are seeking over the long haul.

This implies that for an act to be morally right, the means must "fit" the end. If there is no fit between the means and the end, if the end could be achieved with another means that produces less harm, or if the means ultimately undermines the good sought in the end, then the action itself is wrong.[9]

Normally, in order to find out whether an action is morally right or wrong, we must assess the means in relation to the desired end to see if there is an appropriate fit. And so, for example, we must ask if we would ever kill as a means to repel an unjust and deadly aggressor (yes), or to take revenge for an insult (no). As these examples illustrate, we cannot properly evaluate a means without looking at the intent of the actor. In this way, the assessment of the relationship between intent and means has a kind of action-specific or contextual dimension.

Even so, there do seem to be two sorts of means that most reasonable persons would automatically discard, arguing that there could be no fit between such means and any truly good end. Sometimes the means in question, like *murder,* is known in advance to be an unjust or wrongful sort of action. Thus, while we might consider *killing* as a justifiable means for saving a life, we could not consider murder. (But note that we don't know if an act is murder until we have looked at the fit between the killing and the purpose for which it is being done. Until we've discovered that such a killing is unjustified we can't be sure it is murder.)[10] At other times, however, the means being considered, like rape, the torture of innocents or the use of nuclear weapons against civilians, are so disordered and/or fraught with harm that most prudent persons would argue that such actions could never be appropriate, regardless of intention and regardless of the situation or context at hand.

THE CIRCUMSTANCES

Often enough the "fit" between the means and the intent of an act shows up in the circumstances, the concrete and specific facts of the case or the relevant data of the moral setting in which the act takes place. It is impossible to determine whether a proposed means fits an intention—and thus whether or not the act is morally right—without knowing the circumstances involved.

By looking at the circumstances we might discover that there is indeed another way to restrain the unjust aggressor, which would indicate that killing would not be justified as a means of self-defense. There is no fit. Or we might learn that Mr. and Mrs. Johnson already have six children (two with Down's syndrome), and that natural family planning has been terribly ineffective for them. That might significantly change the moral evaluation of the fit of contraception in that case.

Over the years ethicists have debated whether certain actions could be evaluated morally apart from their circumstances. Some suggest that the universally agreed-upon prohibition of the direct bombing of civilian populations is an example of such an action. But, as you might guess, the counter argument is that such a prohibition has already "factored in" the relevant circumstances, namely that the bombing involves civilians populations. In fact the line between an action and its circumstances is not always easy to draw; they are, in fact, part of the action. Sometimes circumstances are so critical that they determine the moral meaning of the act (such as, that the bombing involved civilians), while other circumstances seem much less significant (such as, that the murder took place on a Tuesday). What does seem clear is that an adequate understanding of the moral meaning of an action needs to include a thorough examination of the relevant circumstances of the case.

THE CONSEQUENCES

What are the likely effects of this action? What benefit(s) or harm(s) will it generate on the personal, interpersonal and social levels? What impact will it have on all three of these levels, not only here and now, but in the long run as well? These questions point to the consequences of an act, another indicator of the moral rightness or wrongness of an action. If we have a call to love others effectively, to really offer help and aid to others, then we must attend to what our acts are doing to them, to what the consequences of our deeds really are.

Clearly we don't wish to act in ways that produce more harm than good, so it makes sense to look at the consequences of our actions, and indeed at the full range of those consequences. Indeed, quite often the full wrongfulness of an action may surface only when the consequences of an action have been examined. To be sure, this does not mean that we look *only* at consequences, or that some combination of particularly good consequences can overcome a bad fit between the means and the intent. It only means, as we've noted, that in order to fully grasp the moral meaning of an act, we must examine all of the consequences involved.

THE ALTERNATIVES

In his essay, Daniel Maguire emphasizes how important it is to investigate alternatives when considering a course of action. It is simply not possible to know whether there is a real fit between the means and the end unless we have explored alternative ways of solving the problem. Was there any other way we could have achieved our goal, any path that involved less harm or did more good? Until we know the answer to such questions, we don't really know if an action was right or wrong. In the medical arena this is common sense. If a patient has a toothache that stems from a cavity, and it is possible to alleviate it by drilling and filling (even though this may not be pleasant), then wouldn't it be wrong to do an extraction? Such is the case with all areas of our moral lives. At times our actions may involve exposure to some degree of harm. Before proceeding with such an action, it is simply the morally responsible thing to do to seek alternatives, to seek ways to minimize the harm in the situation. The judgment of "fit" between intention and means should be made only after all alternatives have been exhausted. Sometimes it may be necessary to do the extraction—sometimes.

Having analyzed these various elements of human action, all of which are crucial in determining the rightness or wrongness of our actions, a concluding word seems in order. It certainly happens that persons (and communities) sometimes seek to do good but end up harming others instead. We make mistakes. We can have good intentions and try to do our best, but fail to do the right thing. Even actions that flow from a good character and good intentions can end up harming others inappropriately. Or it can happen that our actions have a negative impact on others and on the world around us because of ignorance or lack of freedom. In such cases, of course, we may have a diminished degree of culpability or subjective guilt—perhaps none at all.

Still, such an action, from an objective perspective, might well be wrong; harm may have resulted regardless of our intent. This fact should give us some pause, for while it may be a consolation to know that we will not be held culpable for honest mistakes, we need to be concerned about the effects these mistakes have on those around us. Specifically, we must seek to become ever more aware of the effects of our personal, interpersonal and social acts on others. For these acts, like Dr. Jekyll's Mr. Hyde, are out in the world wreaking havoc whether we attend to them or not, and we may be the only ones who can affect them.

In the past, one of the harms of a highly privatized and individualized morality was that we often focused only on those personal acts to which we brought a very high level of personal freedom, understanding and commitment, acts to which we gave a full, and sharply defined consent of the will. As a result, we allowed ourselves to go on blithely ignoring the real harm being generated all the time by our larger interpersonal and social acts. As we will see in the next chapter, there is a need to wake up to what we are doing not only as persons, but as communities.

A Case Study: One of the most significant and controversial events of the twentieth century was the nuclear bombing of the Japanese cities of Hiroshima and Nagasaki by the United States in World War II. How do those actions "stack up" in relation to the elements we have identified that are important for assessing the moral rightness and wrongness of an action?

Some Conclusions—On Moral Actions

1. Actions are important to morality because they express and form our moral character (their subjective dimension) and because of the effects they have upon the world we live in (their objective dimension).

2. The subjective importance of human actions (which take place on the level of deed, habit and fundamental option) is measured by the intention of the agent as well as by the freedom, understanding and commitment persons bring to them. Thus, in determining the subjective rightness of an action (and thus the moral responsibility of a person) we look to the intention, freedom, understanding and commitment of the agent.

3. The objective importance of moral actions (which take place on the personal, interpersonal and societal levels) is measured by the way they help or harm others. Thus, in determining the objective rightness of an action we look to its means, circumstances, consequences and alternatives.

4. It is clearly possible to have actions which are objectively wrong, but for which the agent is subjectively inculpable (innocent of intentional wrongdoing). Still, since there is a duty to find the moral truth about an action, and since errors do harm persons, persons are obliged not only to have good intent, but to make a serious effort to find the truth and "do the right thing."

Chapter Four.
Community: Building Justice

Introduction: Community Character

1. Family Types: When we were kids one of the great joys was spending an overnight at a friend's house, because it gave you a peek inside the world of another family. It was like visiting a foreign country, with its own foods, customs and language. Of all the families we visited there are two whose special feel I remember the clearest: Mary Newcombe's and Steve Lefevre's. Visiting Mary's house was like running away to the circus. Her home was always overflowing with projects, conversation and laughter, and every guest at the dinner table was quickly welcomed into the steady roar of news, entertaining stories and passing plates. Steve's house, on the other hand, reeked of "proper and polite," all full of immaculate rooms, plastic slipcovers that stuck to your back and long silent spaces at the dinner table. It reminded you of a hospital. The funny thing was that, starting when we were in college, Mary and Steve's family "went in" on a vacation house at the shore, and even today you can still tell the difference between July and August in that house. I always visit when the circus is in town.

What is the narrator saying about these two families? Have you ever thought that your family, school or club had a character that was different from that of other families, schools or clubs? How do you think you've been shaped or influenced by the character of your family? How do you think you've helped to shape that character?

2. Robbers: A Social Problem. One day a Samaritan on the way to Jericho came across a man who'd been mugged and left by the road to

die. The Samaritan, being a good man, took the poor fellow to a local inn, where he paid for his lodging and treatment. But going home the next day, the Samaritan came across other victims in the same place, a woman and her small child who had also been waylaid by a gang of robbers. So the Samaritan loaded them on his mule and took them to the inn, again paying for their shelter and care. The third day a very tired (and nearly broke) Samaritan came across a whole family of tourists who'd been attacked by thieves. He put two of the children on his exhausted mule and took the family back to the inn, which was now becoming something of a clinic.

That night the Samaritan and the innkeeper met with the local merchants and chiefs and tried to figure out what to do. Something was very wrong, they all agreed, and they needed, as a group, to come up with some answers. They soon discovered that the local robbers were their own neighbors, poor unemployed peasants who could find no work or food. Since all the farm land was owned by a few families, the poor had no way to feed themselves, and no way to learn a skill because local taxes didn't provide for trade schools. So during the summer they lived off a meager income from fruit and berry picking, and during the winter they roamed the countryside in gangs, robbing tourists and pilgrims, or dying quietly of starvation.

So the merchants and farmers agreed to establish trade schools for the peasants' children and to let the workers buy parcels of land where they could build shelters and raise food for their families. The next year the Samaritan had to pay a tax to the innkeeper to support the local trade schools, but it was cheaper than running his own ambulance service.

What did the Samaritan and his friends learn about the problem they were facing and the sort of solution they would need to formulate? Was the problem just a couple of bad robbers? Could it be solved by just rescuing an occasional mugging victim? What was going on?

Recognizing Communities: The Third Dimension of Moral Experience

The Problem of Overlooking Community

One common mistake we make when thinking about morality is that of "missing the forest for the trees." That is, we are so focused on individual persons and their actions that we often overlook the critical role and impact of the communities we form and belong to, and through which we act in coordinated and influential ways. That turns out to be a serious error indeed, for the "forest" of these communities makes up a third and very important dimension of moral experience. Just as we can't understand the full moral meaning of an action without looking at the person who performed it, so too, we can't have a complete grasp of the morality of persons and their deeds without knowing something about the communities they are shaping and by which they are shaped. For, like saplings, we grow up and produce the fruits of our deeds in the forests of our communities, and both we and our deeds continuously shape and are shaped by the environments of these woods.

Perhaps the reason for this mistake is that too often we forget that persons are not only unique, but social, and that both individuality and community are essential, complementary dimensions of being human.[1] We don't just live and act as individuals. Often it is as *communities* that we both experience and respond to the "moral tug," which (with the help of Enda McDonagh) we have described in chapter 1. Indeed, although their ways of being differ from those of individual persons, communities are also important moral agents, with their own specific character, behavior and influence. For example, in the two stories at the start of this chapter it is clear that the families and communities in question are "more than the sums of their parts." They are integrated, dynamic and organic wholes with lives of their own, related to but distinct from the lives of their members. And it is very clear that the moral call in the second story is addressed not to the individual Samaritan, as good as he is, but to the local community, and it is that community which must respond to this call.

And so we talk about Mary Newcombe's and Steve Lefevre's families as having their own distinctive flavor or character, and we're even willing to judge one of them as better or worse than the other. In fact, we often judge the moral character of whole nations, describing, for example, countries with open democratic structures and/or humane economic systems as good, and states ruled by oppressive dictatorial regimes or divided by racist policies as evil. Furthermore, we are willing to hold these communities responsible for their corporate culture or behavior. So while we would blame the roadside robbers for assaulting travelers to Jericho, we would also point a finger at the unjust economic conditions in the local community. Or when hearing about a corporation involved in a massive oil spill or consumer fraud we are willing to punish not just a few key employees, but the very company itself, because we think corporate policies contributed to these crimes. And finally, we are aware of the influence communities have on the moral formation and behavior of their members. That is why parents want to keep their adolescent children out of fanatical cults, vicious gangs or bigoted groups of any sort. It is also why moral reformers so often try to change not just the hearts and minds of their followers, but also the laws and customs of their societies.

Still, in spite of the fact that in Christian ethics disproportionate attention has sometimes been given to individual actions and persons, the importance of communities has not been without some advocates, particularly in the past century. Whether they were writing about the covenantal society of Israel or the early Christian churches of Corinth and Rome, biblical authors from Isaiah to Paul have railed against unjust or immoral communities and called not merely for personal conversion, but for the social transformation of whole communities. And during the last century Catholic moral teaching has been significantly enriched by a new body of social documents urging Catholics and all persons of good will to work for social justice and structural reform in all sorts of human communities and institutions.[2] Meanwhile, the writings of contemporary feminist and other liberation ethicists urge us to recognize the presence and power of unnoticed social structures oppressing women, minorities and the poor.[3] Finally, the work of family therapy (and indeed of systems theory itself) continues to illustrate the impact of family and group dynamics on the moral development and behavior of persons.[4]

57

The Importance of Community

Communities constitute a critical dimension of moral experience for two reasons. First, as humans, we are both unique and social beings, meaning that both of the concepts "I" and "We," considered separately, are important but incomplete ways of speaking about our identity as humans. As a result, we experience and respond to the moral call *as individuals* and *as communities*. This means that while we are often more immediately aware of the *individual* dimension of moral experience — what "I" am being called to do or be — there is also (and always) an equally real and important *communal* dimension of moral experience — what "We" are being called to do or be. Indeed, as the individual and the community are both essential and complementary dimensions of the human, it is not really possible to have moral experiences which are not communal. Therefore, communities are both *sources* of the moral challenges confronting us and *agents* of our moral response. Put differently, we receive a moral call *from* communities and we need to respond *as* communities.

Second, our human communities have their own distinctive moral character, a character which shapes and is shaped by the character and actions of individual persons. The particular character of our communities will radically affect our ability to respond to the moral call as a community, and at the same time the community's character will shape our individual acts and lives. As we will see below, the ways in which we behave as communities are shaped by, and in turn shape the ways in which we live and act as individuals. We are both students and teachers. In and through — and sometimes over and against — the structures, institutions and systems of our communities, individual consciousness, habits and decisions are formed, and, in turn, we respond, to *re-shape* and *re-form* those very structures. Communities are critical to moral experience because they represent a communal dimension of our lives, a dimension which is consistently interacting with our individual acts and character.

None of this is to argue that individuals and their actions are not important, or that we can be reduced to mere "parts" of communities. As humans we are both individual and communal, and we need to take both of these dimensions of our humanity seriously. Neither completely explains us, nor the full humanity to which we are called.

Moral experience has three dynamic and interdependent dimensions, and an accurate view of morality requires understanding the dynamic balance of these three dimensions. In the past, moralities which have focused too much attention on individual actions have tended to be rigid, authoritarian and legalistic, failing to appreciate the relation between such actions and the freedom, understanding, intention or story of the persons from whom they flowed. At the same time moralities that placed too much stress on individual persons and their intentions tended to overlook the objective reality of our actions. Such "situational" moralities have been overly subjective, providing no coherent or consistent method of decision making. Moralities that forget or misread the importance of communities are just as flawed as those ignoring or overrating the importance of persons or deeds.[5] Authentic moralities are based on an appreciation of the balanced importance of all three dimensions of moral experience: character, action and community.

In the revised version of the good Samaritan story at the start of this chapter what, in your opinion, is the central moral issue that needs to be addressed? Would you have seen that moral issue if you looked only at individual acts or persons? Who is the moral agent that needs to respond to this issue? What happens if we ask one individual, like the Samaritan, to deal with this problem?

Take a few moments and think about two or three communities you belong to (a nation, a church, a race, an economic group, a family, a school, a political party, etc.). First, try to identify some moral obligations or duties that these groups have to its members or other groups. (What moral duties does America have to its members, other nations or the global community?) Second, try to describe the specific moral character of these communities (their institutional virtues and vices).

Individualism

One big reason that we in the United States might tend to overlook the moral significance of communities is that our culture suffers from a serious case of individualism. Individualism ignores the social dimension of human experience and reduces the complex mystery of persons to their uniqueness. Since persons are then seen primarily as individuals with some important but secondary social skills or needs, human communities and their structures are necessarily relegated to the sidelines of morality—mere circumstances or background material. The influence of individualism is widespread in American culture, reaching back at least to our colonial days and expressed in economic and political structures stressing personal liberties over social obligations.[6] And while contemporary Catholic social thought is deeply critical of individualism, there are some ways, especially in the past, in which Catholicism itself embodied and passed along a good deal of this individualism. The manner in which the sacrament of penance has been celebrated (at least until recently) is an example. With so much emphasis on the confession and remission of personal (translate private) sins, it is not hard to see how the immorality of corrupt groups and unjust social structures was so often overlooked. After all, it's probably easier to imagine a camel going through the eye of a needle than an unjust corporation squeezing into the confessional box.[7]

There are three serious problems with individualism's understanding of moral experience.[8] First, by reducing persons to mere individuals it ignores their social character, overlooking the network of social ties which both oblige and nourish them. To paraphrase Shakespeare's Shylock, "Hath not a person neighbors, children, sisters or cousins? And need not a person parents, friends, family or lovers?" Apparently not. Second, individualism is blind to the social systems, structures and institutions which profoundly shape our lives. As a result, it acts as if the moral or immoral behavior of persons were not seriously affected by social forces. One wonders, then, why crime, violence and drug addiction always seem more prevalent where there is poverty, unemployment, discrimination and ignorance. Are these mere coincidences? Third, because it ignores the impact of social forces, individualism offers personal solutions to social problems. Such an approach is not moral, but "moralistic," heaping burdens on people's shoulders without lifting a finger to help. For when individualism urges people to fight oppressive and alienating social systems with only the firm resolve to behave well in interpersonal exchanges, it sets them up for failure for which it implies they have only themselves to blame.

Though not as serious a problem for our culture, it is also possible to overvalue the role and impact of communities by overlooking persons and their free actions. This happens when people reduce themselves or others to mere cogs within a system. When Nazi physicians and military officers excused themselves for barbarous behavior by saying that they "were only following orders," they seem to have forgotten that as human beings with knowledge and freedom, they did not *have* to follow those orders. When wealthy and powerful people argue that admittedly unfair political and economic systems are "simply the way things are" and cannot be changed, they are too modest about the capacity of persons to reform groups and structures. And when groups of persons begin to think of themselves or others as merely victims, they surrender the power and responsibility they have as persons. At the same time, when people think that changing social structures will eliminate all evil and injustice, they have forgotten the importance of good persons and right actions. For we cannot create a society so morally good that there will be no need for virtue or right actions. Thus, whether fatalistic or idealistic, these approaches overlook the role and impact of persons and their deeds, forgetting it is "we, the people," who are always struggling "to form a more perfect union."

In order to understand adequately the communal dimension of moral experience, it is necessary to do three things. First, we need to examine the identity, formation and influence of groups, paying particular attention to their relationship to individual persons and actions. Second, we need to discern what it is that constitutes a "good" community. And third, we need to articulate how it is that good communities are built or achieved.

In Carlos Fuentes's novel A Good Conscience, *Jaime Ceballos, the young nephew of a wealthy Mexican family makes friends with a peasant revolutionary and discovers that his own very religious family has made and maintained their wealth by oppressing the poor. Meanwhile, his uncle Balcarcel drags the young man to the parish priest demanding that he confess his adolescent sexual fantasies, lest he be condemned to hell. What does the uncle's focus on Jaime's individual sins conveniently overlook?*

About thirty years ago our medical technology developed the capacity for organ transplants, and many ethicists wrestled with the morality of transferring a healthy kidney from one person to another. Given

the present health care crisis in America, and indeed the dreadful state
of medical care in many third world nations, can you think of some
social or communal questions we ought to raise about this practice?

The Identity, Formation and Influence of Groups

To say, however, that we are social beings means more than just
acknowledging that we are interpersonal or even relational creatures.
It means we are individual and communal. We don't just *belong* to
families. Instead, as a popular song says, "we *are* family." To return to
our tree metaphor, persons grow up and live and work in the "forests"
of organized groups and communities. Our social nature points to the
fact that we both form and are formed by these groups and their structures. We are these groups and the individuals who make them up.

What are groups and communities? They are stable and organized
associations of persons, allowing their members to develop and flourish as persons and to coordinate their common efforts in beneficial
ways. The communities we form, however, consist not only of their
members, but also of established patterns of communication, behavior
and thought called systems, structures and institutions.[9] Structures are
set patterns of relating between various individuals or groups of members. Family life is an example of a structure in society. Within these
structures there are certain established practices known as institutions.
Such institutions, like marriage, are formalized ways of behaving
which provide a model of how things are to be done in this group.
When groups of structures are pulled together into organized patterns
they form what are called systems.

The key to understanding the dynamic relation among the three
dimensions of moral experience (character, actions and communities)
is to be found in examining the processes by which persons form (and
re-form) communities, and by which successive generations of persons
are themselves formed or affected by these groups and their structures.
Mark O'Keefe, in his text on social sin, offers an excellent sketch of
these processes, breaking them down into three fundamental stages;
persons make groups, groups exist and *groups make persons.*[10]

PERSONS MAKE GROUPS

Over two centuries ago a group of American colonists meeting in Philadelphia decided that they could no longer live under the tyranny of a foreign king, and so they made choices and took actions that led to the formation of a new nation and, in time, to all of its laws, customs and practices. In this way the ideas and choices of these historical persons were brought into the world, or **externalized,** eventually becoming the community we call the United States of America, as well as the established judicial, political and cultural systems, structures and institutions which give it shape. This is the story of every group, for such associations and their structures come into existence or are modified as the result of choices and actions taken by people at some point in history.

GROUPS EXIST

Once persons have formed groups and their accompanying structures, these formations begin to take on a life of their own. In time the United States and its systems, structures and institutions were recognized by persons as real entities, having an identity that endured long after the deaths of the founding fathers. Maps were redrawn and embassies set up in recognition of this new nation, while the executive, legislative and judicial branches of the government went about the daily business of applying the principles of the Constitution and administering the country. In this way the choices and actions of the colonists had become **objectified** as a community with definite structures.

Over time, however, it often happens that such groups are not only objectified as distinctive entities, but are actually **reified** in the minds of many people. This means, for example, that the United States and its structures are seen as realities completely independent of the people who formed and sustain them. In this way it is often forgotten that, to paraphrase Lincoln, this nation and its structures compose "a government of the people, by the people and for the people." The communities, institutions and structures not only need to be recognized and received, but in an ongoing way they need to be *re-shaped* and *re-formed*.

63

GROUPS MAKE PEOPLE

Once these seemingly independent groups and their structures have been in place for a while, successive generations of people come to see them as "the way things are," or "the way things have always been." Like the mountains and rivers, or the stars in the heavens, groups and their structures can come to be seen as part of the natural or God-given order of things. Too often no one thinks to question whether this is the only or the right way to do things. This is because the systems, structures and institutions of the group have been **internalized** by later generations of people, thereby shaping their very patterns of thinking, communicating and behaving. And so the group made by the colonists then makes their grandchildren. This is called socialization.

Two classic fairy tales illustrate the process of internalization. In *The Emperor's New Clothes,* the people around the emperor fail to recognize that he is naked because the power of the state is being used to intimidate them. Politicians and townsfolk are afraid of losing their jobs, so they convince themselves that they really can "see" the emperor's new clothes. It is only a child who has not yet internalized this idea who notices that the emperor is not wearing anything. On the other hand, in *The Ugly Duckling,* a young swan grows up in a society of ducks and ends up internalizing the way ducks think, feel and act, coming to the (erroneous) conclusion that he is in fact a duck. The duck society has definitely gotten inside of his head and formed his consciousness.

Once we understand the ways groups are formed and in turn form persons, we can see the importance of both examining the communities we belong to and working to improve them through reform of their systems, structures and institutions. This means discerning what sorts of communities and structures are good and how we might go about building good (or at least better) communities.

Take two or three communities to which you belong, or have belonged, and describe some ways in which you have internalized certain beliefs, attitudes and/or practices of these communities. Example: Are there some ways in which commercials and advertisements offer a particular view of ourselves and our world? If you put your child in front of the TV for about twenty hours a week for about eighteen years, what sorts of messages do you think s/he might internalize?

As new parents in a community, you are not satisfied with the youth organizations available for your adolescent children. At a neighborhood parents' meeting you are interviewing a person your group is hiring to organize a new youth group. First, what kinds of values or beliefs do you want this group to "teach" or "instill" in your children? Second, what kinds of structures or practices should this group have in order to teach such values?

Justice: The Morally Good Community

A good community might be described as a society whose structures and institutions help persons to flourish. Today we often speak about "healthy" or " whole" communities as opposed to ones that are chaotic and dysfunctional. Of course we also tend to think of peaceful and loving communities as the ideal, contrasting them with violent or cruel societies. And in modern politics we generally describe free and democratic communities as good, likewise condemning oppressive and tyrannical regimes as evil. There is nothing wrong with any of these responses, and indeed they each say something quite true about good communities. But for thousands of years, when philosophers, citizens and prophets have sought to describe the sorts of communities we ought to build and live in, they have cried, above all, for justice. Indeed, the American philosopher John Rawls argues that "justice is the first virtue of social institutions," a notion that finds echoes in both the writings of Western philosophers like Plato and biblical prophets like Isaiah, Jeremiah and Hosea.[11]

Justice in Athens

Beginning with Plato's *Republic* (Book IV), classical and contemporary Western thinkers from Aristotle to Rawls have described the general virtue of justice as the central virtue of social groups and institutions, and have described the good community as the just community. Comparing society to a human body, Western authors have argued that justice might be called the "health" of the good community, providing as it does for a peaceful and harmonious order by governing the workings and relations of all its parts in a reasonable and orderly fashion. Like a good administrator of a household or a talented conductor of an orchestra, justice coordinates the various efforts of all the members so as to provide a reasonable order to the workings of the organism, thus creating harmony out of the contributions of the many. And so Plato describes justice as, "that quality, I mean, of every person doing their own work, and not being a busybody."

What is distinctive about this conductor, however, is that the harmony which the general virtue of justice creates cannot be imposed forcefully on its members, cannot rely on deception or manipulation, and cannot violate the rights of any members of the group. Instead, justice aims at a harmony resulting from the reasonable and moral ordering of society, *a good order that any reasonable and free person would accept.* So, while apartheid in South Africa or slavery in antebellum Mississippi may have seemed harmonious and lawful to the white landowners, neither of these systems was either reasonable or just. In fact, like all unjust communities, both of these societies employed very high levels of violence to maintain their semblance of harmony. Such violence, deception or manipulation are not components of justice, which only requires persons to do their "fair" part, nothing more and nothing less.

Justice, then, is harmony for the whole built upon fairness for each of its members (whether groups or persons). Ensuring this fair treatment of individual persons and groups is the task of the four types of justice: commutative, legal, distributive and social. Commutative justice deals with the fair exchange of goods and services between individuals, while distributive justice ensures that each person or group contributes and receives a fair (proportionate) share of the common good. Legal justice has to do with the individual's obligations to the larger society, while social justice looks to the establishment and maintenance of just and equitable systems and structures in the community. Social justice seeks to provide for the full and fair participation of all persons and groups in the governance of political, economic, cultural and social institutions, and aims at correcting any oppressive and alienating trends within the community. Where there is no social justice, there is probably not much distributive, commutative or legal justice either, and there is certainly not much harmony.

Although this classical notion of justice as the foundation of a harmonious community built upon fairness nicely stresses both the common good and the equality, rights and duties of persons, our modern grasp of justice has often been corrupted by individualism. For, instead of paying attention to the rich social character of this virtue and its commitment to the "health" of the community, we have tended to equate justice with the punishment of criminals and/or the protection of civil liberties, ignoring our larger duty to work for the common good. We have too often reduced "justice" to the work of our criminal courts, forgetting that health, education and welfare are also critical tasks of the just society. It is hard to see how such a narrow vision of justice can provide for a good or healthy community.[12]

As noted, we have slipped into this corrupted vision of justice because the blinders of individualism screen out the social ties that bind us to our neighbors, to the social structures required to create and sustain a just community, and to the special duties we have toward the weakest in our societies. As long as we think that we are, first and foremost, individuals, and that our social obligations are weak, secondary ties, then the heart of justice will always be about defending our personal freedoms and punishing those who harm us. But such a stripped down view of either ourselves or the concept of justice lacks an adequate grasp of the common good, the need for social justice and the importance of compassion and love. Such skeletal justice can define the minimal standards of individual behavior in exchanges between persons, but it cannot construct truly good communities. It pays insufficient attention to the social systems and structures required for a good community and ignores the social obligations we have to all our neighbors, particularly the weakest and poorest in society.

In response to its crime problems America has developed one of the largest prison populations in the world. Admitting that the criminal courts are clearly a part of the work of justice, what other works or systems might be needed to create a more just society?

Justice in Jerusalem

Justice was also an important notion for biblical authors. Indeed, as biblical scholar Gerhard von Rad wrote, "There is absolutely no concept in the Old Testament with so central a significance for all relationships of human life as that of *sedaqah* (justice/righteousness)."[13] This was especially true of prophets like Isaiah, Jeremiah and Amos, who were continuously reminding the Israelites that as God's people they were to imitate Yahweh's steadfast love, mercy and *justice*, which meant they were to treat others as God had first treated them. For, by rescuing them from the Egyptians and making a covenant with them, God had fashioned a holy people out of Abraham's descendants, and as Yahweh's chosen community they were to practice the Lord's own justice by being faithful to their neighbors. In particular, *sedaqah* demanded that they were not to forget the widows, orphans or the poor and alien of the land, for they themselves had once been such folk, and their God had delivered them from slavery, exile and oppression.[14] As the author of Exodus writes, "You shall not wrong or oppress a resident alien, for you were aliens in the land of Egypt. You shall not abuse any widow or orphan. If you do abuse them, when they cry out to me, I will surely heed their cry" (22:21–23).

Therefore, to remember the poor and lowly was not only to show obedience to God, it was to take up the very mantle of justice. Indeed, according to the prophets, Israel's treatment of the *anawim* (Hebrew for "little ones") was the central criteria of its justice and its faithfulness to God. As Jeremiah and Isaiah write,

> Thus says the Lord: "Act with justice and righteousness, and deliver from the hand of the oppressor anyone who has been robbed. And do no wrong or violence to the alien, the orphan, and the widow." (Jeremiah 22:3–4)

> Is such the fast that I choose, a day to humble oneself? Is it to bow down the head like a bull rush, and to lie in sackcloth and ashes? Will you call this a fast, a day acceptable to the Lord? Is not this the fast that I choose: to loose the bonds of injustice, to undo the thongs of the yoke, to let the oppressed go free and to break every yoke? Is it not to share your bread with the hungry, and bring the

homeless poor into your house; when you see the naked, to cover
them, and not to hide yourself from your own kin? (Isaiah 58:5–7)

In later biblical writings, as in the book of Tobit, *sedeqah* became a
demand to give alms for the poor, while Christian authors, such as Paul
and James, continuously reminded the followers of Jesus that they had
a moral obligation to share with the poor and to care for those in the
margins. Indeed, according to the famous last judgment scene of
Matthew 25:31-46, only those who have fed the hungry, clothed the
naked, sheltered the homeless and visited the sick or imprisoned will
enter into God's reign; all others will perish. Justice to the neighbor,
especially the neighbor in need, is critical to salvation.

Within the last century many Catholics and other Christians have
been reawakened to the social demands of God's justice as it appears
in the Bible, and have become increasingly aware of the moral call to
recognize our obligations to others, particularly those in the margins.
Modern popes and bishops, as well as theologians, have argued that
God's call to *sedeqah* makes demands upon us as a believing community and challenges us to reform our social structures and institutions
so that all, especially the poor, will find a place.

Whether speaking about the covenantal community of Israel, the
body of Christ or the family of the human race, what these biblical and
theological understandings of justice have in common is that they do
not flow from an individualistic vision. Instead, these visions of justice
pay attention to the communities in which we live, the deep communal
bonds that tie us to *all* our neighbors, and the social systems and structures required to build justice in these communities. For both biblical
and contemporary authors assert that we are social beings living in
community with others, and that the work of justice depends upon recognizing and honoring the full range of our social obligations, particularly to the poor. Above all this means creating just communities by
becoming just persons *and* by building just systems and structures.

If we were to combine the insights of these differing perspectives,
we might describe a good or just community as having the following
traits. *First,* in a good community system, structures and institutions
exist to serve the complete and authentic development of all persons
and to ensure their full participation in every aspect of the life of the
community. The Sabbath (and banks and governments and churches)
were made for the good of all women and men, and not the other way

69

around. This means, *second,* that these structures and institutions must provide for the adequate protection of personal liberties, for the provision of those basic goods and services required for participation in community life and for the full exercise of each member's authority as a person. It also means that, *third,* all persons and groups will be treated fairly in the distribution of burdens and benefits and the exchange of goods and actions. *Fourth,* systems, structures and institutions will provide for the common good by ensuring the presence of freedom, truth, justice and genuine peace (even solidarity) among its members. And *fifth,* in a good community persons and groups will constantly monitor and reform structures tending to alienate and marginalize the weak and powerless. They will do this by making a commitment to stand in solidarity with, and act as advocates for, the poor and powerless, and by striving to overcome every oppressive and divisive structure.

Imagine that you have traveled back in time to the end of the eighteenth century and that you have a voice in writing the Constitution of the United States. What changes would you make to form a more just society, particularly if you were concerned about practicing biblical justice?

Creating Moral Communities

Our final question has to do with how we can create good communities. Since most of the communities we belong to are already created, it's probably more accurate to say that our question concerns how we shall *reform* or *change* the unjust communities or structures we encounter. For in the real world most of the work of building good communities is primarily a labor of reform. And since any real reform of human communities can only be effected and sustained if the hearts and minds of those making up these communities are also transformed, it should be clear that the work of building just communities must involve a two-pronged process involving both personal conversion and structural transformation.

The personal conversion required to reform communities has been described by some liberation theologians as a "conscientization," a process of being awakened to the demands of justice.[15] This process often begins when we are forced (sometimes rather painfully) to recognize the presence of some social injustice—like segregation or discrimination—in our society. Sometimes we may know about such practices, but as long as they don't seem to cause us any personal consternation, we may keep them on the periphery of our minds rather successfully. Only when we are brought face to face with such injustices—as has happened in recent years to many people in regard to the problem of sexual harassment in the workplace—do such social concerns move from the edge to the center of our consciousness and our conscience.

Once awakened to such issues, we may become willing to address the injustices, finding perhaps that our investigations and work provokes hostility and resistance from those practicing and benefiting from such wrongs. In our day Bishop Oscar Romero of El Salvador discovered that when he tried to address the economic injustices in his country he found himself the target of all sorts of criticism and violence. Often the process of "conscientization" demands that we make a choice to press on or to retreat. Indeed, it is not uncommon that this choice involves picking sides in a confrontation, at least in the sense of standing with those harmed by injustice and against the structures and systems that oppress them. For Bishop Romero this personal conversion meant publicly criticizing his government, celebrating the sacraments with the poor of his country and ultimately being executed as an enemy of those powerful forces oppressing the poor. And in the process of his journey from complacency to solidarity with the suffering, Bishop Romero helped in the work of transforming his community.

At the same time, real reform in communities will not occur unless there is also a transformation of social structures, institutions and systems. As we saw previously in the description of good communities, unjust structures must be changed so that all persons and groups can participate and develop fully within the society so that all their rights are protected and so that they are treated fairly. Achieving such reforms in a society is not an easy process and may involve a number of paths.[16] Still, three steps that are often seen as part of this reform are: (1) publicly proclaiming a prophetic word, challenging and unmasking the myths and lies used to defend or cover up unjust structures and institutions; (2) performing symbolic actions (such as sit-ins at lunch counters or demonstrations against apartheid) that confront unjust structures and

71

force people to make choices; (3) taking political actions to change the actual structures and institutions themselves, and to force others to abide by the new law.

In the work of building just communities the twin processes of personal conversion and structural transformation are essential and interdependent. It is not possible to have one without the other, for each nourishes and supports the other and, indeed, makes the other possible. Structural transformation both depends on and provides a context for personal conversion; any personal conversion which does not lead to structural reform is not only incomplete, but inauthentic. In order to create a just community there must be people who care about justice. At the same time, personal conversion often depends upon the work of structural transformation. For the struggle toward change confronts and educates sleeping consciences to the presence of injustice, while structural changes free both oppressors and victims from the social forces that led them to accept unjust structures and conditions in the first place. Together these interlocking processes form a single path to genuine reform and the creation of good (or at least better) communities.

Building Just Communities—
Some Conclusions

1. The communities we come from, form and constitute are an often overlooked but important third dimension of moral experience.

2. Created and sustained by persons and their actions, communities take on a distinctive character and life through the formation of systems, structures and institutions and, in turn, generate their own significant impact on both the moral formation and conduct of persons.

3. Given the tremendous importance of communities, it is critical to learn the difference between good and bad ones, and to discover how we might go about building the former and reforming the latter.

4. Overall, good communities may be described as rich in justice, and are constructed through personal conversion and structural transformation.

Chapter Five.
Morality and Stories

Introduction: Good Stories

1. "Then we must first of all, it seems, control the storytellers. Whatever noble story they compose we shall select, but a bad one we must reject. Then we shall persuade nurses and mothers to tell their children those we have selected and by those stories to fashion their minds far more than they can shape their bodies by handling them. The majority of the stories they now tell must be thrown out."

Plato, The Republic (Book III, 377c)

Why is Socrates concerned with controlling the storytellers? Why have American politicians so often been concerned about movies and television? Why, in so many countries, is there so much censorship, not just of journalists and reporters, but of cartoonists, film makers and script writers? What is so powerful about stories that we can't even let adults read them?

2. Two thirds of the way through her Friday lecture on the Civil Rights movement the history professor realized that she had lost about half of her audience. In the late afternoon heat several students had stopped taking notes, seven or eight were fighting to keep their eyes open, three were looking out the window, and in the second row Alice Thornton was twirling strands of her hair, checking for split ends. Capping her marker and stepping away from the overhead projector, the instructor pulled up a corner of her desk and said, "Put down your pens. I want to tell you a story about a middle-aged black woman who decided one day that she was just too tired and annoyed to give up her seat to a white man, and in that moment started a protest that ended up

crippling the entire bus system of Montgomery, Alabama and led to the most important transformation of American society since the Civil War. Her name was Rosa Parks, and the way I know about her is that my aunt Meredith was, on that fateful afternoon, seated just two rows behind her. You see, Miss Parks, who was on her way home from....."

The reaction was instantaneous. Napping, notetaking and split end checking came to a dead stop, and as the bemused storyteller regaled her rapt audience with the story of Rosa Parks and the Montgomery bus boycott, she sorely wished that she had good stories for all of her lessons, knowing her students would remember this tale long after they had forgotten her outlines. Why, she wondered ruefully, was that so?

What is it that makes a story so interesting to us, that makes us perk up when we hear one? Why does a well-told story capture us so, and what is going on in us when we listen to it? Even more so, what could we actually be learning when we hear or read a good story?

The Moral Importance of Stories

Is there anyone who doesn't love a good story, who wouldn't put down the paper or stop what they're doing to catch a good tale? Don't we all feel the slight tingle of excitement, the little quickening of attention that comes with hearing the words, "Let me tell you a story," particularly if the storyteller is any good at her craft? "Oh, I've got a story for you," we hear over the phone line, and we're all ears.

Stories engage us, excite us, entertain us. We feel ourselves drawn to them, sucked in by their undertow and pulled all so willingly into their imaginary worlds. They are, in a very real sense, *wonder*-ful, for they engage our wonder and imagination in a way that few other things do, and we have loved them since we were very small children.

And yet, perhaps because they are so enjoyable, so deliciously pleasurable, we often fail to understand just how important and powerful stories are. Indeed, it is just because stories are so entertaining that we can easily forget how much more than entertainment they really can be. Like the people of Troy who opened their city gates to let in the Greeks' "gift" of a horse, we are often lulled by the playfulness and enchantment of stories, thinking that they are simply children's toys, little diversions from the serious world of adults. We say, after all, that they're "just stories," tales one tells to small children. And even our "adult fiction"—our mysteries, romances, thrillers and science fiction, the stuff we read on the plane, the train and the beach—may seem to be little more than fanciful vacations from reality, quick trips to the sandbox of the mind. They're not real, we think, and we just read them to escape. Not much harm or gain in either direction.

But it's a mistake to take stories so lightly, the same sort of mistake that has led many a librarian to put Jonathan Swift's political satire, *Gulliver's Travels,* in the children's section. Indeed, in the Bible (2 Samuel 12:1–15) King David learns what an error it is to underestimate a story when the prophet Nathan regales him with an after-dinner tale about a rich man who murders a pauper's only lamb. Enraged by the injustice of this crime, David roundly condemns anyone who would do such a thing, only to be reminded that his adultery with Bathsheba and the murder of her husband Uriah has made *him* just such a person. The king has been trapped by the story, drawn in by its perfume and deeply stung by its message.

Like many stories, Nathan's little tale of a lamb turns out to be something of a wolf in sheep's clothing, and reminds us that, in spite of their coy wrappings, stories have a tremendous moral power. For good or ill, they can challenge, influence and even transform us. A well-told tale can pierce us to the heart, give us a fresh insight on what the right moral choice might be, or provide the encouragement or motivation necessary to make that choice. Moreover, some stories can show us our character flaws and biases, transform the way we see ourselves and the world, and—every now and then—start a revolution. Surely there is something playful about a story, but a good story ought not be mistaken for a toy.

The major reason that stories are so important to morality is that they express and form (and *re-form*) how we see ourselves and the world around us, both as persons and as communities. Our stories are not just our literature and entertainment; they are our theology, philosophy and politics. In the stories we choose to attend to, believe in and repeat to others, we are expressing and shaping ourselves as persons and communities. Therefore, on the personal and communal levels our stories express and shape our moral character.

If that weren't true, why would Socrates be so concerned about "controlling the storytellers" in the opening passage of this chapter? And indeed, why was the church of the Inquisition so concerned about condemning certain books and stories? Why did Hitler and Stalin burn books and imprison writers? Why were Hollywood screenwriters and directors (but not accountants) blacklisted in the '50s, Why have some public schools banned *Catcher in the Rye* or *Tom Sawyer*? If stories weren't important, what would be so frightening about George Orwell's *1984,* or Ray Bradbury's *Fahrenheit 451*, novels in which a fascist state controls or destroys all of our stories? If stories didn't have any real adult power, why did Jesus so often—and so effectively— teach with them, and why has his story become so important and trans- formative to hundreds of millions of people?

It ought to be clear, then, that stories are important for morality. The remainder of this chapter will explore just how that is so. First, we will discuss what scholars have referred to as the "narrative" quality of experience, including moral experience. This will shed light on just how it is that stories can "work" on us so powerfully. Second, we will examine the importance of stories to moral character. Third, we will discuss the role of stories as moral teachers, the way they can impact not only our minds, but, much more pervasively, our lives. Fourth, we will take note of various kinds of stories; different kinds of stories do different kinds of things. And finally, we will ask "What sorts of stories should we tell and become?" Some stories disclose the truth, others tell lies; some stories help, others harm. How can we know the difference? What kinds of stories are worth remembering and passing on? What kinds of stories do we want our lives to be about?

"The Narrative Quality of Experience": How Stories "Work" (On Us)

It may be tempting to think that the real moral importance of stories is to be found in the point that the storyteller is trying to make, for indeed every story seems to have some sort of moral or lesson to offer its readers or listeners. Certainly many stories do teach something very specific about how we should act or what we should do. How many of us as children were told stories about youngsters who played with matches, didn't look both ways before crossing the street, or accepted a ride from a stranger? And yet, if the central importance of stories was that they taught us what to do in a particular setting, then such tales would simply be a more entertaining way of teaching us something that we could just as well have learned from a law or a lecture, and the real meaning of every story could easily be distilled into a neat little lesson, a bumper sticker or sound bite we could memorize and follow. But that, as we know, just isn't so.

Now certainly some stories, particularly crude and moralistic ones, can be reduced to a single point, but that is because they are not great stories to begin with. Instead, they tend to be terrible stories, told with little imagination and intended mainly to browbeat an audience into accepting some rule or lesson. Such stories are usually accompanied by a wagging finger and the interrogatory, "NOW do you understand what I was saying?!" These stories don't seduce us; instead they are wielded like hammers, and we usually feel beaten up, not transformed, by them.

But just try reducing a really good story to a sound bite! If you have ever been deeply touched or moved by a story of extraordinary power, you certainly know the folly of trying to "sum up" this experience in "a lesson." *Romeo and Juliet* is about the trials of teenage love? *The Red Badge of Courage* teaches us to stand up for our country? Think of how often you have seen a movie which completely failed to capture the rich texture and passion of a novel, or how flat the plot summaries in Cliff Notes are when compared to the actual books. How often have we just come to the end of our patience and said, "Look, I can't explain it. You'll just have to read the story for yourself." Real stories, great stories, have a power which goes far beyond any single lesson. They are far more than an entertaining preamble to a moral.

The real moral power of stories flows from the fact that they *engage* us as persons, and the best of them engage us so fully, so effectively, draw us so profoundly outside of ourselves and get so deep inside our imagination that it is simply not possible for us to be the same persons after such an encounter. They shape our character. Indeed, the result of a good story is not that we now "know something" we didn't know before. It is that we now "see" things as we have never before seen them. Good stories, by altering the inner landscape of our imagination, leave us in a different place. Such stories slip past our logical and linear defenses and, like the rabbit in *Alice's Adventures in Wonderland,* draw us tumbling and falling into their world. And because they engage us at the level of our imagination, stories do not simply *inform* us, rather, they *transform* or *re-form* us.

In recent years scholars from a variety of fields have attempted to analyze just how it is that stories are able to do such things to us, just how it is that they work on us. In an important article about this in 1971, Stephen Crites named and described what he called the "narrative quality" of experience. We human beings, he argued, can't help but experience our lives as an ongoing story. Life is "durational." Our experience in every moment of our lives is shaped by our capacities to remember and to anticipate.[1] To say this more simply, there is always a story going on: our story. Although most of the time we may not attend to it very consciously, in every moment of our lives we are attempting to act and live in a way that makes sense in relation to who we have been (memory) and who we hope to be (anticipation).

If what Crites and others are suggesting is true, then it may explain (partially at least) why it is that stories engage us so fully and so powerfully. The fact is that *we ourselves are "storied" people.* In the circumstances in which we find ourselves, we "characters" are always attempting to make sense out of things, to interpret our personal, interpersonal and social experience in light of our previous life stories and the stories we hope to fashion. What we hear in the stories that are told to us, then, are echoes of our own lives, echoes not just of who we are and have been, but also of who we might be. Because all stories are about persons (whether they appear as humans, animals or aliens) wrestling with crises or trying to make sense of their lives, every story can become our story; we hear a piece of ourselves in the story of another.[2] In this way a really good story doesn't just offer a report of events or the description of someone else's experience, but an *invitation* to consider—even to experience imaginatively—the implications that their narrative holds for *us*. A good story invites us to get inside of it, and to allow it to get inside of ourselves. Inside a really good story we end up wondering not just what will happen next, but what *ought* to happen in our own lives.

Theologian Robert McAfee Brown has described this "meeting of stories" this way:

> This, it seems to me, is how we must approach literature that seeks
> to instruct, to inform, to challenge, to liberate. Its importance to us

is that on some level it "touches" us. However different the story on the lap of the reader is from the story going on in his or her life, if the reader can trust the author, the two stories will meet at some point and the reader's own life story will be up for reexamination.[3]

In really great stories we "meet," are confronted with, sometimes riveting accounts of our own humanity, accounts that often stretch— and sometimes shatter—the comfortable and constricted ways in which we see ourselves and our world. Indeed, the best of our stories are forever carving out a richer, meatier grasp of what it means to be human, unpacking in all its depth both the depravity of which we are capable and the full humanity to which we are called. Great stories show us parts of our humanity, or indeed hidden potential within us which we might not have considered otherwise. In that way they enrich our sense of who we have been, who we are now and who we might become. Imagine, for example, a world in which we did not know the things that *Robinson Crusoe, Huck Finn, Pride and Prejudice, Les Miserables, The Color Purple* or *The Grapes of Wrath* have shown us about ourselves. And, what might be worse, imagine a world in which we did not feel the tug or invitation these stories offer.

Many stories, of course, are too thin or flat—pencil sketches bearing a single insight, a lone message for one particular listener, time or place; and before long we outgrow and discard such tales like yesterday's news. But other stories seem to thrive with the passing of time, offering fresh and undiscovered insights, perspectives and questions. These stories deserve the name "classics," because they continue to bear fruit reading after reading, generation after generation, in culture after culture.

In the second story at the beginning of this chapter, a teacher tells her bored students the story of Rosa Parks, the Montgomery bus boycott and the Civil Rights movement. Assuming that this story is being told to a group of mostly white students more than thirty years after the events in question, what could a well-told story hope to do for these students? Does such a story have any implications for their lives? Can you think of any great stories (fiction or fact) that would offer the same benefit to this audience? What are they, and why do you consider them important?

79

Stories Express Who We Are

Since we ourselves "are" stories, it makes sense that stories would represent the best way to speak about who we are, and, in fact, stories may be the best way to speak about the moral meaning of our actions, as well as our moral meaning as persons and communities. This is not to say that other kinds of speaking or writing are not both important and helpful, but only that a full grasp of moral experience is probably not possible without some use of stories, or that stories, especially good ones, bring something unique and special to our understanding of morality.

As human agents, our actions are part of the ongoing conversation we are having with God, ourselves and our neighbors, and, as we saw from the chapter on actions, we can only make full sense of these deeds and choices when they are situated within the unfolding story of these conversations. In the words of H. Richard Niebuhr,

> ...the questions we raise about [our actions] are not only those of their rightness or wrongness, their goodness or badness, but of their fitness or unfittingness in the total movement, the whole conversation. We seek to have them fit into the whole as a sentence fits into a paragraph in a book, a note into a chord in a movement in a symphony....[4]

The full moral import of our actions, in other words, can only be grasped when they have been placed within a human story. We cannot fully grasp the moral identity of our actions without appreciating the specific moral demands and challenges God and our neighbors have placed before us, the intentions and motives from which our acts spring, the specific means chosen (and/or discarded) to achieve our ends, the concrete circumstances surrounding the actions and the consequences which our deeds have produced. And, of course, if we had all of that information about an action, plus a sense of how the agent moved into and through her choices, we would have a story, for only a story could do all of that for us. As Stanley Hauerwas writes,

> A story, thus, is a narrative account that binds events and agents together in an intelligible pattern. We do not tell stories simply because they provide a more colorful way to say what can be said in a different way, but because there is no other way we can

articulate the richness of intentional activity—that is, behavior that is purposeful but not necessary. For as any good novelist knows, there is always more involved in any human action than can be said. To tell a story often involves our attempt to make intelligible the muddle of things we have done in order to have a self.[5]

In a similar fashion, stories are an excellent way to speak about our character. We recognize this when we remember, as theologian Timothy O'Connell points out, that persons have a fourth dimension: time. "But to understand (persons) more completely, we must also watch them move. Human life is temporal life, changing life. There is a past and a future, and they are at least as important as the present."[6] And the only way to adequately express this movement through time is in narrative. So perhaps it's not too surprising that we not only spend our lives attending to and internalizing various stories, weaving them into the fabric of the story we call our self, but that we also spend our lives living out and authoring that same story.

The fact that we are "storied" creatures and that stories are the best way to express our character can be seen in two ways. First, if we really want to know someone's character, if we want to know *who* someone is—whether that someone is our "self" or someone else—we must ask for their *story,* not just for a list of the facts of their life, or even a description of their virtues and vices, but their biography. For to really know someone we need to know the warp and weave of their life, the ebb and flow of it; we need to see them unfold or wither as the hero, villain or victim of that life. (To be prudent, of course, we should let them tell us their own story *and* ask for corroborating versions from others who know them well. For since none of us can know ourselves fully, and most of us ignore or overlook some pretty critical things about ourselves, our full story needs to be a twice-told tale.) Second, another way in which we can know someone's character is by listening to the tapestry of stories they tell about themselves and others. Indeed, sometimes the keenest insights into someone's character comes from listening to the types of stories they tell and retell. Isn't that why psychologists often give folks pictures and ask them to make up stories about them? Our stories express who we are.

And this is just as true on the communal level, for here too our stories give a good indication of our corporate identity. Both our own story as a people and the stories we tell ourselves and our children give a fairly good indication of our communal character. For certainly we can get a pretty fair grasp of who America is by listening to the stories of all its peoples, as well as the peoples it has dealt with. And just as clearly we can learn something about ourselves as a nation by attending to the stories we are forever telling and retelling on television, in our movie theaters, on the best-seller list, and in our popular songs. As Bernard Brandon Scott argues, "Understand how a society tells its stories and you understand that society and, even more, the options for existence imagined in that society."[7] After all, don't the classic American stories (such as westerns, thrillers, mysteries, and, of course, Horatio Alger tales) reveal a society committed to integrity, fair play, competition, freedom and initiative, as well as a community infected by individualism, violence and consumerism? And even more, don't these stories reveal the scope of our imagination about such issues? Our stories don't just show what we do; they reveal what we can imagine doing.

Think for a moment about your family, and then try to answer this simple question: "What is your family like?" First, use a list of adjectives (as many as you need) for the description. Then tell a story that "captures" at least a good deal of what your family is like. Which method of description seems most effective? Why? Repeat the same exercise for a friend and then for a social group of which you are a part (church, family, etc.).

Stories As Moral Teachers

From what we have said so far it seems that stories teach us morality in two ways: first, by forming and *re-forming* our personal and communal character, and second by giving concrete directions about how we ought to behave in a particular setting. The power of stories is to be found in their capacity to engage our moral imagination, to shape or reshape our hearts and minds, and to enlighten us about what we ought or ought not do.

On the level of character, stories help to teach us by developing our sympathetic imagination.[8] That is, the best stories increase the capacity of our hearts, and they do this by giving us a chance to walk around inside someone else's skin. As Jean Louise, "Scout," says in Harper Lee's prize-winning novel *To Kill a Mockingbird,* "Atticus was right. One time he said you never really know a man until you stand in his shoes and walk around in them." And Lee's novel, like any great story, lets us do just that: walk around inside other people's shoes, feel the blessings and bruises of their lives, and experience the slings and arrows they face each day, *especially* those which we ourselves might unknowingly have caused. Like young Prince Edward in Mark Twain's *The Prince and the Pauper,* or Ebenezer Scrooge in Charles Dickens's *A Christmas Carol,* the listeners of a good story find themselves suddenly experiencing the joys and sorrows of people they rarely notice. Good stories pull us outside of ourselves and put us inside the hearts and minds of people we overlook, people we know nothing about, sometimes even people we *think* we know so very well. In this way these tales increase the range and depth of our sympathies, helping us to recognize the humanity of our neighbors and to uncover the full implications of our own humanity. Our world and our hearts are made larger by such stories.

Of course this change of heart must lead to new attitudes and intentions, for stories with real moral power don't just leave us *feeling* different, producing some cathartic bath of tears or warm afterglow. Instead, great stories, by shifting the interior landscape of our character, by altering our reference points, affect the stances we take in the world, the things and persons we value, the commitments we make and our basic intentions about who we want to be and how we hope to act. Good stories shape our identity and affect our loyalties. So it is that by the end of both *The Prince and the Pauper* and *A Christmas Carol,* Prince Edward and Scrooge don't just *feel* differently about the poor and suffering around them, they have themselves, as a result of the stories they've heard, become new persons, and are behaving differently in the world. As an example of this sort of transformation, there is the disclosure that Lyndon Johnson made to one of his biographers. Johnson, the man who pushed some of America's most sweeping antipoverty programs through Congress, acknowledged that it was reading Steinbeck's *Grapes of Wrath* that had opened his eyes and his heart to the experience of the poor in America. Any story that can do that—not only touch a heart, but impact a nation—is quite a story.

At the same time, good stories shape our character by stripping us of our self-deceptions and uncovering our biases. Like the small child who cries out at the end of *The Emperor's New Clothes,* good stories strip away our illusions and awaken us to the fact that we are not nearly as perfect nor as innocent as we think. Clearly Nathan's little lamb story does this to David, holding up a mirror to the "good" King's adulterous and murderous behavior, and unmasking the lie of his innocence and moral superiority. And indeed, every great story echoes Nathan's accusation, reminding *all* of us that "That man is *you!*" For stories don't shape our moral character by pointing out *other* people's flaws, but by uncovering *our* self-deceptions. And if we think a story was intended to teach someone else a painful lesson, we have probably wasted our time listening—or, more honestly, *not* listening—to it.

Take, for example, the parable about the Pharisee and the Publican in Luke 18:9–14:

> He also told this parable to some who trusted in themselves that they were righteous and regarded others with contempt: "Two men went up to the temple to pray, one a Pharisee and the other a tax collector. The Pharisee, standing by himself, was praying thus, 'God, I thank you that I am not like other people: thieves, rogues, adulterers, or even like this tax collector. I fast twice a week; I give a tenth of all my income.' But the tax collector, standing far off, would not even look up to heaven, but was beating his breast and saying, 'God, be merciful to me, a sinner!' I tell you, this man went down to his house justified rather than the other; for all who exalt themselves shall be humbled, but all who humble themselves will be exalted."

Almost all of us know some folks who remind us of that rather haughty Pharisee—people who think they're better or more moral than the rest of us. Do we not take some pleasure in having parables like this one prick their balloons? These are pompous, hypocritical and judgmental folks who are always telling us about their generosity, their brilliant children, their charitable activities, all the while tearing down others and complaining about other people's failings. "Thank goodness we're not like that," we might say. But is that not the point of the story? If a good story leaves us feeling pretty smug, it's unlikely that it's had any real effect on us, or that we've even got the point.

Stories can also offer us concrete examples of how (and how not) to behave in different situations. The stories we are told, remember and pass on sometimes present us with virtuous persons whose general behavior or character traits we ought to admire and emulate (or vicious persons whose conduct and habits we should avoid), as well as many concrete illustrations of right (or wrong) actions. Thus, stories we hear from our parents and teachers often have heroes and villains whom we are encouraged to model ourselves upon (or not). The Bible, history books, legends and popular fiction are full of tales about persons whom the authors of these works offer as examples of how we might *be*. Be like Jesus, Moses and Ruth, but don't be like Judas, Attila or Hitler. At the same time, many of these stories offer examples of what we should (or shouldn't) *do* in concrete situations. So we have stories of truth telling, forgiveness, courage, self-sacrifice, compassion and hard work. All these stories suggest how we ought to act, both generally and in particular settings. Indeed, much of William Bennett's recent work, *The Book of Virtues,* offers examples not only of virtuous people, but of right actions. Good stories can both suggest who we might be as well as what we might do.

You and your two young children (three and four years old) are going on a long journey that will keep you isolated for many years. You can take five stories with you to read to the children as they grow up. Pick several well-known stories (from scripture, plays, novels, films, folktales or other sources) which you think would be good for their moral education. First, what are the stories you chose for them? Second, if you can, try to say (1) how you think these stories will help to form your children's character, and (2) what specific lessons you would hope they might learn from these stories. Third, after your children have turned twenty-one, what five stories would you offer them as adults? Why these?

Some Different Sorts of Stories

Not all stories are the same. The stories we hear and pass on come in a variety of forms, and each type of story does something different.[9] For example, *myths* are stories that take the complexity of our experience in

85

the world and seek to create an understandable way of perceiving and relating to that world. In this way myths offer us what is known as a worldview, and seek to provide us with a place and a role in that world. Often myths try to explain our origins, identity and ultimate destiny in the form of a coherent narrative. Thus both the creation story of the first two chapters of Genesis and the big bang theory are myths.

Two other kinds of stories are *apologues* and *satires,* each of which responds to myths in its own way. Apologues are stories that defend established myths about humanity, theology, politics or science. Thus an apologue seeks to show why a particular myth is true, or to give illustrative examples of this myth. So, for example, Western tales about lonely but brave frontiersmen or women support American myths about rugged individualism, while stories about boatloads of pilgrims landing on Plymouth Rock undergird the myth of America as a New Jerusalem. At the same time, *satires* attack and ridicule prevalent myths, lampooning the worldview presented by them and attacking the practices and beliefs associated with such myths. In our own time, political cartoons have become one very popular form of satire, such as the *Doonesbury* strip, which regularly attacks and ridicules many of the popular myths of both church and state. If there is a conservative belief in America, Gary Trudeau has probably satirized it, while Rush Limbaugh has done that for nearly every belief held sacred by liberals.

A fourth type of story, one we will be seeing more of later, is the *parable*. Like satires, parables are an attack upon the sacred myths of the listening person or community, but their assault is not frontal. Parables, like the best of stories, work precisely because they seem at first to be such innocent, even tasty little morsels, but, in fact, unfold in a fashion that ultimately undermines the audience's most sacred assumptions. For example, the parable of the "good" Samaritan (Luke 10:29–37) accepts the "rule" that we are to love our neighbors, but then goes on to transform radically just what that rule might mean. The hero of the story, it turns out, is not only a foreigner, an outsider, but a despised enemy of the Jews (probably the first hearers of the parable). "Neighbor," in other words, might be someone we least expect, but worse, someone from whom we would hardly be inclined to receive assistance. The "rule" *love your neighbor* is not the same after this parable. The parable upsets the comfortable world of the listeners, stretching their moral imaginations. That is what a good parable can do.[10]

What Sorts of Stories Should We Tell and Become?

Throughout this chapter we have been talking about the moral power and importance of stories, but what about their *truth*? As should be obvious, this question is not primarily about the factual or historical accuracy of a story, for some of our greatest stories have been works of fiction, and hardly anyone would think of dismissing *The Odyssey* or *Crime and Punishment* because they weren't "true" stories, true in the sense of accurate accounts of historical events. The truth of these stories is a different kind of truth. The truth of *The Odyssey,* for example, has something to do with its ability to name and describe—in a way that is so true to life—the strivings and stirrings of the human heart, as well as to touch what our full humanity is all about.

By contrast, we all know stories that distort the real meaning of what it is to be human, stories that offer corrupt and self-serving versions of the full humanity to which we are called, stories that lie about who we are and who we are summoned to become. We have called such stories lies, propaganda, rationalizations, excuses and/or self-deceptions, and they have been used to defend all sorts of biases, abuses and a myriad of injustices.

The malice or wrongness of some stories is obvious. Looking back at D. W. Griffith's epic 1915 film *The Birth of a Nation,* it's hard not to be scandalized by a racist narrative that lionized vigilante Klansmen and portrayed African Americans as cowards and fools. At the same time, it's discouraging to recall how the vast majority of Hollywood westerns blithely ignored the United States' systematic destruction of the Native American way of life, all the while portraying these people as villainous "savages." Within Christianity it is clear that some of the stories we have told ourselves about the Jews killing Jesus, or about Arabs sacking Jerusalem have been used to support, if not justify, all sorts of heinous crimes, not the least of which was the Holocaust. More recently, it is clear that some of the stories we are currently telling ourselves about America's right to foreign oil, or indeed to our present levels of consumption, constitute no small threat to the survival of the planet. Dangerous and self-deceptive stories abound. To put it mildly, some stories help, others stories harm.

So how can we tell the difference? Unfortunately, it is not always so clear which stories are true or right, and so we need to have some tools or criteria by which we might discern those stories that do indeed invite us to become more fully human, and those that do not. Clearly this is a difficult process. To be sure, we ought not dismiss certain stories because they make us uncomfortable, upset our accepted ways of looking at reality, or challenge some of our most sacred assumptions. As the American novelist Tim O'Brien has argued, the truest stories are usually the ones that neither fit neatly into our expectations nor raise our level of comfort.

Stanley Hauerwas offers some helpful reflections to guide us in this process of discernment. He suggests that a "fruitful way to begin thinking about this question, or perhaps to better identify what kind of question it is, is to ask what kind of story must I have to speak of myself truthfully."[11] What sorts of stories will bring us closer to an appreciation of the full humanity to which we are called? What sorts of stories will help us to draw closer to that humanity? Hauerwas argues that we are in need of stories that will help us overcome our ongoing tendency toward self-deception, stories that will help us to recognize the commitments our humanity demands of us, and stories that will help us fulfill those commitments.

And so we need to ask, "Where are our stories leading us; what kinds of practices or attitudes are they protecting or undermining; what sorts of biases or advantages are they preserving or challenging? Are they helping us to uncover the full depths and demands of our humanity, or are they letting us off the hook, insulating us from our own consciences?" We need to get inside of our stories and discern just where they might be taking us.

Concretely, there are a number of questions we might ask of the stories we encounter. First, how do these stories help us to recognize the full humanity of all persons, including the powerless, the stranger and the enemy? Second, how do these stories help us to take seriously the paradox of our own humanity, of our tremendous gifts and terrible flaws? Third, how do these stories help us to step back from all sorts of violence—against ourselves, our neighbors and our world? Fourth, how do these stories offer a check to everything in us that does not want to know the truth, that does not want to grow, to stretch, to be faithful? And fifth, how seriously do these stories engage and consider the stories of other persons or communities, including the tales of our enemies and the stories of the victims of our indifference and/or oppression?[12]

Along with such questions, however, we need to remember that the process of discerning true stories is a communal one, for we can never hope to overcome our biases and self-deceptions on our own. Until the landowners are checking their stories with those of the campesinos, indeed until they are listening with an open heart to the campesinos' stories, there can be no truth. Until bishops have heard the stories of women, until Christians, Jews and Arabs have heard one another's stories, none of our stories can be true.

Finally, for Christian persons and communities the process of discernment demands that all stories must be held up against the central stories of Scripture, and in particular the story of Jesus Christ. For our story only makes sense in response to the story of God, and in light of the God made flesh in Jesus. God's story is the one that makes the deepest but richest demands of us, and at the same time Jesus' story is the one that reveals the fullest depths and riches of our humanity. For Christian people Jesus is the beginning and end of our story, and thus the story against which all of our stories must be cast. But *that* is for the next chapter.

Some stories help, some harm. Some tell the truth, some lie. Give three examples of helpful, truthful stories: one that was helpful/truthful for an individual person, one for a family and one for a community. Now give three examples of harmful, deceitful stories: one that was harmful/deceitful for an individual person, one for a family and one for a community. The conclusion of this chapter offered criteria for discerning a truthful from a deceitful story. Do you have other criteria to suggest?

Morality and Stories — Some Conclusions

1. Stories are not just for entertainment. In the stories we choose to attend to, believe in and repeat to others, we are expressing and shaping ourselves as persons and communities.

2. **We are "storied" people,** always attempting to interpret our per-

sonal, interpersonal and social experience in light of our previous life stories and the stories we hope to fashion.

3. In the stories that are told to us, there is an *invitation* to consider the implications that the narrative holds for *us*. A good story invites us to get inside of it, and to allow it to get inside of us, perhaps even to transform our stories and our selves.

4. Good stories can teach us morally by touching our imagination and pointing out not only who we have been and who we are now, but who we might become.

5. Some stories help, others harm; some tell the truth, others lie. Discernment is needed in order to determine which stories invite us to become more fully human and which do not.

Chapter Six.
Christian Stories and
Christian Morality

Introduction: The Place of the Story

1. "From the moment Zuni people arrived on the surface of the earth, the emergence place, the water, the soil and the first plants, animals and birds they encountered became important in use and symbol. The narratives that tell of this time play a vital role in Zuni religion. The narratives hold power in themselves and are sacred....We tell the stories at the end of each year to call our ancestors to us, to remember who we are, and to prepare for the future....They are still preserved by special caretakers and this is why stories of our emergence must be recounted in secret." (Zia and Zuni Pueblos, New Mexico. Taken from a plaque in the Museum of Native American Peoples, Albuquerque, New Mexico.)

Why would the people of the Zia and Zuni pueblos hold on to these stories? Why would such stories play a critical role in their religion? What do these stories do for the people of these pueblos? Why do they tell and listen to them in such regular rituals? What would happen to these people if they lost or abandoned these stories?

2. "The most important part of the Liturgy of the Word consists of the readings from sacred scripture and the songs occurring between them....In the readings, which are interpreted by the homily, God speaks to his people, reveals to them the mysteries of redemption and salvation, and provides them with spiritual nourishment; and Christ himself, in the form of his word, is present in the midst of the faithful." (General Instruction on the Roman Missal, no. 37)

Why did the bishops of the Second Vatican Council (1962–1965) place so much importance on the biblical readings we hear each Sunday? What importance could these letters, stories and prayers have to us as a community? What would our community be like without these stories or without our regular reading of them to each other? Why would the bishops believe that God could be present in the telling of these stories? Do other faiths believe such things? Why?

The Influence of Christian Stories

As we've already seen, our stories are excellent ways to *express* and *shape* our moral vision. Well-told stories reveal who we are and have an impact upon who we are becoming. Drawing us out of ourselves, they invite us to enter into conversations with them, to be challenged and changed by their vision, to reexamine and *re-form* the story of our lives. At the same time, they often offer us some specific insights into the kinds of actions we should perform and the kinds of persons we should become.

In a similar fashion, our moral vision, and indeed our personal and communal character as Christians is expressed and shaped by our sacred stories, particularly the Jesus story. In fact, these stories are critical to our making sense of Christian morality. This doesn't mean that there is no place for rules or norms in Christian ethics, or that such an ethic pays no attention to reason, experience or tradition; only that Christian stories are an essential source of our morality, shaping our moral consciousness and offering lessons about virtue and right actions. Indeed, one could argue that without these stories Christian morality would not even *be* Christian, because it wouldn't be grounded in the acts and events that formed the Christian community.

For nearly two thousand years, Christianity and Christians have been shaped and nourished by our sacred stories, with each generation of believers receiving them as a trust and handing them on as a life-giving heritage. In fact, these very stories have helped to make us Christian. For as we have told and remembered these stories—particularly in our eucharistic liturgies—they became vehicles for us to proclaim and to celebrate our faith as a Christian community, and continue to form and educate ever new communities of disciples.

These stories have offered us an effective instrument for proclaiming our Christian faith; also, taken collectively, they are an important resource for faith building. As Christians we tell and remember these stories, and yet it is in that very telling and remembering that we are becoming the disciples of Christ. Indeed, these sacred stories have been a living tapestry into which we have woven the threads of our own lives, finding in these larger patterns a shape and meaning which makes us Christian. For by immersing ourselves in these stories we have, as St. Paul notes, "taken on Christ," in this way being schooled and formed by those perspectives, intentions, affections and loyalties that make us Christian.[1]

This tapestry of sacred stories which shapes our Christian consciousness is, like Joseph's fabled coat, a fabric made up of many colors. It includes the inspired narratives of the Hebrew Scriptures, those holy stories of God's wondrous creation of the world, of our fall into sin and of Yahweh's enduring covenant with Israel. Into this garment are woven numerous tales of God's endless fidelity to her/his promises, limitless compassion for the poor and suffering and boundless forgiveness of repentant sinners. At the same time, this tapestry also consists of the myriad stories of men and women whose lives have been changed by God's saving words and acts. As we can see from the statues, frescoes and stained-glass windows decorating our chapels and cathedrals, tales about prophets, apostles, martyrs, virgins, ascetics, pilgrims, confessors, servants of the poor and a variety of other kinds of saints are an integral part of our living heritage of Christian stories.[2] For each of these narratives not only reveals something about the God who touched these lives, but also offers an example of how we might respond to God's invitation to rewrite our own stories.

At the heart of this tapestry, however, have been the New Testament stories we have received from and about Jesus, both those parables and narratives about God's reign which Jesus recounted to the early disciples, as well as the ultimate story God told us in the life, death and resurrection of Jesus. At its core the Christian moral vision has been formed and nurtured by Jesus the *storyteller* and Jesus the *storytold*.[3] For not only were the early followers of Jesus so transformed by their encounter with the stories and story of Jesus that they went out to proclaim the good news to the ends of the earth, but as successive generations of disciples have recounted and remembered these sacred stories in our eucharistic celebrations, the Christian community around the world continues to be fed and invigorated by the Word of God made flesh. Indeed, as we saw in one of the introductory quotes above, we believe that God speaks to us, and that Christ is present among us in the proclamation of our most sacred stories—in our liturgical readings from both the Hebrew Scriptures and the New Testament.

> The Church has always venerated the divine Scriptures as she venerated the body of the Lord, in so far as she never ceases, particularly in the sacred liturgy, to partake of the bread of life and to offer it to the faithful from the one table of the Word of God and the Body of Christ.[4]

Obviously, the point of this chapter is going to be that the Bible is an important resource for the Christian moral life. Before proceeding, ask yourself, "Does this seem true in my experience?" Has the Bible been important for your moral life? If so, how? Have specific passages had an important influence upon you? If so, explain how. If the Bible has not been important for your moral life, why not?

The Importance of Scripture and the Jesus Story

So it is that for Christians the Scriptures are our stories *par excellence*. For these are the holy stories which disclose God and make Christ present to us in their telling, if we but have "ears to hear." They are described as "the Word of God" because in them we hear the story of God's self-revelation, of God's encounter with the human, and of our vocation from God. God speaks to us, Christ is present to us, and the Spirit of God is sent among us in our reading of the Scriptures. At the same time these stories are also, for Christians, the story of who *we* are, locating us as they do in our most fundamental relationships: with the divine, with our neighbors, and with our own humanity. And so it is by revealing God and ourselves to us that these stories shape our character, making radical demands upon us, not simply by telling us how we should act and what we should do, but by pointing out the sorts of persons and communities we are called to become.

It is in the hearing, remembering and seeking to be faithful to these sacred stories that we come to know who we really are as Christians, and indeed that we are constituted as a community of Christians. For the church is not only the guardian and steward of Scripture, it is also the community formed and nurtured by those same stories. As Stanley Hauerwas has argued, the moral authority of Scripture is that it "provides the resources necessary for the church to be a community sufficiently truthful so that our conversation with one another and God can continue across the generations."[5] Scripture provides us with a living memory, a memory rendering us capable of being an authentic Christian community.

> For the scripture forms a society and sets an agenda for its life that requires nothing less than trusting its existence to the God found through the stories of Israel and Jesus. The moral use of scripture, therefore, lies precisely in its power to help us remember the stories of God for the continual guidance of our community and individual lives....The narrative of scripture not only "renders a character" but renders a community capable of ordering its existence appropriate to such stories. Jews and Christians believe that this narrative does nothing less than render the character of God and in so doing renders us to be the kind of people appropriate to that character.[6]

If this is true of Scripture, it is particularly true of the Jesus story, for as the author of Hebrews (1:1–2) has written, "...long ago God spoke to our ancestors in many and various ways by the prophets, but in these last days he has spoken to us by a Son." Jesus, as the Gospel of John argues, is the Word of God made flesh.

> In the beginning was the Word, and the Word was with God, and the Word was God. He was in the beginning with God. All things came into being through him, and without him not one thing came into being....And the Word became flesh and lived among us, and we have seen his glory, the glory as of a father's only son, full of grace and truth....No one has ever seen God. It is God the only Son, who is close to the Father's heart, who has made him known. (John 1:1–3, 14, 18)

For Christians this means that the Jesus story is God's most articulate self-disclosure to us. God tells us her/his story best in Jesus, and

95

so we encounter God most powerfully in this story. Indeed, God's reign is not simply proclaimed but also initiated in the story of Jesus. At the same time Jesus, the Word made flesh, is also radically and fully human, having taken our form and become like us in all things but sin. In fact, Jesus is the truest story of our humanity, told without any of the distortions of evil or sin. The Word made flesh reveals our deepest and richest humanity, and is thus a "gift and call" to that humanity. As Richard Gula writes,

> Jesus the Christ sums up the divine invitation and the human response in a way which makes him the new covenant, the fullness of what the Christian moral life ought to be. We look to Christ, then, as the model of the sort of persons we ought to become and the sort of actions we ought to perform....The stories of Jesus and about Jesus portray most explicitly what life looks like for one who is wholeheartedly committed to God.[7]

The Jesus story, then, becomes paradigmatic for all Christians. It is a story in which the liberating, forgiving and reconciling grace of God reaches out to transform us, and we respond to this story (and indeed to the stories of Jesus) by becoming disciples, by becoming persons and communities whose whole lives are being reshaped by God's revelation in the life, death and resurrection of Jesus. We are challenged and invited by this story to take Jesus as our *alpha* and *omega,* our beginning and our end, to model our lives upon his, and like Jesus, to take part in helping to fashion the reign of God. Discipleship means not simply that we change our behavior, but as we will see in the chapter on conversion, that we take on new hearts and minds, that our perspectives, affections, beliefs, intentions, attitudes and fundamental loyalties be transformed so that they have Christ as their center.

Of course it may not always be so easy to determine beforehand the exact shape of this discipleship, to know just who we are called to be or what we are obliged to do. This will require prayer, reflection, consultation and discernment, and our vocation as disciples will be largely shaped by our history and culture. Still, it is fairly clear that being a disciple of Christ means living our lives in a way that centers upon and is radically loyal to the Jesus story. We get a sense of what such discipleship might look like in Colossians 3:12–17.

As God's chosen ones, holy and beloved, clothe yourselves with compassion, kindness, humility, meekness, and patience. Bear with one another and, less if anyone has a complaint against another, forgive each other; just as the Lord has forgiven you, so you also must forgive. Above all, clothe yourselves with love, which binds everything together in perfect harmony. And let the peace of Christ rule in your hearts, to which indeed you were called in the one body. And be thankful. Let the word of Christ dwell in you richly; teach and admonish one another in all wisdom; and with gratitude in your hearts sing psalms, hymns and spiritual songs to God. And whatever you do, in word or deed, do everything in the name of the Lord Jesus, giving thanks to God the Father through him.

What does the phrase "the Jesus story" mean to you? How might the cultural or historical situation of a person or a community have an impact on how he or she might say what "the Jesus story" actually is? For example, how might a Christian person suffering from AIDS (as well as those caring for him/her) tell "the Jesus story"? How might Christian African American slaves in the Deep South in 1840 have told or sung about "the Jesus story?"

The Challenges of Using Scripture As a Moral Resource

As we've noted, Scripture is the classic and authoritative text for Christians. A classic, as William Spohn notes, is a work which, although composed in a particular time and place and addressed to a specific audience and set of issues, has a voice and a message so rich with human meaning that it is not spent or exhausted in being spoken once, but rather continues to have something important to say to the larger human community long after its original audience has passed away.[8] Scripture is our classic text because in its pages Christians down through the ages and in all sorts of settings have continued to find a wellspring of God's prophetic, liberating and salvific word, a word that addresses us today with the same vibrancy and urgency with which it was first spoken over two millennia ago.

97

Meanwhile, to consider the Bible authoritative for Christians is to argue, as Richard Gula does, that:

> Scripture is a normative criterion of judgment in Christian moral- ity because Christians believe that in the events recounted there, preeminently in the life of Jesus, God's intentions for human liv- ing are revealed. Hence, the authority of the Bible for morality is that it is the word of God, the privileged, though not exclusive, source of our knowledge of God and of God's intention for us.[9]

While we acknowledge the classic and authoritative character of Scripture, and admit that it should and does shape our character and actions in a radically powerful and unique fashion, we still do not know just *how* this happens, or indeed what we should hope for when we turn to Scripture. How are we to listen to, be shaped by, and apply Scripture? How are we to know who the Word of God is calling us to be, or what it is calling us to do, especially when we are confronted with so many interpretations—often in disagreement with one anoth- er—of the moral meaning of Scripture? And how are we to be morally shaped or directed by texts whose authors lived in a world so very dif- ferent from our own, who accepted practices (slavery, polygamy, holy wars) that we reject as immoral, and who had no concept of some of the major issues facing us today (nuclear war, overpopulation, global economics)? These are just some of the challenges that face us as we struggle to discern how Scripture is to shape our moral character and conduct, or how we are to make use of this moral resource in shaping our character and conduct as Christians.

One of the reasons Scripture presents such a challenge to Christian ethicists is the richness of its language. For the Bible is not one book, nor is it one sort of writing, and so it does not speak with a single the- ological or ethical voice. Instead, Scripture is a symphony of literary forms, an extended conversation composed of a chorus of voices speaking out of a variety of historical and cultural contexts and a num- ber of theological perspectives and addressing a broad spectrum of moral questions. In the pages of Scripture we hear (among others) the plaintive songs of the psalmist, the stern commands of the lawgiver, the chanting repetition of the genealogist, the irony of the satirist, the courtly voice of the king's historian, the thunderous railing of the prophet, the wonder of the storyteller and the discourse of the essayist.

98

As a result, the Bible does not offer us a single (or monotonous) theological or moral vision. Instead, as Allen Verhey has written, "Biblical ethics is unyieldingly diverse....The one God of Scripture assures the unity of biblical ethics, but there is no simple unitive understanding even of that one God or of that one God's will."[10] Rather, each of the members of this chorus has their own distinctive take on our relation to God and God's demands upon us to this creation, thereby producing an incredibly rich orchestration, one that would be seriously impoverished if we tried to reduce it to a simple melody line.

The richness of Scripture's language also means that the Bible doesn't shape our moral vision in just *one* way. Indeed, because Scripture has more than one voice, it speaks to us in a variety of modes: commands, prayers, stories, songs, and so forth. And, as Spohn notes, as a result of this "irreducible plurality of literary forms in the Bible...we enjoy an irreducible plurality of the theological uses of scripture in ethics."[11] This means that it is always a mistake to try to reduce the Bible to a book with only one kind of moral authority, with only one way of forming our moral character. That is the flaw in trying to understand the Bible as a book of laws or rules, even though Scripture contains many ethical norms and commands. It is also the problem with trying to use any single approach in grasping the full moral authority of Scripture. Thus Spohn and others have argued that there are at least six ways of understanding how Scripture speaks to us, and that we ought to resist the temptation to reduce this list to just one. At various times the Bible might serve as: (1) an expression of God's command in our lives, (2) a moral reminder, (3) a call to liberation, (4) a revelation of what God is doing in our world, (5) a call to discipleship and (6) an invitation to respond to God's love.[12]

Given the multiplicity of theological and moral visions present in Scripture, it's not surprising that one can find so many differing (and often conflicting) approaches and responses to the various moral problems addressed in the Bible. Whether we are in search of a single unifying moral theory which holds together all the differing ethical positions found in Scripture, or simply looking for consistent teachings on specific questions of human sexuality, politics, medicine or economics, we are unlikely to be satisfied with what we find. Does the Bible presume a particular philosophical approach to ethics? Does it presuppose a certain model for decision making? What, after all, is *the* biblical teaching on monogamy, war, wealth or the proper treatment of aliens? It is simply not possible to discover a completely consistent or coherent set of ethical teachings within the various books of Scripture.

The final difficulty which confronts us in our attempts to unpack Scripture's moral meaning comes from the fact that biblical ethics is not identical with Christian ethics. For what we have in Scripture are people in historical and cultural settings quite different from our own trying to respond to God's call by facing and resolving very specific problems— their problems, not ours. And while we can certainly learn a great deal from the ways in which these Hebrews and Christians understood and sought to be faithful to God, we cannot become moral by imitating their behavior or copying their answers. For our political, cultural, social and economic contexts, as well as our grasp of important issues like humanity, sexuality, society and technology are so profoundly different from that of the people in Scripture that we simply cannot rely upon them to supply us with all of life's important ethical questions or answers. Imagine, after all, if we followed biblical teachings on slavery, capital punishment, polygamy or holy wars. And what would we do if we had to turn to Scripture for teachings on the morality of international trade agreements, arms control, nuclear proliferation or the medical technologies reshaping the ways in which we live and die?

Formulating a Response to These Challenges

In the past Christians have tried to solve these challenging problems in a variety of ways, the two most popular (and troublesome) being a sort of biblical fundamentalism and proof-texting. Concerning the first, some Christians have envisioned the Bible as a book of moral rules or commands which might be applied quite literally to contemporary questions, discarding any differences in the historical or cultural settings in which such rules were written, and ignoring the larger literary fabric of Scripture. Concerning the second, some Christians have—in a practice called proof-texting—selected passages or incidents in Scripture and offered them as biblical proof of a stance they had already reasoned or come to by some other means.

There are a number of problems with both fundamentalism and proof-texting. First, they ignore the literary, theological and moral richness of Scripture, attempting as they do to reduce the entire Bible to a single, univocal text. Second, they fail to take the narrative quality of Scripture seriously, overlooking its primary role as a former of character in favor of a secondary function as a source of moral directions. And third, in their own way each of these approaches ignores the difficult but unavoidable task of interpretation, preferring to assume that the moral vision(s) of biblical texts can be applied directly and effortlessly to contemporary issues, or—even worse—overlooking the ways in which proof-texters and fundamentalists use their own interpretive criteria when selecting "authoritative" biblical passages. In this way proof-texting and fundamentalism fail to take either Scripture or our present setting seriously.

Along with Hauerwas, many Christian ethicists agree that the first step in understanding the moral significance of Scripture is to remember the narrative character of the Bible, that is, to remember that even those parts of Scripture which are not stories are part of the sacred narrative that formed God's holy people.[13] Focusing on this narrative quality of Scripture is important because, as we've already noted, stories educate us in a way that is fundamentally different from principles. Unlike rules, narratives are not primarily aimed at teaching us moral lessons about the permissibility or impermissibility of particular behaviors. Rather, they are geared at reshaping our very imagination, at remapping the inner terrain of our intentions, affections, attitudes and loyalties. Thus, acknowledging the narrative character of Scripture means that for Christians the primary moral significance of the Bible is to be found in the way it shapes and nurtures our personal and communal *character*. This is not to say that we cannot find moral norms or rules of importance in Scripture; indeed we can. But as critical as these norms are to our moral formation, they are secondary to the Bible's central significance as a story shaping our character, and that each of these commands can only be understood when placed in the context of the larger narrative in which they are found. The Bible is not first and foremost a rule book, but a large and incredibly rich narrative.

And how are we to make use of this narrative? The ethicist Kenneth Himes has pointed out a set of processes by which we might be able to discern just how Scripture ought to shape our moral vision, and how we can know what it might be calling us to do or become. In order to take both Scripture and our present situation seriously, Himes notes that we need to attend to four different, but interrelated tasks: the exegetical, hermeneutical, methodological and theological.[14]

First, we need to examine and understand the biblical text. Thus, our exegetical task is to investigate the original setting and meaning of the texts in question, to determine, as much as possible, the passage's literary form or genre, the intent of the biblical author and the way that this message would have been heard or received by audiences at the time. What did a specific command, narrative or idiom mean to the people who first heard or read this passage? What was the historical, cultural, religious and/or legal setting in which this passage took place or made sense? As part of this exegetical task we might ask, for example, just what the author of Genesis 19 (which relates the story of the attempted rape of Lot's guests by the men of Sodom) is railing against—homosexuality or inhospitality? Or we might investigate the context or intent of the command in Exodus 21:24 that we exact an eye for an eye and a tooth for a tooth.

The second task before us is *interpretation* (*hermeneutics*, i.e., the "science" or study of interpretation), namely, the project of discerning just what the messages of these texts might mean for us in our present situation. How are these "classical" texts to be applied to settings so profoundly different from those they were originally constructed to address? As we attempt to make sense of and respond to the pressing moral questions of our day, how are we to understand and make use of biblical passages and texts? So, for example, in our present struggle to sort out the meanings of human sexuality, to address contemporary questions relating to homosexuality and gender roles, which biblical passages ought we to consult or consider authoritative, and why? Given our present understanding of the nature and causes of a homosexual orientation or the mutuality and equality that ought to characterize marital relationships, what are we to make of the condemnations of certain homosexual acts in Leviticus 18:22 and Romans 1:26–27 or the instructions in 1 Peter 3:1–6 directing women to be submissive to their husbands?

We cannot adequately answer these hermeneutical questions until we have first developed clear rules and methods for unpacking Scripture's moral meaning, for understanding and selecting relevant or authoritative biblical passages, and for dealing with the differences, disagreements and gaps we encounter in the Bible's moral teachings.

Furthermore, given the rich complexity of Scripture, it is not likely that we will find any single method capable of unpacking the moral meaning of the Bible. With all of its differing literary forms and theological and moral visions, Scripture helps to shape our character and guide our moral decision making in a number of ways, and so we will need a *methodological* approach to Scripture which recognizes the richness and complexity of the Bible and embraces a number of overlapping interpretive strategies.

Ethicist James Gustafson has sketched out such a methodological approach:

> Scripture witnesses to a great variety of moral values, moral norms and principles through many different kinds of biblical literature: moral law, visions of the future, historical events, moral precepts, paraenetic instruction, parables, dialogues, wisdom sayings, allegories. They are not in a simple way reducible to a single theme…(thus) the Christian community judges the actions of persons and groups to be morally wrong…*in the light* of appeals to this variety of material.[15]

So Gustafson and others argue in support of a "great variety" approach to Scripture, recognizing the need for a flexible range of strategies in interpreting the differing biblical materials, in this way honoring the rich complexity of the Bible and the numerous ways in which its differing literary forms and moral voices challenge, enrich and shape our moral character and inform our moral decision making.

Still, if we allow Scripture to speak to us with its full range of voices, if we recognize the authority or at least legitimacy of a number of differing theological and moral positions within Scripture, how will we keep from being overwhelmed by the chaos? How are we to know *which* biblical teaching on war, capital punishment, slavery or marriage to apply? How are we to argue against biblical citations offered in support of nuclear war or racism? Indeed, what are we to say in response to those scriptural sayings which seem to tolerate, justify or even command forms of behavior we consider to be immoral?

Along with Gustafson, a growing number of Christian ethicists have suggested that one way of negotiating the great variety of moral messages found in Scripture is to read the Bible more "contextually," seeking out those deeper theological and moral "themes" running through and unfolding within the pages of Scripture and relying upon a configuration of these themes to interpret both specific biblical passages and the contemporary moral issues we are attempting to resolve. So it is that Timothy O'Connell has argued that in our use of Scripture as a moral font we should attend to such themes as; covenant, kingdom, repentance, discipleship, law, love, the beatitudes and eschatology,[16] while other writers have pointed to the importance of notions like creation, incarnation, liberation and social justice.[17] By relying upon this loosely constructed network of critical biblical themes, the argument goes, we will have a framework for interpreting the Bible's moral message.

According to this approach, then, we need to listen to Scripture just as we would a great symphony, with one ear paying attention to the deeper themes or movements running throughout the piece, and the other focusing on particular voices or passages. Thus, instead of basing our moral evaluation of homosexuality or capital punishment exclusively on the small number of scriptural passages addressing these specific issues, we would listen to these admittedly important texts against the backdrop of major biblical themes like covenant, sin, incarnation, love and discipleship. Such themes would offer us a context for understanding and interpreting these passages, and for judging how they ought to apply. By using these major biblical themes as tools for interpreting both the contemporary moral issues we face and the particular Scripture passages which seem to address them, we would be able to make use of Scripture's moral authority in a way that recognizes both its complexity and integrity.

Using such an approach, however, would mean that we could no longer hope to find the answer to a moral question by simply looking up an appropriate passage in the Scriptures. Instead, we would need, through study, prayer and reflection, to enter into a sustained conversation with the Bible, becoming familiar with its plots, themes and voices, getting a sense of its general shape and deeper truths. And that, of course, could prove to be quite a daunting project. Indeed, if we were really honest with ourselves, we would soon recognize that we could not hope to accomplish the exegetical, hermeneutical and/or methodological tasks alone, for they not only demand thoughtful reflection and prayerful discernment, but also require a good deal of expert knowledge and judgment about all sorts of historical, biblical, theological and moral issues. No reasonable person would attempt to do this without help, nor should they.

Instead, in order to adequately grasp the moral meaning of Scripture, we need to be part of a church with the resources and experience to take on these tasks—even more, a church which has itself been entrusted with, as well as nourished and shaped by, Scripture for nearly two millennia, and which has sought to understand and to be faithful to God's Word in all sorts of settings and contexts. For a critical part of the process of understanding and being shaped by Scripture is belonging to and being immersed in the *ongoing narrative* or "tradition" of the Christian community. By such immersion in the larger narratives of the church we place ourselves in a privileged position for hearing and understanding the Word of God, gaining access to the wisdom and experience of persons and communities challenged and converted by the Word of God, and benefiting from the protection and inspiration of the Holy Spirit. Our reflections and understandings are thereby grounded in the authority of this living and engraced community of storytellers and story rememberers. So it is that we can only authoritatively tell and remember these narratives in the context of the community of disciples to whom they belong, and who are continuously shaped and nurtured by them. For understanding the Bible means belonging to the faith community to whom it is addressed and being in dialogue with the tradition of that church.

At the same time, we can only understand Scripture's moral message or meaning for us if we are also in conversation with our present context, particularly with what reason and experience are showing us about the human condition. For the Word of God is not an abstract reality, but a word spoken *to someone*. And if we are to know the meaning of this word, we need to understand well the community of persons being addressed by this word. This means that we need to pay close attention to our experience and to all that human knowledge and science can tell us about that experience. We need to look long and hard at what is actually going on in the world, at what people are doing and at what is happening to them and creation as a result. It also means that we need to use our minds and our reason to probe and understand the human condition, to discover the meanings of our experience and to bring the fruits of our experience and reason into conversation with our church's tradition and the stories of Scripture. For while **Scripture** is a

105

critical source of our moral formation, it is not the only one. Rather, it needs to be read and understood in conjunction with what we learn from *experience, reason* and *tradition.*

Unfortunately, figuring out just how this fourfold conversation ought to be constructed and how our understanding of Scripture ought to inform and be informed by what we learn from experience, reason and tradition is not an easy thing. There are no simple mathematical formulas for accomplishing what Himes has described as the theological task. Nonetheless, there is some general consensus about two things. First, most Christian ethicists agree that Scripture plays a critical and unique role in our moral formation, particularly in the way that it shapes and informs our basic worldview, loyalties, attitudes and intentions, and that any *Christian* morality which is not grounded in and shaped by the central narratives of Scripture is not worthy of that name. Second, any serious attempt to form a Christian conscience or ethics must pay sustained attention to all four voices in this conversation, meaning that it must be deeply and consistently schooled in the lessons of *reason, experience, tradition* and *Scripture.* Thus, even if there is not a consensus about exactly how this ought to be done, most ethicists agree that Scripture, the classic and authoritative text of the Christian community, is a unique and critical source of our moral formation, a source which cannot be ignored and which must be held in tension with and informed by three others.

1. In your own words, what are some of the obstacles that one must face in using the Bible as a resource for Christian morality? What are some of the ways to deal with those obstacles?

2. In your own words, what is "fundamentalism"? Give some examples. In your own words, what is "proof-texting"? Give some examples.

*3. Try to think of at least one example of a topic on which the "wisdom" from the **Scriptures, tradition, reason** and **experience** might differ. How might the tension resulting from those differences be resolved?*

Eight Central Biblical Themes

Although a growing number of contemporary Christian ethicists and biblical scholars agree with Gustafson's proposal to read Scripture contextually, identifying a list of central biblical themes which in turn shape and guide their moral reflections, hardly any two authors come up with the same list of themes. Still, perhaps, we ought not to be surprised or disappointed at this lack of a sharply defined consensus, seeing it rather as further proof of the rich complexity and vibrancy of God's word, a word which, like the householder in Matthew 13:52, is always bringing out from the "storehouse things both old and new." All the same, a number of the same or very similar biblical themes do continue to surface in the writings and reflections of various authors, and while the following list is by no means exhaustive, it does offer a preliminary sketch of key scriptural notions informing and shaping Christian morality. These include: creation, sin, covenant, incarnation, resurrection, love of neighbor, discipleship and reign of God.

Creation. In the creation narratives of the first two chapters of Genesis, we learn about the great and loving God who brought the universe and humanity into being, about the glory, grandeur and graciousness of this one God, about the goodness and splendor of all of creation, and about the miracle of our having been fashioned "in the image and likeness" of that God.

At the same time, these texts also offer us a picture of the humanity we were created for, a life in loving harmony with our God, our world, our neighbors and ourselves. In this way the creation narratives call us to respond to our creator God with gratitude and trust, to show reverence and respect for our neighbors and ourselves, and to exercise a loving stewardship towards all of God's creation.

Sin. Unfortunately, as the story goes, our ancestors did not remain in Eden very long. In Genesis 3–11 we hear the tales not only of Adam and Eve's fall from grace, or Cain's murder of Abel, but of a deepening wickedness in the human spirit, a malice which ultimately produces the tower of Babel and invites God's punishing flood of the earth. These and other stories, like Israel's worship of the golden calf (Exodus 32), David's adultery with Bathsheba and murder of Uriah the Hittite (2 Samuel 11), or Judas's betrayal of Christ (Matthew 26:47–50) point to the awful tragedy of our sinfulness. Time and again biblical passages describe this sinfulness as a personal and communal rebellion against God, a calloused indifference and malice towards our world and our neighbors, and a corrosive self-destructiveness within our very humanity. Within Scripture sin is revealed as a fourfold alienation, disordering

107

our relations to God, creation, neighbor and self; as well as a cancer corrupting our character and distorting our individual acts, interpersonal relations and social structures. Broken, exiled and crushed by this sinfulness, we are deeply wounded and in desperate need of help.

In this way biblical stories of sin point to our need to repent and seek forgiveness, to make amends and to turn back to the Lord our God. They indicate the need for personal and social conversion, for penance and reconciliation. Even more, however, the treatment of sin in Scripture makes it clear that we have a God who wants to help us in this process, who stands ready to show mercy and forgive our sinfulness. Like the woman in Luke's parable of the lost coin (Luke 15:4–7), far from being willing to abandon us, God is eager to scour the earth in hopes of finding a single sinner and bringing her/him safely home. Thus, even in the heart of the story of sin we learn of God's mercy. As St. Paul notes, "where sin abounds, grace abounds all the more."

Covenant. It is particularly in God's covenant with Israel that we see this unwillingness to abandon us to our sinfulness, where we witness the divine mercy and fidelity that is offered again and again to sinners who have not merited such graciousness. In the book of Exodus God not only liberates the Hebrews from their Egyptian oppressors and delivers them to the Promised Land, but enters into a covenant with the children of Abraham and Sarah, making an unswerving commitment to be faithful to them. "They shall be my people and I will be their God."(Jeremiah 24:7) And in spite of numerous failures and sins on Israel's part, Yahweh honors this commitment. God is faithful.

At the same time, the notion of covenant also points to God's radical demands upon us, reminding us that being constituted as God's people is not some cheap grace, but generates serious moral obligations. So, for example, we see that in the Decalogue (Exodus 20:1–17), the Holiness Code (Leviticus 17–26) and the writings of the prophets that the God who has led the Hebrews out of bondage has also laid down the law for them, spelling out just what it means to be in a covenant with Yahweh. Their lives and their conduct are to be different now. They are to abandon all forms of idolatry, worshiping only the one true God. Furthermore, they are to behave justly and mercifully in all their commerce and dealings with other persons and communities. But the justice and mercy they practice, however, is not to be that of the Egyptians or Canaanites, but of the God who heard their cry in the night and sent Moses to liberate them from their shackles and deliver them from their exile. To the Hebrews, honoring their covenant with Yahweh never means simply offering holocausts and sin offerings, but treating widows, orphans and strangers as God once treated them when they were poor, oppressed and marginalized.

Incarnation. In the life of Jesus, however, the covenantal fidelity of Yahweh goes one step better, taking on our very flesh and blood. Born into the world as one "like us in everything but sin," Jesus immerses himself completely in our human condition, feeling the full weight of our hopes and fears, our joys and sorrows. As the prologue from John's gospel notes, "The Word was made flesh and lived among us."

As a result of the incarnation, then, we have an even stronger sense of God's boundless love for us, of God's radical intimacy in our lives. For here is a God who has not simply created and watched over us, but actually taken on the full breadth of our experience and walked around in our skin. Here is a God who has embraced our embodied lives and made them sacred, who has eaten and drunk with sinners and tax collectors, touched and healed the sick and lame, grieved and wept with the bereaved and railed against the structures and attitudes that crush the weak and poor and hungry. After the incarnation, then, it is not possible for Christians to accept any dualism that fails to attend to the holiness of our bodies, or any politics, economics or theology that disregards or ignores the embodied sufferings of the naked, the hungry, the sick or the imprisoned, or any social structure or system that oppresses, alienates or marginalizes these bodies. Everything about our human condition must now be taken seriously and must now be part of our loving response to God.

Death and Resurrection. The story of Christ's death and resurrection is at the heart of our Christian faith. Indeed, it would be impossible to separate our faith from this belief. At its core the story of the dying and rising of Jesus expresses our faith that God has indeed saved us from our sinfulness, that in his life, death and rising Christ has liberated us from the power of sin and death, reconciled us to God and created a new destiny for us. Furthermore, our faith in the bodily resurrection affirms that we have experienced redemption as embodied spirits, and that the power of God's redemptive grace permeates every dimension of our lives, and so, as St. Paul notes in Romans 8:35, "nothing therefore can come between us and the love of Christ."

It is impossible to face the miracle of the resurrection without experiencing both a heartfelt gratitude for the miraculous and unbounded love embodied in this event, and a profound hope in this offer of redemption. For Christians the resurrection is both a sign of God's incredible and efficacious love for us, and a reason to hope.

Discipleship. Just as the people of Israel had experienced Yahweh's covenant with them as making radical demands that would change their lives forever, so too those persons who encountered the life, death, and resurrection of Jesus felt a call to leave all else behind and follow after Christ. This call to discipleship took a variety of forms. Some, like the rich young man in Luke 18:18–27, were invited to surrender their property and worldly possessions. Others, like the tax collector Zacchaeus (Luke 19:1–10) were called to repent from lives of sin and corruption. Still others, like some of the scribes and Pharisees, and even some of Jesus' close friends, were challenged to abandon their self-righteousness and moral indignation towards other sinners. What united all of these calls to discipleship was a single demand that anyone encountering the Jesus story should be willing to drop whatever it was—sin, power, wealth, rank, innocence, righteousness, even friends and family—that stood between them, and follow after Christ wholeheartedly.

The call to discipleship, then, is a call to leave everything else behind and follow after Christ. It is a call to make Christ the *alpha* and *omega* of our lives, to recognize that he is the way, and the truth and the life, and that being a Christian means making Jesus the central focus of our own stories. Discipleship, then, means that we are to fashion our lives in the image and likeness of Christ, that we are to take on Christ in our lives, not just imitating his words and deeds, but being transformed in our hearts and minds and communities, being born again in Christ. At the core of this life of discipleship is the command to love as Jesus loved and to make way for the reign of God.

Love of Neighbor. At the heart of Jesus' life and preaching was the command to love, and indeed in Matthew 22:37–39 Jesus reduces the teachings of the law and the prophets to the twin commands to love God and love our neighbor, inferring that it is in our love of neighbor that we best express our love for God. Neighbor love for Jesus, however, is neither romantic nor conventional. Instead, such love has a decidedly concrete and radical flavor to it. For the love Jesus calls us to cannot remain a sentiment locked in our hearts, or an affection reserved for those we enjoy or are attracted to. The neighbor love Jesus requires of us puts food in the bellies of the hungry, clothes on the backs of the naked, roofs over the heads of the homeless and arms around the bodies of the sick and lonely. At the same time this neighbor love challenges us to tear down every wall separating us from those we do not recognize as our neighbors or friends, demanding that we love not just those who are good to us, or those who can do us some good, but that we reach out especially to those who hate us, to those who cannot possibly return our generosity.

Through his example and parables Jesus challenges us to love concretely and radically. Going against every sort of convention, he breaks bread with all sorts of strangers, sinners and untouchables, modeling a love that will not be contained, that will not be restricted to some narrow vision of neighbor or friend. Meanwhile it is impossible to hear parables such as the good Samaritan (Luke 10:29–37), Dives and Lazarus (Luke 16:19–25), or the unforgiving servant (Matthew 18:23–35), and not recognize the radical love that God demands of us, a love that embraces enemies and strangers, that reaches out in solidarity to the poor and oppressed, that forgives trespasses and injuries. Compassion, mercy and forgiveness are names for this love, which, as Jesus is fond of reminding us, is the same love we have first been shown by God.

Reign of God. At the same time the reign of God is also at the heart of Jesus' life and preaching. Indeed, as we have noted, the Jesus story doesn't just proclaim the breaking in of God's reign, it actually initiates it. In the life, death, and resurrection of Jesus a certain wondrous transformation of the human community has already begun, and God's reign, like a mustard seed, or the leaven in a loaf of bread, is already at work among us.

Of course, the reign of God is not like other kingdoms. In fact it may be the antithesis of principalities or nations as we know them. For, unlike them, it does not owe its allegiance or authority to military might, economic wealth or cultural status. It does not rely on structures or systems based upon fear, greed or force. As a matter of fact, it is not even a place, a nation or a society. Instead, the reign of God is the hearts and minds and structures of humanity being transformed by God's redemptive love. It is the human community being molded by this love into a family where peace, love, compassion, forgiveness and justice reign supreme. For this reason, the proclamation of God's reign summons Christians everywhere to work for the personal and social transformation of our world and to live in hope of the reign already begun but not yet fulfilled.

We have named and discussed eight biblical themes important for Christian morality. Which of these eight seem to be the most important ones to you? Why?

Not even all scholars agree on this list of eight. Would you like to tamper with the list? Do you have additions or even deletions you'd like to make? If so what would they be?

Conclusions—
Christian Stories and Christian Ethics

1. One primary source of Christian and Catholic ethics is the tapestry of Christian stories found in Scripture, the lives of the saints, the tradition of Christianity, our liturgies, hymns, stained-glass windows and statues.

2. Scripture is the source of Christian stories *par excellence* and a primary font for the moral education of Christians.

3. Christian stories in Scripture and elsewhere offer moral education through character formation and concrete directions or guidelines for specific issues. Character formation occurs through offering believers ways of seeing, feeling, thinking and acting towards the world.

4. Figuring out just how Christian morality ought to be shaped and informed by Scripture is a challenging task, one that requires personal and communal practices of reading, studying, and praying the biblical texts, immersion in the living tradition of the faith community and ongoing conversation with the best efforts of human reason and experience.

Chapter Seven.
Conscience: "Doing the Truth"

Introduction: Cases of Conscience

1. Valerie and Michael are in a place they had not intended or wanted to be—at least not yet. Both in their second year at the local community college, Val, twenty-six, and Michael, twenty-four, are two people who have finally gotten some direction in their lives after more than a few false starts in dead-end jobs and troubled relationships. Together for two years, they had managed to improve their grades and credit ratings enough to secure entry into a four-year program at the state university. Things were finally turning around.

But now Val is pregnant. Apparently her form of birth control wasn't as reliable as hoped. She is stunned. How can she possibly have a baby now, just when things are starting to break for her—for them? But then again she can't really imagine having an abortion either. She took that approach once before in her junior year in high school and doesn't think she could bear doing it again.

Michael will have to be told. Will he bolt, urge an abortion, promise to stand by her? Oh God, why can't this just be a bad dream?

What does Valerie "bring with her" into this moral situation? Where might she turn for help or wisdom in determining a course of action? The decision she must make is very personal. Is it also private? Is it communal or social as well?

2. Aunt Mabel, age seventy-four, suffered a severe stroke five weeks ago and has been in the intensive care unit since then—hooked up to a ventilator and a maze of other high-tech gadgets. The doctors want to press forward, insisting that "she may make her way out of this." Her

nieces and nephews are not sure. Some of them feel there is no point to such aggressive treatment, that Mabel wouldn't want any of it. Others are shocked by the suggestion of "letting her go."

Who are the "players" in the decision at hand? Is Aunt Mabel still one of them? Where might the decision makers turn for wisdom? It seems like a group of people are involved in the decision-making process. Does that make it harder or easier?

3. The parish council of a suburban church is struggling. The issue?—whether to proceed with plans to build a parish social and athletic center (primarily for the children of the parish) or whether to intensify their support for their central-city partner-parish, which faces closing its school unless increased financial support is obtained. Through the interventions of several council members, the conscience of the community has been pricked. Where should their priorities be? What's at stake? *Who's* at stake?

What does it mean to say that a community has a conscience? What does this particular group—the parish council—bring with them into this decision-making process? What difference might their Christian faith make for what they decide? Where might they turn for moral wisdom? How does a group make a judgment and a decision?

"Doing the Truth"

So far in this book we have done two things. First, we examined the dynamics of moral experience by considering the importance of character, choices and community. Second, we investigated the narrative dimension of morality, the ways in which the stories we learn, remember and pass on help to fashion our personal and communal character, shaping our perceptions, affections, loyalties and intentions, teaching us what it means to **be** good and to **do** the right thing. Specifically, in the last chapter we offered a rough sketch of the way some of the central stories or themes of Scripture have shaped the moral life of Christians.

We have, then, a general sense of the kinds of persons and communities we are called to be, a rough idea of what it means to be fully human and to be Christian. We are to be virtuous, meaning especially that we are to be responsible, just and loving. We are to recognize, respect and respond to our neighbor, and to construct and reform our communities so that they are just and moral. We are to immerse ourselves in and be shaped by the great tapestry of stories in Scripture, particularly the Jesus story, which calls us to a life of discipleship, repenting of our sinfulness, loving our neighbor and making way for the reign of God.

What we still need, however, are the answers to two very important questions. First, HOW DO WE KNOW WHAT IS THE TRULY RIGHT THING TO DO IN A PARTICULAR SITUATION? In other words, how are good people — including good Christian people — to discover and determine their specific moral obligations within a concrete set of circumstances? How are the people in the three stories at the beginning of this chapter to decide what they ought to do or, indeed, what aids can any of us draw upon when trying to determine which course of action is right or wrong? What resources and processes can we employ when seeking moral wisdom about a particular decision? *How* do we discern exactly *what* our response to the God-given call to be fully human and loving ought to be in the concrete, confusing and often messy situations of our lives?

Traditionally we have answered this first question by arguing that we are to rely upon CONSCIENCE — that it is in and through the exercise of conscience that we are able to both *discover* and *do* the right thing. Indeed, to borrow a phrase from Enda McDonagh, it is our conscience which enables us to "do the truth," not just to seek out and find the morally right option, but to choose it as well.[1] For the mature and well-developed consciences of good persons give evidence of their moral character, integrity and wisdom, express their hunger for goodness and truth, reveal their skills at moral reflection and discernment, and empower them to seek out and embrace the good which must be done.

Still, that leaves us with a second important query. HOW ARE WE TO COME BY A **GOOD** CONSCIENCE? That is, how are we to become people of conscience? How are we to develop and/or build the moral sensitivities and skills required of conscientious people? How are we to form our consciences so that when we find ourselves confronted with all sorts of moral crises and problems, we have the tools and resources to face and sort out these dilemmas in a moral fashion? What is the process of conscience formation?

These are the questions we will address in these next two chapters, "Conscience" and "Conscience Formation," examining first just what a conscience is and how it works, and then looking into how a good one is formed (or *re-formed*). In this chapter our investigation of conscience will proceed in three steps. First, we will describe exactly what it is we mean by conscience, discarding some popular but generally unhelpful images, unpacking some important reflections from Scripture and the Second Vatican Council and offering a reflection on the *conscience of communities*. Second, echoing the work of several contemporary Christian ethicists,[2] we will sketch out the three distinct but interdependent dimensions of conscience, illustrating how each dimension flows from and enriches the other two, as well as how each is critical to the ongoing development of a healthy conscience. Finally, we will offer some thoughts on the sanctity and frailty of our consciences, as well as some prudential guidelines for living with a fallible conscience.

Images of Conscience

We begin our discussion of conscience by saying three things that it is not. First, conscience is not a **separate** person or voice whispering moral directions in our ears. It is, as Sidney Callahan notes, neither Jiminy Cricket nor a guardian angel telling us what to do.[3] Rather, conscience is an aspect of who we are; we **ourselves** are our conscience when we attend to God's call to be good by seeking to discover and do what is right. Nor is conscience some **infallible moral code** already programmed into our brain. For while most of us may have a desire to be good and a general sense of right and wrong, we often don't know just what the right action is. Instead, on many issues we have to struggle to inform and develop our conscience, to learn what we ought to do. Our conscience, then, is both our developing sensitivity to the good and our ever-unfolding capacity to discover what we should do. Finally, the conscience is not a **stern critical voice** shouting "shoulds" at us, threatening us with punishment and feelings of anguishing guilt if we disobey. It cannot be identified with either our "gut feelings" or our superego.[4] This is not to say that emotions are not important to conscience or conscience formation, for indeed they are. Still, our conscience is more than just our emotions. It represents our best efforts to integrate all our ways of understanding human experience into a moral judgment about what is right and wrong, and, beyond that, it is a commitment to do the right thing.

When turning to Scripture for insights about this topic, one of the first things we note is that the ancient Hebrews had no word for conscience. Instead, what we find in the Hebrew Scriptures is a discussion of the ways in which God speaks to us in our "hearts."[5] In Jeremiah 11:20 and 17:10 "heart" refers to who we really are in the inner sanctum of our being, so that when we read that "God probes the *heart,*" we are being told that Yahweh knows our true moral identity. Furthermore, this "heart" is where we encounter God's word and feel the tug of God's call, so that the psalmist warns us, "O that today you would listen to his voice! Do not harden your *hearts,* as at Meribah" (Ps 95:7–8). Even more, Ezekiel 11:14–21 and Jeremiah 31:31–34 inform us that God's law is not simply addressed to us, but has actually been transcribed into our very "hearts." If we listen to our "hearts," then, we will hear God's call, indeed, we will find God's law. Finally, our "hearts" are also the place we hold up a mirror to ourselves, the locus of our deepest moral judgments about our own deeds and lives. So, for example, Job examines his own "heart" and finds it does not reproach him (Job 27:6). Still, our "hearts" can be mistaken, even corrupted. As suggested in Psalm 95, through indifference or malice they can become calloused and hardened to God's word, thereby leading us into sin and destruction.

Many of these ideas are repeated and unpacked further in the New Testament, particularly in St. Paul's much more explicit treatment of *syneidesis* (conscience), a Greek term he borrows and significantly reforms in his writings. Here conscience refers to an innate capacity of all persons—indeed, one grounded in our very ability to reason—for discerning and following God's moral commands, for discovering and knowing the difference between right and wrong. As Romans 2:14–15 informs us,

> When Gentiles, who do not possess the law, do instinctively what
> the law requires, these, though not having the law, are a law to

> themselves. They show that what the law requires is written on
> their hearts, to which their own conscience also bears witness.

Indeed, this conscience is described as a steady guide, helping us to judge rightly both the past deeds and courses of our lives as well as the moral quandaries before us. In 2 Corinthians 1:12 Paul's conscience assures him of the rightness of his conduct, while in 1 Timothy 1:18–19 the apostle to the Gentiles instructs his young friend to "fight the good fight, having faith and a good *conscience*. [For] by rejecting *conscience,* certain have suffered shipwreck in the faith."

At the same time, this conscience, which enables us to know and follow God's law and make judgments about our own deeds and lives, can—through scrupulosity or sinful indifference—be wrong and lead us astray. In 1 Corinthians 8:7–12 Paul discusses the weak and erroneous consciences of certain Christians scandalized by the eating of meat sacrificed to idols, while the author of Hebrews 10:22 urges that we approach God "with a true heart in full assurance of faith, with our hearts sprinkled clean from an *evil conscience*."

One way to prevent our conscience or heart from leading us astray, suggests the author of 1 John 3:18–23, is to keep God's commandments, to believe in Jesus Christ and to love our neighbor. In this way we can be certain that we live in God, and God in us.

> Let us love, not in word or speech, but in truth and action. And by
> this we will know that we are from the truth and will reassure our
> *hearts* before him whenever our *hearts* condemn us; for God is
> greater than our *hearts,* and he knows everything. Beloved, if our
> *hearts* do not condemn us, we have boldness before God; and we
> receive from him whatever we ask, because we obey his com-
> mandments and do what pleases him.

At the same time, the New Testament reminds us of the ways in which the Holy Spirit instructs and protects our conscience. In John 14:16–17, 25–26 Jesus promises to send his disciples another Advocate, the Spirit of truth, a Spirit who "will teach you everything and remind you of all that I have said to you." Thus, in Romans 8:26 Paul tells his audience that "the Spirit helps us in our weakness," enlightening and directing our "hearts."

And so, having discarded some unhelpful images and reviewed

biblical reflections on this topic, what, finally can we say about conscience? What would we say that conscience is? Perhaps the best contemporary synthesis of Catholic thought on conscience is to be found in the Second Vatican Council's Pastoral Constitution on the Church in the Modern World.

> In the depths of our conscience, we detect a law which we do not impose upon ourselves, but which holds us to obedience. Always summoning us to love good and avoid evil, the voice of conscience when necessary speaks to our hearts: do this, shun that. For we have in our hearts a law written by God; to obey it is the very dignity of the human person; according to it we will be judged. Conscience is the most secret core and sanctuary of a person. There we are alone with God, whose voice echoes in our depths. In a wonderful manner conscience reveals that law which is fulfilled by love of God and neighbor. In fidelity to conscience, Christians are joined with the rest of people in the search for truth, and for the genuine solutions to the numerous problems which arise in the life of individuals and from social relationships. Hence the more right conscience holds sway, the more persons and groups turn aside from blind choice and strive to be guided by the objective norms of morality. Conscience frequently errs from invincible ignorance without losing its dignity. The same cannot be said for the person who cares but little for truth and goodness, nor for a conscience which by degrees grows practically sightless as a result of habitual sin.[6]

What then can we say about conscience? Four comments suggest themselves. First, the biblical literature and the Vatican document referred to above both describe conscience in terms of a law and an inner voice. That is, we experience conscience as a command, but not one that imposes itself upon us as a stranger or a tyrant, but, rather, one that resonates in our very hearts. The voice of conscience speaks to our hearts, and we recognize it as our own. The genius of the biblical notion of heart, therefore, is that it reminds us both that our conscience is the inner sanctum where we hear God's call to be good and do what is right, and that this call summons us to be our best selves, to be fully human persons and communities. As a result, conscience is the "place" within us where we face ourselves most profoundly and honestly, and the "place" where we discern how God calls us to do the truth.

Conscience is us as we struggle to discern and respond to the "moral tug."

Second, note that the bishops describe conscience as a "search." In and through our consciences Christian persons and communities, and indeed all people of good will, search for the truth about what it means to be good and to do the right thing. *Search* suggests that there is something dynamic and unfinished about conscience, that it involves a process of responding to the moral "tug" described by Enda McDonagh, a process of going out and looking for moral wisdom. If that is true, then being people of conscience doesn't mean "having the answers," but rather being willing to go out and look for them. Thus, complacency or arrogance cannot be a part of conscience. Indeed, those who are complacent, who think that they have such a complete grasp of the truth that there is no further need to search, are far from conscience. Conscience is about seeking; those who have arrived need not apply.

Third, note the religious imagery about conscience: "a law written by God," "the sanctuary of a person," the place where we are "alone with God." A sanctuary is a holy place, a place where one encounters mystery, where one goes to pray, and especially to listen. How fitting those images are for conscience. Conscience is our capacity not only to seek for the good, but to encounter God; not only to inquire about our moral obligations, but to discern how we might respond to the gracious gift and challenge of God's love.

Fourth, and most overlooked, there is a need to recognize the personal *and* communal character of our consciences. For although the bishops referred to conscience as "the most secret core and sanctuary of a person," they also noted that "in fidelity to conscience, Christians are *joined with the rest of people* in the search for truth....Hence the more right conscience holds sway, *the more persons and groups....* strive to be guided by the objective norms of morality." This would seem to indicate that the work of our personal conscience is always part of a larger quest for moral wisdom, always in conversation with, if you will, the "conscience of a community."

Admittedly, the notion of a "community conscience" might strike us at first as a little strange, particularly given our description of conscience as a person's inner voice and sanctuary. Even more, so many of our public moral debates have been framed in terms of a conflict

120

between the individual conscience and the common good that we could be forgiven for thinking that conscience is a very private, very individual affair. Still, there are good reasons to speak about the conscience of a community and to recognize that focusing exclusively on individuals gives us a very skewed sense of conscience.

First, as we saw in the chapter on community, moral experience is both personal and communal, meaning that we hear and respond to God's call *as* persons and *as* communities. So it is not surprising that in Scripture God's invitation to conversion is not addressed simply to individuals like Moses or Paul, but to whole communities. In the writings of the prophets *all* of Israel is chastised for being unfaithful and challenged to repent, while Paul calls the Christian communities in Corinth and elsewhere to reform their sinful ways. It is as persons *and* communities that Israel and the Christian churches hear God's word addressed to their "hearts" and turn to examine the course of their lives.

Second, given what we have already noted about the importance and influence of social structures and systems, it makes perfect sense that we would need to look not just at our individual acts but also at what we are doing *as* communities.[7] In other words, that we should examine our community's conscience. But what we might have missed is that we would need to examine that conscience *as* a community; that is, to discern and reflect on God's call and our response not just as individual persons, but as a community of persons, with a broad variety of perspectives and voices. In determining the morality of our national policies regarding armaments or welfare, we need to listen to the voices of the poor and the marginalized, as well as the bright and well educated. And in making moral judgments about health care, education or employment, we require not only the consciences of a few moral individuals, but the conscience of a nation, fully engaged and actively discussing matters in a way that no single individual could. For communities too need to make moral decisions, and they need to do so *as* communities.

None of this is to suggest that there are two separate and opposed consciences to which we must attend, my own pocket-sized personal conscience and the larger institutional-sized conscience of the community. Rather, it is to argue that there can be no description of conscience that is exclusively individual or social, that does not recognize

121

the personal and communal dimensions of moral experience, that does not acknowledge that we discern and choose the good and the right as persons and communities.

"Heart," "Search" and "Holy": three images for conscience. Drawing on a film or a novel with which you are familiar, identify and describe a person, group or community whose moral life/conscience seems to indicate that they "had heart." How did that moral agent "search" for wisdom? In what way was that moral agent's conscience holy?

Three Dimensions of Conscience

Building upon an insight of Timothy O'Connell's, numerous contemporary Christian ethicists have described conscience in terms of three distinct but interdependent dimensions that Richard Gula has named: **capacity, process** and **judgment**.[8] Using Gula's language, we will explore the ways in which our personal and communal consciences include: an unfolding **capacity** within us for moral goodness and rightness; a **process** we go through preparing us to discern concretely what is the right thing to do here and now; and the **judgment** we make about our moral obligation in a given situation. Let us elaborate.

CONSCIENCE AS CAPACITY

The first dimension of conscience refers not to something we do or produce, but to our general hunger for and orientation to the good. In the concrete it is our capacity to recognize and respond to the moral "tug," our drive to and skill at becoming good persons and just communities by doing the right thing. Traditionally this capacity has been referred to as our **antecedent conscience,** that enduring habit, shape or state of our moral selves before we confront a particular choice or problem. It is the condition of our moral appetite to be good, to do what is right and to build justice.

Although all healthy human beings have such a capacity for goodness and rightness, the specific ability to discern and respond to the moral "tug" is different in each of us, and grows or declines with our moral character. For our capacity to hear God's call, figure out what we need to do, and actually choose the right course of action is not a static, but a dynamic, reality. Indeed, our conscience is not unlike a moral "muscle" or faculty that is strengthened and sharpened through regular use. Certainly most of us would acknowledge that our drive or talent for honesty or justice or chastity is not what it was twenty years ago, perhaps not even what it was two months ago. Rather, the course of our lives and the choices we have made have, in shaping our moral character, also shaped our ability to recognize moral values, make moral judgments and struggle after the good.[9] As a result, in each of us our antecedent conscience is a unique and developing capacity to face and resolve moral questions and challenges.

And since this capacity to hear and respond to the moral "tug" is both personal and communal, we can also speak about the antecedent conscience of a community or nation. So, for example, in the opening vignettes of this chapter we read about a parish council and church community facing a moral question about how to allocate and spend its funds. That parish, as a community, will need to draw on its corporate vision, values and virtues—its antecedent conscience—as it tries to discern concretely the good that is to be done. And, given their specific structures, cultural attitudes and moral commitments, some communities will be better or worse at wrestling with particular moral issues, at doing the truth. Certainly the antecedent conscience of South Africa is in better shape today regarding the question of race than it was just a few years ago, to no small degree because the community of that nation engaged in a difficult and sustained struggle to reform its moral vision and practice.

And how does our being Christian affect our capacity to know and do the truth? How does our immersion in the Christian faith shape our antecedent conscience? Clearly that conscience is shaped and formed by our reading of Scriptures, our celebration of the sacraments and our attending to church teachings, for one cannot live the Christian life and not see and intend the world differently. But even more than that, Christians believe that God has written a new law in our hearts, that Christ has given us a fresh capacity to hear God's call and to respond to it with love. And this New Law of the Gospel is, as St. Thomas Aquinas writes, none other than the grace of the Holy Spirit.

> Now that which is preponderant in the law of the New Testament, and whereon all it is efficacy is based, is the grace of the Holy Spirit, which is given through faith in Christ. Consequently we must say that the New Law is in the first place a law that is inscribed in our hearts, but that secondarily it is a written law.[10]

Thus, the antecedent conscience of Christians is shaped by the free and unmerited gift of the Holy Spirit. What Christian persons and communities "draw upon" as they confront moral issues is the living and loving Spirit of God, a Spirit that Christ has sent to dwell among us, to engrace and protect us, and to challenge us to respond to the moral "tug" which that Spirit bears.[11]

Consider Valerie, whose moral situation began this chapter. Do you have any "glimpses" of her antecedent conscience? What will she draw on as she faces this situation? If you were her friend or parent, what sorts of resources would you want her to have?

The capacity of our conscience, like moral character itself, grows and develops. A personal question: What does your own "moral reservoir" look like today? If you had to face a difficult moral decision tomorrow, what are the moral strengths and weaknesses you would bring with you into that "grapple"? How different are you in this regard from how you were five years ago?

CONSCIENCE AS PROCESS

Once we encounter a particular moral issue or problem, however, our consciences are suddenly aroused, called into action, and we enter into a process of "moral reasoning" or "moral science,"[12] seeking to determine just what the right or moral course of action might be. This is the second dimension of conscience, what might be called our conscience as process, or even our **actual conscience.** Thus, when the family members of Aunt Mabel face decisions about her medical treatment, they will need to engage their actual conscience, seeking to inform themselves as fully and reasonably as possible about all the facts and values of the case, attending to all the issues and concerns that need to be attended to, and taking enough time to dialogue, reflect and pray about the issues before them. In this way they can hope to move toward a reasonable judgment and a responsible decision, to make good use of their conscience.

Paying attention to both our heads and hearts, our actual conscience is our best attempt to grapple with the moral issues at hand and, as Aquinas noted, to use our practical intellect to sort out exactly what we ought to do in the here and now.[13] Like Aunt Mabel's relatives, our task is not just to come up with a set of abstract rules about medical care, but to decide what ought to be done in this particular case. *What medical treatment is appropriate or right for Aunt Mabel here and now, or, how should the general norms and guidelines about the use and nonuse of life-sustaining medical treatment be applied in Aunt Mabel's situation?* Guided by the virtues of prudence, courage and humility, we need to sort through the often competing and conflicting factors and move toward a concrete moral judgment.

Because we are trying to apply general moral principles to a very particular setting, our actual conscience has a kind of "bipolarity" about it.[14] In making our decision we need to pay attention to both the unique elements of this case and those things it has in common with other similar situations. Every moral experience has a certain uniqueness, which we ignore at our own peril. Indeed, moral experience is always situational, and if we fail to pay attention to the particularities of the situation at hand—whether we are talking about an issue of sexuality, medicine or justice—we can fall into legalism, an inflexible compliance with laws and rules that all too often overlooks and/or disregards what is actually going on. At the same time, moral experience also has a certain commonality about it. We are not moral islands, and this is not the first time someone has faced a similar choice. If we pay close attention we will surely notice that this situation is *like* other situations we have faced, and indeed that our moral experiences are *like* the moral experiences of others. If we ignore these similarities, or the shared wisdom and norms that have been developed in response to other cases like this one, conscience becomes a synonym for moral privatism, and moral life becomes a by-product of subjectivism. Instead, our conscience needs to honor both the uniqueness and the commonality of the situations we confront. That can result in a certain amount of tension, but it can also lead to more balanced and accurate judgments.

And just what should the workings of our actual conscience look

125

like? How ought we to go about the process of determining the moral course of action? While there are a variety of possible approaches to making moral decisions, we suggest five critical (and sometimes over-lapping) steps: (1) gather relevant information, (2) identify the moral choice to be made, (3) seek counsel, (4) reflect and pray and (5) eval-uate alternatives.

Gather relevant information. Good decision making begins with investigation, and this is no less true of moral decisions. The first task of the actual conscience is to identify all the relevant facts of the case, asking a series of what Daniel Maguire refers to as "reality-revealing" questions.[15] Who is—or ought to be—involved in making this deci-sion? What are the relevant circumstances surrounding this choice? What sorts of options do we have, and what would be the short and long-term consequences of each of these alternatives? What types of means are being considered to achieve our objectives? In Aunt Mabel's case we might ask who has the right or duty to make decisions on her behalf? What sort of medical information do we have about her prog-nosis, and what do we know of her wishes, values, special needs or emotional and financial resources? What are the realistic options regarding treatment, recovery or long-term care, and what would the effects of these choices be?

Identify the moral choice. Our next step is to get a clear idea of the moral choice(s) before us. To do that we have to have some sense of the ethical issues involved in this case, as well as an understanding of how various options would contribute to (or detract from) our full humanity. Are we choosing to kill Aunt Mabel or to let her die with dignity? Would this treatment save her life or prolong her dying? What are our moral obligations to the sick and/or dying? What are our rights and/or responsibilities when acting on behalf of the incompetent? Who gets (or has) to make this decision? We need to have a sense of the rel-evant ethical goods, issues and principles which apply to this case, and we need to begin to ask just how these various goods and issues oblige us to act in this particular setting.

Seek counsel. Making a good moral decision also means getting good advice. We seek the advice of experts in various fields, of people who have experience dealing with this or similar problems, of people whose judgment we have learned to trust, and of people who have a right to participate in the discussion because they too will be impacted by its outcome. Clearly, in Aunt Mabel's case it would be prudent to seek advice from her physicians, as well as input from other medical and health care professionals. But it would also makes sense for family members to try and discover her wishes, to listen to each other and to seek counsel from their pastor, the hospital chaplain, a medical ethicist and/or someone who has had experience in caring for the dying.

At the same time Christians believe that they can also turn to Scripture and tradition (church teaching) for counsel, and so, along with the advice of those whose experience and wisdom gives them special insights, we find ourselves turning to the Bible and the church for ethical guidance and direction. Indeed, given what we have said about the presence of the Holy Spirit in the Christian community, it is hardly surprising that Catholics should hold that the teaching authority of our church (the *magisterium,* from the Latin word *magister,* meaning "teacher") should have a special place among the sources of moral wisdom to be attended to in making ethical decisions. For it is the role of the bishops (including the pope, the bishop of Rome), as Spirit-guided pastors and teachers, to articulate the beliefs, values and norms of the community as they impact specific issues in our lives. Naturally, these teachings need to be presented in ways that help us both to recognize their "deeply reasonable" character (Paul VI makes this point in his 1968 letter concerning the regulation of birth[16]) and to apply them intelligently to the situations at hand. The bishops of Vatican II have reminded us that in forming our consciences "the faithful ought to diligently attend to the teachings of the church."[17] Such "diligent attention to the teachings of the church" does not mean that the *magisterium* replaces our conscience, but that church teachings are designed to guide and serve the critical processes of our actual conscience, and that we are to approach such teachings with humility and openness. In other words, the appropriate attitude of faithful Catholics to such teachings is not one of blind obedience, but humble and diligent attentiveness.

Reflect and pray. Often enough our best decisions are made after we have had some chance to let them stew inside us for a while, when we have slept on them, taken some time aside with them, or spent a few hours in prayer. Given some time to mull things over, to sort out our feelings and to let our intuitions bubble to the surface, we can make better decisions, decisions that feel truer and are easier to live with. As

Christians we know that Jesus often spent time alone thinking about things and praying to God, and spiritual authors in the church have always stressed the importance of prayer as a way of listening to God and sorting out our conflicts. Clearly, if the purpose of our conscience is to discover what God is calling us to be and do, then we need to take some time in prayer when confronted with major decisions.

Evaluate alternatives. As we sort through the decision-making process, our conscience will discern a number of possible choices we might make, and we will need to monitor and evaluate these options, testing them against the ethical values and principles we have discovered, comparing them with each other and running them past the counsel we have received. We may test them against our gut feelings, our best insights and church teachings. Or we may see how they fit with the direction of our lives or the message of Scripture. What is critical is that we explore, attend to and evaluate these options to the best of our abilities. (And as we will see, this evaluation does not necessarily stop once we have reached a decision.)

Identify a person, family or community that has faced a difficult moral judgment and decision. (Use the three vignettes that opened this chapter to "prime the pump" of your imagination.) How did each of these moral agents seek moral wisdom? Were there "pieces of wisdom" that turned out to be truly wise and others not so wise? Why? What norms or guidelines did each moral agent encounter? Were they helpful? Why? Why not?

CONSCIENCE AS JUDGMENT

Once we have moved through the moral decision-making process of actual conscience, we need to make a concrete judgment about our specific moral obligation in this case, about **the truth that is to be done** in this specific situation. This dimension of conscience, our conscience as judgment, has also been referred to as our **command conscience.** For having made a firm judgment about what we ought to do in a particular situation, we experience that judgment not as mere counsel or advice, but as a command. Indeed, we experience an unconditional obligation to follow this judgment of conscience, for to betray such a judgment and to disobey this command would be to violate our own character and moral identity. Put differently, it would be to choose intentionally to do wrong, to be bad and to turn against full human personhood. In religious terms, it would be to sin.

It is not surprising then that Aquinas argued that we must obey our conscience over all other voices, or that, as we have seen, the bishops at Vatican II contended, "to obey it [our conscience] is the very dignity of the person; according to it we will be judged." Indeed, in their treatment of conscience in The Declaration on Religious Liberty, the bishops went on to note that, "in all their actions, human persons are to follow their consciences faithfully....they are not to be forced to act in a manner contrary to their consciences, nor to be restrained from acting according to their consciences." As theologian James Hanigan says about conscience, it is "the ultimate, subjective norm of morality."[18]

This means that our command conscience is our best moral judgment concerning the right course of action to be taken in this setting. It is what we believe in our hearts about what must be done, about what we are called to do here and now. It is not some egotistical flexing of our will, some attempt to impose our desires and opinions on the world around us. Rather, it involves our most serious effort to understand and do the moral truth. In this judgment we make our best determination of how the various assortments of moral norms and rules apply in a particular case, which of the competing goods and values take precedence and/or need to be protected, and what course of action ought to be followed. At the same time this judgment is also our decision to *do* the good we have recognized, to commit ourselves to the only course of action that makes any sense to us, to be faithful to God's call as we hear it. Clearly we must obey such a judgment.

At the same time, it should also be fairly clear by now that the judgment we reach in command conscience will only be as good as the ground it is built upon, meaning that a well-formed antecedent conscience and a studious, thoroughgoing actual conscience will produce a far better judgment than one reached by an immoral or lazy person. Our obligation to follow our conscience is not just a duty to obey the judgments we reach; it is also a responsibility to commit ourselves to the ongoing formation of our antecedent conscience, and to the painstaking and difficult work of the actual conscience. We know ourselves that when looking for help in making moral decisions we are unlikely to trust the judgment of persons we think of as lazy, calloused, indifferent or biased, and we would certainly be cautious about relying on information or data that has not been critically examined and carefully thought through. It only makes sense, then, that we should be wary about claiming that we are just following our conscience when in fact we have made no real effort to know and do the truth, but are simply acting on some relatively uninformed and unexamined opinions or feelings. Even a well-formed command conscience can be mistaken, and Aquinas argues that such an erroneous conscience still obliges us. But Catholic teaching also makes it abundantly clear that such a judgment is to be the fruit of hard work, dialogue, study, reflection and prayer. It is our duty to make certain that our command conscience is that judgment we reach after having made our very best efforts to know and do the truth. Otherwise, we will certainly not have been following our conscience.

Judgments of command conscience need to be based upon balanced attention to the particularity and commonality of moral experience. Name and describe a moral situation in which the quality of a person's, family's or community's moral judgment seemed to become derailed because of too little attention paid to particularity. Describe another situation that involved too little attention to commonality.

Conscience: Sacred and Frail

Echoing the bishops of Vatican II, the recently published *Catechism of the Catholic Church* argues that we are obliged to follow faithfully what we know to be just and right in all we say and do (no. 1778), meaning that we are bound to follow our conscience, for if we were to do otherwise, we would condemn ourselves (no. 1790).[19] Moreover, the *Catechism* further argues (nos. 1790–1793), that we must act in accord with what our command conscience has judged to be true, even if that judgment is objectively wrong. Indeed, if we follow our conscience in good faith—even if we are mistaken about what ought to be done—we are not culpable of any wrongdoing, while if we violate our conscience—no matter how erroneous it later turns out to be—we will be guilty of sin. For the truth is that our conscience is sacred. That "most secret core and sanctuary of a person...(where) we are alone with God," is, in the end, the best guide we have, and the one we must follow.

Still, for all its sacredness our conscience can be wrong. We can be in error regarding the objective morality of an action or decision, and even well-intentioned people make serious mistakes that harm themselves and/or others. As we saw in the chapter on moral actions, even when we are subjectively innocent of any malice, we can still be making choices that are objectively wrong, choices that do not lead to a fuller humanity, but rather detract from it.

One implication of the possibility of an erroneous conscience is that we should be very wary of making moral judgments about other persons. The mere fact that someone's behavior seems to be objectively wrong does not mean that they are guilty of any sin or malice. As the bishops note, "conscience frequently errs from invincible ignorance without losing its dignity." Being wrong is not the same as being evil.

At the same time, the possibility of an erroneous conscience should give us some humility about our own moral judgments, for being certain does not always mean being right. We need to remember that we are all capable of making mistakes in our moral judgments, and that these errors can produce very harmful effects for ourselves and others. There may have been Christian plantation owners who really didn't know there was anything wrong with slavery, but that didn't make the experience of the men and women who lived and died under their tyranny any less awful. And there may be parents who think it is all right to beat their children, but that doesn't prevent those youngsters from being seriously harmed by such treatment.

At the very least, we need to continuously monitor our moral judgments, particularly when our actions produce significant harm, or when our positions are challenged by people of good will. We cannot afford to be complacent about our judgments, but must be vigilant in examining the short- and long-term consequences of our actions. We must also be humble in getting counsel and feedback from others, not seeking corroboration of our own positions or judgments, but pursuing the honest truth regarding what we have done. In particular, we should seek out and learn from the wisdom and advice of the larger community. We should attend to the counsel of experts, of people with experience, of Scripture and of the church. Only a fool would try to negotiate the moral life alone or seek to make important decisions without

131

listening to the wisdom of others, and certainly no reasonable Christian would believe that she or he could find the moral truth without the guidance and support of the Bible and the church.

Our consciences are sacred, so we must follow them. But they are also frail, so we must monitor them.

Conscience—Some Conclusions

1. Conscience is hard to define, as the many diverse images for conscience suggest. Some of those images are troubling because they image conscience as some*thing* separate from human moral agents. The biblical image of "heart" may be one of the best images because it captures the truth that conscience is "within us," a "part" of who we are.

2. Conscience as capacity, or antecedent conscience, refers to the ability within moral agents that enables them to strive for moral goodness through doing what is right. It is the enduring habit, shape or state of our moral selves before we confront a particular choice or problem. It is our general desire or will to be good, to do what is right and to build justice.

3. Conscience as process, or actual conscience, refers to the processes moral agents employ to seek moral wisdom in the situation at hand, and to determine what that situation has in common with other moral experiences. By seeking moral wisdom, moral agents try to inform themselves as fully and reasonably as possible, attending to all that needs to be attended to as they move toward a reasonable judgment and a responsible decision.

4. Conscience as judgment, or command conscience, is a judgment—the concrete, practical (and hopefully wise), moral judgment—about what we must do here and now. This judgment and the "internal command" to act in accord with it is command conscience. We are obliged unconditionally to follow this judgment of conscience.

5. Especially because of the individualism that is so much a part of American culture, it is important to emphasize the communal nature of conscience. While not a guarantee that we will always do the right thing, "community connectedness" can go a long way to help us overcome moral blind spots.

Chapter Eight.
Conscience Formation

Introduction: Forming Our Hearts

1. In Carlo Lorenzini's classic nineteenth-century children's story *Pinocchio*, made popular to American audiences by Disney's 1940 animated film, a good fairy breathes life into a wooden puppet and informs the little creature that if he wishes to become a real boy he will need to prove himself to be truly good. Unfortunately, this turns out to be no small challenge for Pinocchio, for the foolish and self-centered puppet-boy has serious difficulties with both honesty and self-discipline, and on more than one occasion it seems as though he will never reach his goal. Still, at the end of Disney's film, Pinocchio overcomes many of his moral flaws and exhibits tremendous love and heroism by risking his own life to save his "father," Gepetto. And because he has finally transformed himself into a loving person, the blue fairy rewards the little puppet by turning him into a real boy.

What do you think the story of Pinocchio says about the process of growing up? Are there ways in which real boys and girls go through some of the changes Pinocchio experiences? Do children grow into more loving persons? What does it mean to "grow up"? How does this happen? Can you think of other stories where children, if they do not become "real boys and girls" like Pinocchio, do become more human or humane?

2. In *Schindler's List,* Steven Spielberg and Thomas Keneally tell the story of an Austrian war profiteer who comes to Krakow in hopes of making a financial killing by exploiting Jewish slave labor, but ends up experiencing a change of heart. At the start of the film Oscar

Schindler is portrayed as an unbelievably calloused opportunist, constructing his financial kingdom out of the misery and horror of the Holocaust, bribing Nazi officers and extorting Jewish merchants with the same slippery charm. Still, something begins to happen to Schindler as he is forced to acknowledge and deal with the unfolding terror of the death camps. He experiences a radical transformation, and in a fascinating study of character development Keneally's novel and Spielberg's film show how the war profiteer who once bragged to his wife that he would leave Krakow with two trunks full of money and jewelry ends up giving away all his wealth and risking his life to save the lives of eleven hundred Jews.

What do you think goes on inside someone going through a change like this? Is it really possible for a person like Oscar Schindler to become so brave and compassionate? Why, or why not? Can you think of other stories or events that show the moral development or growth of a person? Have you had any experiences in your life of moral growth or decline?

3. In the musical production of Victor Hugo's *Les Miserables,* police inspector Javert continuously reminds the former convict Jean Valjean that "a man like you can never change," proclaiming to all who will hear that a criminal such as this will never be anything else than a felon or an outcast. But Javert is wrong, and in the course of Hugo's novel Jean Valjean is transformed from an embittered ex-con to a generous, courageous and loving father and friend. Nor is *Les Miserables* unique in affirming that men and women can and do change, for character development is at the heart of every great story, and whether the protagonist—like Pinocchio, Schindler or Jean Valjean—grows into something of a moral hero, or—like Macbeth, Faust or Darth Vader—is seduced by the power of evil, our stories affirm and celebrate the fact that we can and do grow (or decline) as moral beings.

And while novels and plays tend to celebrate the transformation of individual persons, history gives us evidence of moral development and decay in communities as well. Certainly the story of slavery, segregation and racism in America reveals a community whose moral development was severely deformed, while the history of the Civil Rights movement and legislation in the '50s and '60s gives proof that a society can grow and recover morally, even if it still has a long way to go.

All of these stories and history remind us of a number of things: first and foremost, we can and do develop morally as persons and communities, and this development is reflected in the unfolding maturity of our consciences. For, as we have already noted, our consciences are not separate from us, but rather represent our own capacities to discern and respond to the moral "tug"; and so as we develop into morally responsible beings it makes sense to say that our consciences are maturing and strengthening as ethical guides. Second, while every minimally healthy person seems to have at least the rudiments of a conscience—that is, some innate capacity to reason and act morally and to grow into a moral adult—not all of us grow at the same rate, or to the same degree. Indeed, some persons never seem to move beyond the most primitive levels of moral development, while others achieve a level of conscience formation characteristic of virtuous, loving and principled adults. Finally, the actual progress and state of one's moral development (or the maturity of one's conscience) is profoundly affected by two things: the communities in which we find ourselves and the free choices we make in response to those settings. Thus, we can shape the ongoing formation of conscience by paying attention to where we are and what we do.

If these points are true, of course, the work of conscience formation is absolutely critical to the task of morality, and we have a need and an obligation not just to make the right decision in a particular case, but to make certain that our conscience continues to grow and mature over time. For our moral judgments and actions will only be as good as our conscience, and if we are not constantly working to improve (or repair) our conscience, to become ever more mature and loving persons, then we will very likely stagnate at some early stage of moral development and be guilty of significant moral failure. Indeed, if we fail to attend to and work at the ongoing formation of our conscience, we could remain moral infants or adolescents the rest of our lives, never maturing into real adulthood, but doomed instead to become moral "couch potatoes," persons increasingly incapable of making mature and difficult moral judgments and choices.

But just what are the processes by which our consciences are

135

formed, malformed and/or reformed, and how are we to go about building healthy and mature consciences, or repairing unhealthy and immature ones? To answer those two questions we will try to do four things in this chapter. First, we will take a brief look at the capacity of our consciences to grow (or decline), asking what this ability tells us about our consciences and, indeed, about ourselves as moral beings. Second, we will see what the work of developmental psychologists like Jean Piaget, Erik Erikson and Lawrence Kohlberg tells us about the process of moral development, and thus, conscience formation. Third, we will try to sketch out just what a morally mature conscience might look like, so we can get a better idea what conscience formation should be aiming at. And fourth, we will offer some general suggestions for engaging in the process of conscience formation, in the hopes that these might help us in the lifelong quest of becoming moral persons and communities.

Our Developing Conscience— A Deepening Appetite for the Good

In our discussion of the three dimensions of conscience we noted that our "conscience as capacity," or antecedent conscience, was the enduring habit, shape or state of our moral selves that we brought to ethical judgments. We also noted, however, that this capacity to discern and respond to the moral "tug" was different in each of us and that it grew or declined with our moral character. If, then, we continuously attempt to lead moral lives, facing and addressing ethical problems and challenges to the best of our ability and critically reflecting upon our moral successes and failures, our consciences should develop into ever more mature and useful moral guides, particularly if we find ourselves in a morally supportive environment or community. Thus, if we are fortunate enough to grow into ethical adults we should no longer be relying upon the same youthful consciences which guided us through our childhood. Instead, our adult moral judgments should reflect a greater degree of maturity, compassion and wisdom than we were previously capable of.

Of course the development or growth of our consciences is not automatic. It is certainly possible for someone's conscience to be still-born, stagnate or even regress. In both our literature and daily lives we occasionally encounter characters so profoundly deprived or devastated in their physiological makeup and/or early childhood development that they lack even the basic rudiments of conscience. Shakespeare's monstrous *Richard III* and our own Charles Manson may well be examples of just such persons, sociopaths whose moral compass seems irreparably destroyed. At the same time, many more ordinary, law-abiding citizens never seem to move beyond a childish obedience to rules or parental authority. Indeed, they seem incapable of developing adult consciences or, for that matter, any deeply held moral convictions of their own. Perhaps that is why our history books and dramatic works are so often littered with crowds and mobs of "guilty bystanders," gray masses of humanity willing to go along with or ignore whatever evil and injustice seems to come their way. And, finally, people sometimes experience moral decline, their consciences regressing as they are seduced by evil. This is the stuff of tragedies like *Macbeth, Faust* or, perhaps, Judas Iscariot.

In spite of these examples of moral stagnation and failure, however, it does seem that most persons at least begin life with the capacity to grow into ethical adults, even if not all achieve this goal. This means that the vast majority of us are provided with the basic building blocks of conscience, and that this conscience, if appropriately nurtured and supported by environment and strengthened through regular use and good choices, can develop into a mature and useful guide for moral decision making.

In his book, *Christian Conversion,* Walter Conn attaches a great deal of importance to the fact that our consciences can grow, or that we can develop morally. He believes that this dynamic capacity reveals that conscience is not just the ability to make decisions about ethical questions confronting us in the present moment, but represents instead a deep and abiding hunger within us to move beyond ourselves, a moral appetite constantly urging us on beyond all our limits and boundaries, calling us to stretch ourselves beyond our selfish and petty concerns, reaching out for others, for the moral good and ultimately for God.

> As one's moral reasoning develops from an egocentric, preconventional orientation, to a social, conventional orientation, and finally to a principled orientation, one progressively moves more and more beyond one's self and one's narrow interests toward

137

ever greater and wider values. And this is the basic reality of conscience: a radical drive of the personal subject to reach out
beyond himself or herself to others in the realization of value.[1]

For Conn to describe conscience as "the radical drive for self-transcendence…(or) the developing dynamism of the person for self tran-
scendence," means that in the inner sanctuary of the conscience the
voice of God is not just calling us to act rightly in this or that matter,
or to obey any particular precept or command. It means that conscience is not just a capacity to make an ethical judgment about any
particular case, but, rather, that the law of God written in our hearts,
which we call "conscience," is in fact a summons to realize our full and
authentic humanity. The "moral tug" coming from the heart of conscience is the tug of our unfolding vocation. For in the recesses of the
conscience God is not just telling us what we should *do,* but reminding
us who we are called to *be.*

Echoing what Enda McDonagh has said about the "moral tug," Conn
argues that in that most secret core of our being we are haunted by a
moral siren summoning us to become more and more fully human, to
transform ourselves into increasingly loving and principled adults,
indeed, to become saints. Throughout our lives our conscience not only
guides us through difficult moral choices, it also goads us on, challenging and prodding us, showing us where we need to be and reminding us
of what we have not yet become. As Tennyson wrote in his poem
Ulysses, it calls us "to strive, to seek, to find, and not to yield."

At the same time, this unfolding nature of conscience, this capacity
for moral development also tells us something about our very nature as
persons. For if Shakespeare was right in arguing that we all play a
series of different parts in life, it does not seem that we move through
these stages like tourists randomly visiting shrines. Rather, we appear
to grow and unfold through them, summoned, as John Macquarrie
argues, by a "humanity of which we already have some idea or image
because of the very fact that we are human at all, and that our nature is
to exist, to go out beyond where we are at any given moment."[2] Our
unfolding conscience reminds us that *we* are unfolding, that we are
being summoned to grow into the full human personhood that is our
destiny and vocation. It is also, as St. Augustine would tell us, a
reminder that in the very core of our being we are being summoned to
be with God, and that it is only by responding to that call that we will

find ourselves or our happiness. The capacity of conscience to unfold and to stretch us morally is a compass needle pointing and directing us to our full humanity and to communion with God.

Moral Development and Conscience Formation

Developmental psychologists like Jean Piaget, Erik Erikson and Lawrence Kohlberg have examined the ways in which we grow and mature as persons—cognitively, affectively and morally—and in the process have significantly enriched our understanding of the workings and development of the conscience.[3] To start with, their research has helped to corroborate a number of earlier insights regarding conscience: (1) that conscience is a universal human phenomenon and that all but the severely devastated have the basic capacity to develop into moral beings; (2) that conscience develops as we grow and is radically transformed in the passage from infancy to mature adulthood; (3) that this development is deeply affected by the communities we live in and the choices we make; and (4) that the development of conscience involves not just cognitive or affective maturation, but the growth of the whole person as a moral being. Further, their findings have significantly added to our understanding of just how the processes of conscience formation take place. They have discovered: (1) that moral development occurs in a series of predictable and identifiable stages; (2) that these stages build upon and transcend the work of previous stages; (3) that each new stage represents a structural change in the workings of conscience; and, (4) that the successful passage from one stage to another depends upon negotiating a crisis and/or accomplishing a specific task.

Relying on the work of developmental psychologists and other sources, psychologist and ethicist Sidney Callahan argues in her text, *In Good Conscience: Reason and Emotion in Moral Decision Making,* that current research tends to support the idea that conscience and its development is a universal human phenomenon.[4] Indeed, in spite of our cultural differences and moral disagreements, most of the psychological evidence Callahan reports on suggests that persons in every society have the basic cognitive and affective skills and drives required for a moral consciousness, and, further, that current brain research may

139

indicate that we humans are hard-wired for moral rule making in the same way we are preprogrammed to learn languages. Even more, she notes that cross cultural studies on moral development indicate that there are more similarities than differences in the ways our consciences are shaped and formed, indeed, that persons everywhere are structured to grow and develop morally in much the same fashion.

Callahan also notes that after our genetic makeup it is environment, particularly that of early childhood, which most influences the formation of conscience. Thus, the communities into which we are born and in which we grow are tremendously important in helping to shape our moral selves. Still, that doesn't mean that we lack any capacity to influence and direct the formation of our consciences through the free and deliberate choices we make. Rather, echoing what we have seen elsewhere, Callahan writes that, "reasoning, emotions and behavior can be shaped by free, intentional acts...(and) normal, nonimpaired individuals in average, expectable environments have freedom and flexibility to be the constructors of their own characters."[5] Ronald Duska and Mariellen Whelan make the same point in their text on the work of Piaget and Kohlberg, arguing that moral development is the result of our free and conscious interactions with our social environment, that we shape our moral identity and conscience through our own free responses to what is taking place around us.[6] Once again, we see the dynamic and interdependent relationship of character, action and community.

The greatest asset of Callahan's work, however, is her grasp of the importance of affections for moral development and the inadequacy of any understanding of conscience formation which reduces this process to cognitive growth alone. Again and again in her work Callahan stresses that full and authentic moral development must embrace and integrate both the affective and cognitive dimensions of the person.[7] For far from being an impediment to moral growth or reasoning, our emotions can enable us to know and care about the good in ways that enhance our fullest development as ethical beings, and the formation of a truly mature conscience must include not just the capacity to think clearly, but the passion and commitment to act well. This is, in part, why Conn, in his analysis of Lawrence Kohlberg's study of moral development, argues that, "while conscience manifests itself in a judgment of what the subject should do in a particular situation, it is always a judgment of the whole person, integrally cognitive and affective."[8]

Through the work of Lawrence Kohlberg and others we have also learned that moral development seems to occur in steps, and that our consciences mature as they move through a series of fairly predictable and identifiable stages, each one building upon the work of its predecessors and laying the groundwork for stages to come. Relying upon Jean Piaget's study of the cognitive and moral development of children, Kohlberg identifies six stages of moral growth, which he has grouped into three pairs, described as the preconventional, conventional and postconventional levels of moral development.[9] In the earlier, preconventional stages (1 and 2), children do not really grasp or attend to society's moral rules, but understand right and wrong as a matter of avoiding punishment or obeying their parents. Later, adolescents moving into and through the conventional stages (3 and 4) take much of their moral vision from their peer groups or from the conventions of the larger society. What is right, then, is what others are doing, or what the law commands. It is only in the postconventional stages (5 and 6) where the moral adult is able to grasp and act upon universal principles of justice no matter what others think or command. Here one "does the truth," not because one's parents or the state have ordered it or because everyone else is doing it, but because one really understands and desires to "do" this truth.

Moving through these various stages, however, is not just a matter of learning new information, of discovering fresh ethical principles, rules and norms, or even of learning how to balance competing rights and duties or means and consequences. Rather, moral development is a process of learning to see, think, feel and act differently, and advancing from one stage to another involves a structural change of our perceptions, affections and behavior. Far more than the accumulation of fresh ethical insights, or even the mastery of the complexities of ethical decision making, our growth as moral beings involves the ongoing transformation of our very hearts and minds and habits. As we move from stage to stage and level to level we are being changed from children into adolescents and finally, if we are fortunate, into adults.

Finally, as we have already implied, the movement from one stage to another is not automatic, but requires that we successfully negotiate a series of crises and/or accomplish a number of specific developmental

141

tasks. For we need to participate in our own moral development, and we do this by making significant decisions about the kinds of persons we want to become, choices at the level of our character.

As both Erik Erikson and Kohlberg have pointed out, our growth into adulthood is achieved by our resolving a series of developmental challenges, successfully completing the work of each successive stage and moving on to take on greater and greater challenges. Each stage prepares us to enter the next, but that entry depends on our learning new ways of seeing, thinking, feeling and acting. As St. Paul writes, to be an adult we must first be children, but then we must put away the things of our childhood and enter into adulthood. So the child becomes the parent of the adolescent, and the adolescent the parent of the adult, but each of these birthing processes involves change and struggle and transformation. The child learns to obey the moral rules and norms of parental authority and to respect the rights of others, the adolescent learns to attend to the values of the group and to cooperate with others, and the adult learns to love and do the truth for its own sake. Along the way we struggle to develop a sense of self, purpose and competence, we learn to relate with others as friends and peers, and finally we develop a capacity to reach beyond ourselves, caring for and loving others with grace and wisdom.

A Morally Mature Conscience: What Would It Look Like?

Even though moral development and conscience formation seems to take place in fairly predictable and identifiable stages, we know from experience that all morally mature consciences are *not* identical. Instead, much like the differing body types of individual athletes, the fully formed adult conscience of any saint, hero or truly good person is, like each one's character and story, genuinely unique. Though they are both famous for their compassion for the poor, the conscience of Gandhi is not a carbon copy of the conscience of Dorothy Day, nor is the courageous conscience of Rosa Parks a clone of the conscience of Abraham Lincoln. Nor should they be, for there is no single, one-size-fits-all definition of what a mature conscience should look like. Rather, every fully developed and healthy conscience, like every great work of art, has its own unique shape and story.

Nonetheless, it is possible to recognize some significant similarities among the consciences of different saints and heroes, as well as some important distinctions separating persons with mature and immature consciences. We can, without much effort, tell the difference between the raw, undeveloped conscience of a child and the wise, compassionate conscience of a mature adult; and, if given enough observation time, we can often separate the saints from the sociopaths. Hitler and Jack the Ripper would not long convince us that they are companions of Francis of Assisi or Mother Theresa. So, even if each morally mature conscience is unique, it tends to resemble the consciences of other moral adults in some significant ways. Callahan offers a brief description of some of the shared traits of mature consciences.

> A person with a highly developed conscience has certain characteristics. The more morally developed self is a self more and more consciously integrated, more and more capable of self-direction, and more and more committed to the good and the right in personal acts. A morally developed person of good conscience can readily and easily activate and integrate her or his reasoning, intuition, and emotions, in order to effect good and right outcomes.[10]

What is clear from Callahan's description as well as from our earlier discussion about conscience formation involving the development of the *whole* person, is that a person with a morally mature conscience possesses not only a set of critical cognitive powers, but also a number of humanizing affections, and a variety of virtuous habits. For the capacity to understand and reason through difficult moral problems is insufficient if one lacks a genuine commitment to the good and a concern for others; conversely, all the good intentions in the world are ineffective if one lacks the wisdom to make good moral judgments or the actual ability to "do the truth" when it is hard or unpopular. Thus, to be persons with highly developed consciences requires that we possess and integrate a number of *moral insights, moral passions* and *moral skills*.

Moral Insights. A person with a well-developed conscience has, of course, an adequate knowledge of good and evil, of basic moral values and disvalues, rights and duties, as well as a sharpening grasp of various ethical theories, principles, norms and rules. At the same time such a person also possesses an understanding of how moral decisions or judgments are to be made, knows the importance of an agent's intent and motive, and has the ability to weigh and balance the various circumstances and consequences of an action against the means or methods being considered.

Even more than this, however, persons with a highly developed conscience are able to call upon a finely tuned moral intuition and a creative moral imagination. This allows them to tackle the most important and critical mental work of moral decision making, which is, first, to figure out just *how* to look at a problem, *how* to describe what is going on, and then, and *only* then, to decide what needs to be done. For persons with a mature conscience possess what we have called elsewhere a sympathetic moral imagination, a way of seeing the world that allows them to recognize and attend not only to their own narrow concerns, but to the rights and needs of others as well. Indeed, they have the capacity to walk around a question and to see it from the inside, the outside and the underside. They can step back from and examine their personal and social actions from a variety of perspectives and angles, ask themselves just how such conduct or practices might affect others—particularly the voiceless—and thus spot moral evils and injustices that others tend to overlook or ignore.

Because they are willing to take a long, hard look at moral experience, because of their increased capacity to see the truth around them, these highly ethical persons have the ability to ask what action or practice would treat *everyone* fairly, to consider the possibility that they are being influenced by bias or prejudice, and to critically examine their own conscience, checking for errors. This capacity of their moral intuition and moral imagination explains why saints and moral heroes are so often the first to speak out against immoral practices like slavery, oppression and unjust discrimination, for they notice and are pained by the malice of these behaviors long before their contemporaries. It also explains why persons with a highly developed conscience are always testing their own moral perceptions and judgments, always seeking the deeper moral truths, no matter what the cost.

As a result, then, of possessing such cognitive abilities or moral insights, persons with a highly developed conscience are able to recognize what is really going on in a given setting, to discern which

144

universal moral principles apply to this problem, and to judge what ought to be done.

Moral Passions. Along with these cognitive powers, however, persons with a mature conscience must also possess and be able to call upon certain affections, to tap into those humanizing emotions which attract them to the good and provide them with the energy to choose and commit the right act, even when it is difficult or costly.[11] For as we all know from experience, it is often easy to know what the right thing to do is and to advise others to do it. It is quite another thing to actually choose to do it ourselves, and if we do not love or care about the good, if we feel no compassion or empathy for the sufferings of others, if we are unable to sustain our feelings of anger at injustice or our love for goodness, it is unlikely that we will find the power to do what must be done.

Persons with a highly developed conscience have, first of all, a growing capacity to care about and be attracted to the good. In the same way that a baseball fan loves a well-executed double play or an afficionado of great music is enthralled by the haunting melodies coming out of a Stradivarius, the morally mature person feels a deepening attraction and affection for the good and a revulsion for evil. We recognize this deepening appetite in the lives of our heroes and saints, for as they mature morally and personally they are increasingly drawn and attracted to goodness, falling in love with it and giving up all other values or concerns. And, coincidentally, we can also recognize the *absence* of this affection in our villains and criminals, for as their consciences collapse and regress we can detect a certain hardness of heart in them, a growing indifference and callousness, even a kind of moral deafness. They do not do the good because they do not care about it.

Since, however, it is impossible to love the good, or God, without also loving those around us, it should be clear that persons with a highly developed conscience must also be persons with a good deal of compassion, and indeed it would be hard to imagine a saint or moral hero who lacked compassion or sympathy for her or his fellow human beings. Rather, in our literature, Scripture and history, persons of extraordinary conscience have always been people who were deeply moved by the sufferings of the weak, the poor and the stranger, and who were angered by any injustice worked against them. For morally mature persons are not just people who allow their lives to be governed by universal principles of justice; they are also, even primarily, people with the capacity to empathize with the experience and sufferings of others, people with the ability to feel compassion for the voiceless, the stranger, even the foe. Such people want to treat others fairly, to do the right thing by their neighbors, because they love them.

Finally, persons with a highly developed conscience are able to tap into and sustain their moral passions, to integrate compassion, sympathy and empathy so deeply into their character that it is a part of them, like breathing. For many of us may occasionally "feel" something for the poor or weak, or be momentarily offended by some injustice we read about in the papers, and in solitary moments we may experience an attraction to the good. But morally mature persons can rely upon such affections sustaining them in their commitment to do good in season and out of season. Their love of the good, of God, of their neighbor is not a passing, ephemeral emotion; it is a piece of who they are.

Moral Skills. Still, knowing the truth, even loving the truth, is not the same as "doing the truth." If conscience is our capacity to discern and *respond* to the "moral tug," then persons with a highly developed conscience will always need to be persons of virtue. They will need to be persons who can act upon their knowledge and affections, who can make and sustain commitments, who can transform their judgments and desires into decisions and, ultimately, into behavior. And in order to do this they will require those moral skills and habits which enable them to choose and perform right actions. They will need, in other words, to develop and practice virtue.

In the chapter on character we discussed some of the ways in which virtues like courage, prudence and justice help us to become fully human persons and to form a good moral character, and as Christians we believe that faith, hope, and—most of all—love, are the critical virtues which enable us to live out our vocation and draw near to God. In the same way, these and other virtues also help us to build a highly developed conscience; for, after all, it is only persons of good moral character who are capable of having such a conscience. Certainly we would not expect an immoral and calloused person whose character has been misshaped and malformed by a variety of vicious habits to be running around with a highly developed conscience. We would not ask a thief's opinion regarding a person's right to private property, or trust a liar's judgment about our obligation to tell the truth. So how could

146

we think that the maturity of our own conscience is not dependent upon our practice of virtue?

In the end, then, the mature conscience is characterized by the presence of certain moral insights, passions and skills, and persons with such highly developed consciences have integrated these cognitive powers, affections and virtues into their very being in such a way that it shapes how they perceive and respond to the "moral tug."

How Are We to Form Our Conscience?

Just as our character is shaped and influenced by both our actions and the communities to which we belong, so too we form our consciences through the decisions and choices we make and the social environments in which we find and place ourselves. Indeed, one might well argue that, as persons, our consciences are always being shaped and formed by the interaction between our deeds and developing character, and by the conversation between ourselves and the consciences of the communities around us. Therefore, if we want to know just how to go about forming a good conscience we should, as we have already noted, pay attention to what we do and where we are.

As we saw in the chapter on moral actions, our choices and decisions are both *expressive* and *formative* of our character, for our deeds not only reveal something about the kind of moral persons we already are, but they also help to shape the sort of ethical persons we are becoming. Our choices are generated by character, and, in turn, lead to the ongoing formation or transformation of that character. Given the expressive *and* formative character of our actions, then, it would make sense that a good moral education should not only include learning to judge the rightness or wrongness of our actions, but should also teach us how to construct a moral life by identifying and selecting those deeds and habits which would, ultimately, lead to the formation of a good character and conscience. We ought to spend at least as much time learning *how* to become good as we do learning how to judge *what* we have done in the past. In other words, ethics ought to be as educational and medicinal as it is juridical and legal.

Unfortunately, because Christian ethics (especially within Catholicism) has tended to focus so much of its attention on the moral analysis of actions, trying to determine the rightness or wrongness of our deeds, and/or to establish the degree of our culpability or inno-cence in committing them, it has often overlooked the way in which those same actions help to shape character and conscience. As many critics have pointed out, Christian ethics has tended to be much more juridical than medicinal, meaning that not much attention has been given to conscience formation. As a result, while textbooks in Christian ethics are normally quite helpful in guiding us through diffi-cult moral decisions or evaluating the morality of different actions, they do not usually offer a plan for personal moral development. Instead, with their case studies and moral analyses, they have tended to look more like law books or tomes in critical thinking than guides for moral development or conscience formation. Indeed, it is only in recent work being done in virtue ethics that we find an increasing amount of attention being paid to the ways in which we can give shape to our moral lives and character through the decisions we make, the habits we develop and the larger narratives in which we immerse our-selves.[12]

Nonetheless, the issue of moral formation was certainly not ignored in Christian theology. Numerous authors in the field of spirituality, as well as the founders and reformers of religious communities and insti-tutes, and countless directors of novices and postulants were deeply concerned with and gave a great deal of attention to the question of character formation, recommending a variety of exercises and prac-tices for the moral and spiritual development of their charges.[13]

In reviewing the writings of these authors as well as the rules or guidelines used in the formation of religious candidates, three things become clear: (1) that the three most consistent practices recommend-ed for moral and spiritual development were study, prayer and service of others; (2) that ongoing moral development was not an accident, but resulted from a sustained and intentional effort, often guided by a spir-itual and moral mentor; and (3) that such development depended upon the presence of a moral community capable of bearing and transmitting ethical values and vision to the young persons in question. In reflecting on the ways in which we hope to form our own consciences it would be good to pay some attention to these three insights.

First of all, what sorts of actions or habits would help persons to grow into moral and spiritual adults? Study, prayer and service are the practices recommended time and time again by Christian authors concerned with the moral and spiritual development of their charges. Students, disciples and novices were repeatedly encouraged to acquaint themselves with the Scriptures, the teachings of the church and the writings of the saints. They were challenged to use and develop their mental capacities and understanding of the world through regular and disciplined study of both sacred and secular authors. And they were not to cease their studies with the end of their formal education, but to make learning a lifelong habit, and to continue to allow their moral imaginations to be expanded and shaped by the teachings and stories of saints and heroes. At the same time, they were also directed and taught to develop their prayer lives, which were to include both a daily practice of quiet and thoughtful meditation and reflection, as well as regular and joyous participation in the common prayer and worship of the church, particularly the Eucharist. In this way their directors and instructors hoped that they might develop—among other things—a rich interior life, a deepening love of God, a growing capacity for critical self-examination, a rich vocabulary of praise, wonder and thanksgiving, and a spiritual resource from which to draw during life's trials. They also hoped that these young people would immerse themselves in the tapestry of the Christian story and stories being celebrated and confessed in the liturgies and sacraments of the church, thereby shaping their hearts and consciences in the image and likeness of Jesus and the Christian community. Finally, these young people were, like Jesus' disciples, sent out from their houses of religious formation to serve their brothers and sisters around the neighborhood and globe. Whether by feeding the hungry, visiting the sick or some other corporal work of mercy, this practice of service was to teach them compassion, empathy and love for their neighbors.

And indeed, even today, outside the walls of religious houses or novitiates, it is hard to imagine three practices better suited to our own ongoing moral development. Regular habits of study, prayer and service to others would certainly go a long way in helping us to develop the requisite moral insights, passions and virtues of a mature conscience. For such actions not only help us to learn more about the good and right, but immerse us in a vision and a community that shapes our character and imagination while allowing us to practice and perfect those good habits that we call virtues.

The second thing these writings make clear is that conscience formation needs to be a lifelong and intentional activity, preferably done with the tutelage and guidance of a mentor or mentors. Just as many contemporary Americans would not think of trying to negotiate the various passages and challenges of adulthood without some regular help from a therapist or counselor, so too spiritual authors and formation directors counseled their audiences to seek the guidance and direction of a confessor or pastor who might mentor them through life's moral and spiritual challenges. Thus Catholics were traditionally encouraged to have "regular confessors," who would come to know the story and shape of their lives and could, therefore, help to guide them through temptations and struggles with sound and appropriate advice.

If it is true that, as Callahan writes, "the process of moral development is like...engaging in some lifelong value-oriented educational psychotherapy, or like being in the novitiate of a religious order," then we need to be more intentional about entering into this process of conscience formation in a conscious fashion, and, in particular, about seeking out helpful guides to direct us through life's moral white waters.[14] Our ethical and spiritual development into fully human persons is the most challenging and significant journey of our lives, and only the very foolish would undertake such a trip without seeking guidance or direction from more experienced and knowledgeable travelers. Thus, if we are committed to forming our consciences well, we must, like Dante Alighieri in *The Divine Comedy,* find ourselves plenty of wise and virtuous Virgils (the great poet-author of *The Aeneid*) to guide us on our way. In Disney's *Pinocchio* Jiminy Cricket tells our young hero that he should let his conscience be his guide, but first he will need some good and prudent persons to guide him in the forming of that conscience. Parents, pastors, teachers, coaches, counselors, mentors and good friends are all resources for the ongoing formation of conscience, as are the teachings and wisdom stored up for us in the writings of great women and men who have gone before us.

Finally, it seems clear that most spiritual authors, founders of religious congregations and directors of novices seek to form conscience and character by immersing their charges in the life, stories and celebrations of a particular moral community. Moral education is seen as something that takes place primarily by incorporating these young persons into the common life, moral values and ethical vision of the religious congregation or church, thereby "teaching" them to become responsible, adult members of the community. And indeed, if we think about it, we recognize that most conscience formation takes place by grounding students and pupils in the larger conscience of the community—that we learn from what we see and do and experience.

The reason for this, as the ethicist and theologian Timothy O'Connell argues in an upcoming work on the transmission of ethical values, is that it is ultimately communities that are the bearers and transmitters of moral values and ethical vision, and thus our moral education and formation takes place primarily through our being immersed in and shaped by (hopefully) healthy and moral human communities.[15] Feminist moral theologian Anne E. Patrick makes a similar point in *Liberating Grace: Feminist Explorations in Catholic Moral Theology* when she notes that such extraordinary persons of conscience as Joan of Arc and Thomas More were themselves deeply influenced and shaped by the communities and contexts in which they found themselves.[16]

As we have seen elsewhere, communities shape our moral development and conscience formation in two ways: through their structures and their stories. The political, economic, cultural and religious structures of our communities influence our moral imagination by teaching us how to see, feel and think about the world around us. If we grow up with prejudice and discrimination embedded into our social structures, we are more likely to think it right and good to see and treat others as our inferiors. If we live in a society governed by consumption and competition, we are far less likely to see the need to struggle for solidarity with those who are weak, or to act with compassion toward those who are poor. At the same time, it is also the stories of our communities that help to form our moral imagination, and indeed some have argued that the work of conscience formation is largely the work of our storytellers, our artists, liturgists, playwrights and musicians. For these storytellers expose us to moral challenges and difficulties outside our own experience, causing us to wrestle with the larger and deeper human questions of life and to learn from our heroes and saints by walking around inside the problems they have faced.

This means that if we are serious about forming good consciences, we must give a great deal of attention to the sorts of communities we belong to, create or join. If our communities are the bearers and transmitters of moral values, then we must be intentional about the sorts of friendships we develop, the kinds of peer groups we join, the types of clubs or groups we belong to, and the communities in which we abide. For these groups and associations will help to shape how we grow and behave. It also means that we need to attend to the types of stories we read, watch and listen to, to the sorts of liturgies and entertainment in which we participate, and to the ways in which these stories and dramas shape and influence the moral imagination. Good conscience formation demands that we attend to both our real and imagined friends and communities, for each has the capacity to shape who we are becoming.

It also means that if we are intent upon forming our consciences as Christians we will need to immerse ourselves in the life of the church. For if the Christian community is to shape character and conscience through its structures and stories, then we must share in the common life of this community, celebrate its sacraments and liturgies, learn its stories and break bread with its members. In the last chapter we argued that Catholics need to diligently attend to the church's *magisterium* (teaching authority) when informing their consciences about a particular question. But the truth is that along with its official teachings the church brings an abundance of other resources to the task of conscience formation. Indeed, our moral development is as deeply shaped by the great narratives of Scripture, the gospel accounts of the life, death and resurrection of Jesus, or the stories of countless saints and heroes as by any particular collection of official teachings about moral issues. Long before we have reached the age or inclination to wade through the carefully reasoned arguments of an official document, our moral imaginations have been influenced by the liturgies and sacraments we celebrate, the psalms and canticles we sing, and the brothers and sisters with whom we seek to pray and be reconciled.

Conscience Formation—Some Conclusions

1. We can and do develop morally as persons and communities, and this development is reflected in the unfolding maturity of our consciences.

2. While all minimally healthy persons seem to have at least the rudiments of a conscience—that is, some innate capacity to reason and

act morally, and an ability to grow into moral adults—not all of us grow at the same rate or to the same degree. Our individual moral development is influenced by our physiological makeup, the communities we belong to, join or form, and the free choices we make in response to these settings.

3. The process of forming a morally mature conscience seems to occur in a series of stages and is accomplished as persons negotiate or resolve significant developmental crises in their lives. Also, because this process involves the moral development of the whole person, it requires the acquisition of certain critical moral insights, moral passions and moral skills.

4. The work of conscience formation is a lifelong project requiring attention to the sorts of choices we make, the habits we develop and the communities we belong to. In particular, our moral development is enhanced by regular habits of study, prayer and service, by careful attention to the friends we make and the groups we join, and by immersing ourselves in stories, liturgies and dramas that allow us to exercise and expand our moral imagination.

Chapter Nine.
Moral Norms: Seeking Moral Wisdom

Introduction: Commitments, Commands, Criteria

1. "The Lord spoke to Moses, saying: "Speak to all the congregation of the people of Israel and say to them: You shall be holy, for I the Lord your God am holy. You shall each revere your mother and father, and you shall keep my sabbaths: I am the Lord your God. Do not turn to idols or make cast images for yourselves: I am the Lord your God....When you reap the harvest of your land, you shall not reap to the very edges of your field, or gather the gleanings of your harvest. You shall not strip your vineyard bare, or gather the fallen grapes of your vineyard; you shall leave them for the poor and the alien: I am the Lord your God....When an alien resides with you in your land, you shall not oppress the alien. The alien who resides with you shall be to you as the citizen among you; you shall love the alien as yourself, for you were aliens in the land of Egypt: I am the Lord your God." (Leviticus 19:1–4; 9–10; 33).

2. "I know you don't see the point; I'm sure you feel you don't need all these rules, that you can make it on your own, but trust me," urged Lisa, "trust me." Lisa is Angela's sponsor in Alcoholics Anonymous. Lisa has been a recovering alcoholic for over twenty years and has been a sponsor for many others. Over the years she has heard the insistence of lots of Angelas, the insistence that they don't need all the *dos* and *don'ts,* the rules and regulations of the AA program—rules about meetings, phone calls and lots of other things. People who have just become sober, who have just come out of treatment, are often con-

vinced that they don't need all the program prescriptions of AA. Lisa has learned that they are wrong, just as she was twenty years ago. "Trust me, Angela; there's a wealth of wisdom here, wisdom born from the experience of many before you. Work the program; it will work for you."

3. "By euthanasia is understood an action or an omission which of itself or by intention causes death, in order that suffering may in this way be eliminated... [N]othing and no one can in any way permit the killing of an innocent human being, whether a fetus or an embryo, an infant or an adult, or one suffering from an incurable disease, or a person who is dying. Furthermore, no one is permitted to ask for this act of killing, either for himself or herself or for another person entrusted to his or her care....

"...However, is it necessary in all circumstances to have recourse to all possible remedies?....It will be possible to make a correct judgment as to the means by studying the type of treatment to be used, the degree of complexity or risk, its cost and the possibilities of using it, and comparing these elements with the result that can be expected, taking into account the state of the sick person and his or her physical and moral resources....It is also permitted, with the patient's consent, to interrupt these means, where the results fall short of expectations. But for such a decision to be made, account will have to be taken of the reasonable wishes of the patient and the patient's family, as also of the advice of the doctors who are specially competent in the matter. The latter may in particular judge that the investment in instruments and personnel is disproportionate to the results foreseen; they may also judge that the techniques applied impose on the patient strain or suffering out of proportion with the benefits which he or she may gain from such techniques." *(The Vatican Congregation for the Doctrine of the Faith, Declaration on Euthanasia, 1980).*

The paragraphs above display different types of moral rules or norms. Examine those norms for a few moments and then begin to ask some questions about each of them: (1) What is the source of authority of the norm? (2) How is the norm worded—does it tell us how to be? How not to be? What to do? What not to do? (3) How absolute or flexible is the norm? If you were going to propose any revision in the norm what would it be?

155

At the beginning of chapter 3 we suggested that although the place of action in the moral life has perhaps been overemphasized, action is nevertheless a critically important part of morality. The same thing is true in regard to norms. Rules and norms have often been given too prominent a place in the moral life, so much so that sometimes morality has been equated—sadly and simplistically—with the following of rules. Anyone with even a little bit of life experience probably agrees that morality is more complicated than that. Sometimes we find ourselves in a "place" where there don't seem to be any established norms. And sometimes the norms we do have don't seem to fit the problem we are facing; indeed, its author or authors don't seem to have considered this particular situation at all. And sometimes—as Rosa Parks' refusal to obey the norm that directed her to the back of the bus dramatized— the norm itself may be the problem. So, no, norms are not the whole of morality.

Even so, because we are not "moral islands," because we live in communities, because we can and do learn from one another, because we can and must strive to contribute to the "moral quality of life" of one another, moral norms and rules are important for morality. Even with their dangers and limitations, any view of the moral life that does not account for the rightful place of norms is, in our view, fatally flawed.

In this chapter we will do two things: First, we will discuss the *what and why* of moral norms. Just what are moral norms in the first place, and why are they important for morality? These are important questions to address at the start. Second, we will distinguish several different *types of moral norms:* some that point out the kinds of persons we ought to strive to become, and others that point out actions that we ought to perform or to avoid.

Moral Norms: What and Why?

Just what are moral norms? And why are they important? To begin with, **moral norms are the general or specific instructions directing persons and communities toward virtue and/or right action.** The purpose of moral norms is to guide us in the task of becoming fully human (good) persons. Unlike the rules of cooking, driving or house building, moral norms are not just guidelines for building a better mousetrap or learning a skill or craft, but actually provide the structures for building better human beings and more humane communities. Thus, moral norms tell us (1) the kinds of persons we need to be if we are going to become good, and (2) the kinds of actions we need to do (or avoid) if we want to do the right (or wrong) thing. Second, **moral norms teach the moral wisdom and experience of the community in short propositional statements prescribing or forbidding certain habits or actions.** We can teach the moral experience and wisdom of the Christian community to our children in a variety of ways, including, among others: (1) stories, (2) moral reasoning and (3) having our children learn from their own experience. We can also teach by using the short, pithy lessons of moral norms, which attempt to express the "bottom line" of our experience and wisdom in a concise direction or command. Such norms are usually formulated as positive ("Treat all persons fairly") or negative ("Don't cheat others") directions or commands, and do not include illustrations or explanations. And, third, **moral norms seek to preserve and protect those basic human goods or values which help make life fully human. They also seek to preserve a sane hierarchy or order to these values.** Since it often happens that we need to make hard choices between or among competing human goods or values like truth, life and/or freedom, moral norms offer guidelines for deciding how we should act in such complicated moral situations.

Some moral norms are very general in nature. Often this type of moral instruction is not directed toward concrete behaviors to perform or avoid, but rather toward the kinds of virtues or character traits persons and communities should strive to develop if they hope to become more fully human. "Be patient; be kind; be honest; avoid laziness; get rid of bitterness; do not speak harshly to one another": these are commonly invoked moral norms that are general in nature since they do not indicate precisely what kind of action would constitute being patient or honest; nor do they indicate which actions should count as lazy or harsh. Even so, such moral norms are worthwhile; they indicate the kinds of virtues or character traits we would do well to acquire. "Do unto others as you would have others do unto you" is a golden rule, not because it is tell us exactly what to do in every situation, but because it embodies an attitude or moral disposition worth acquiring.

Other moral norms are much more specific: "Obtain the informed consent of the patient before doing an invasive procedure." "…[W]hen you reap the harvest of your land, you shall not reap to the very edges of your field, or gather the gleanings of your harvest. You shall not strip your vineyard bare, or gather the fallen grapes of your vineyard; you shall leave them for the poor and the alien" (Leviticus 19:9–10). Specific moral norms such as these specify concrete actions to perform or avoid. This type of norm attempts to protect or promote some basic good or value: respect for the freedom or autonomy of patients in the first case, and care for our needy neighbors in the second. Note that the more specific this type of norm becomes, the more likely we are to be aware of possible exceptions. Put differently, the more specific an action-centered norm is, the less absolute it is likely to be. For example, any physician or nurse with even a minimum amount of experience knows that there are exceptions to the norm concerning informed consent. Emergencies arise that call for decisive, immediate lifesaving action, and that do not allow time to secure consent from patients or their families. Even so, such situations should be recognized for what they are: exceptions to a good norm, one that makes sense because it tends to protect and ensure the dignity and well-being of patients.

As the above examples illustrate, moral norms are often directed not only toward individual moral persons but toward entire communities. Thus the norm about informed consent is an action guide for individual health-care professionals and, at the same time, it is enshrined in the policies and codes of ethics of health-care institutions and communities. Similarly, the norm given to the Israelites about not picking their vineyards bare so that the poor and hungry might find something to eat is not simply instruction for individual farmers, but a clarion call about the kind of community Israel is to be. Moral norms make sense in the context of community. They lift up the values and commitments of the community itself and not simply its individual members.

Some reflections about the norms of the Christian community are also important. Theologian Richard Gula defines moral norms as "the criteria for judging the sorts of persons we ought to be and the sorts of actions we ought to perform in faithful response to God's call to be loving."[1] The Christian faith—the Christian story as we have described it in chapter 6—provides members of Christian communities with the type of criteria Gula describes, criteria for discerning the kinds of persons we ought to be and the kinds of actions to perform or avoid in light of God's love for us and our call to respond in love to God and neighbor.

To elaborate on this, it may be instructive to distinguish between the central and most fundamental Christian norm (singular) and the norms of Christian communities (plural).

The fundamental norm of the Christian is not a written law. In fact it is a person. Years ago, theologian Bernard Haring, in the foreword of his very influential book, *The Law of Christ,* said it this way: "The principle, the norm, the center, and the goal of Christian Moral Theology is Christ. The Law of the Christian is Christ Himself in Person. He alone is our Lord, our Savior. In Him alone we have life and therefore also the law of our life."[2] The life of Christ, in fact the very person of Christ, is **the** fundamental norm of Christian living. This is hardly a new idea. It is what St. Paul had in mind when he said that we bear Christ himself, especially his dying and rising, within our very being (Galatians 2:19–20). It is why those baptized into the Christian community are given new garments and are told to "put on Christ." It is what Thomas à Kempis (d. 1471) was stressing in the fifteenth century in his very influential work, *The Imitation of Christ.* And it is what contemporary theologian William Spohn is trying to get at when he writes that Jesus Christ is the norm for Christian living:

> ...I propose that Jesus of Nazareth functions normatively as a *concrete universal,* the central paradigm in Christian ethics. His particular story embodies a paradigmatic pattern which has universal moral applicability. We move imaginatively from his story to our new situation by analogical reasoning. The concrete universal guides three phases of moral experience: perception, motivation, and identity, since it indicates: (1) *which* particular features of our situation are religiously and morally significant; (2) *how* we are to act even when *what* we should do is unclear; and (3) *who* we are to become as a people and as individuals.[3]

We will have more to say about some of the details of Spohn's thesis in chapter 10's discussion of various modes of moral reasoning. For now the point is simply this: the life story of Jesus Christ serves as the central and fundamental norm for Christian living. As Spohn notes, this does not mean that it is always easy to move from our understanding and interpretation of the story of the life of Christ to an application to the complex contemporary moral issues we sometimes face. As we shall see later on, the work of the moral imagination (requiring disciplined prayer and discernment[4]) is not an exact science. Even so, Christ is the centerpiece. With Bernard Haring, we believe that Christian moral living begins and ends with Christ.

But in addition to the singular norm of the Christian life that is Christ himself, there are many other norms for Christian living articulated by the various Christian churches. As the centuries have passed, the Christian communities have had to face an amazing spectrum of ever-changing moral issues: whether or not it is right for Christians to be involved in the military; whether or not it is right for Christians to gain interest on loans; whether or not it is right for a married couple to engage in sexual intercourse known in advance not to be procreative; whether or not it is right to remove a "feeding tube" from a person in a permanently unconscious state, etcetera, etcetera.

Where have the Christian communities looked for insight into such questions? They have looked to the *Scriptures* to help ground them in a Christian vision that would help them recognize moral values while offering some general clues to the rightness or wrongness of various actions. They have looked to the previous teachings and wisdom of Christian people (*tradition*) for insights and guidelines as to what should be done. And, along with those of good will beyond the boundaries of the Christian community, the followers of Christ have tried to reflect upon the meaning of *human experience* by relying upon the best efforts of *human reason.* By attending to and integrating these four sources of moral wisdom they have sought to discover what sorts of behavior are appropriate for Christian living.

Some Christian communities, such as the Roman Catholic Church, have an official teaching office (Catholicism calls this the *magisterium,* exercised by the pope and the other bishops in communion with him) whose charge it is to give voice to the norms and guidelines of the community as a whole. Other Christian communities do not have such a central and official teaching office. Accordingly, the moral teachings of such churches may well be much more difficult to identify; diversity is often a mark of the moral teachings of such churches. In any case, as we have explained in chapter 7 in our discussion on conscience, the teachings of the churches, including those of the Roman Catholic

Church, are not meant to be a substitute for our responsibility to form our consciences as authentically as possible and to take responsibility for our own moral judgments and decisions. The moral norms of the church are in the service of conscience; they are not its enemy.[5]

Why, then, are moral norms important? For two reasons: (1) Moral norms help to pass on the ethical wisdom of the human community, giving us concrete and/or general guides helpful in facing moral situations and problems which others have faced before us; and (2) moral norms help us to preserve, protect and prioritize competing values and goods in complicated moral situations.

Moral norms are important because, as we emphasized in the chapters on conscience and conscience formation, we do not live our lives in isolation from one another, and indeed if we attempt to do so, we probably do not live them well. We are **social** animals, which means that we share life with others and that we learn and grow through life in community. Norms, then, are a reminder of both the common or shared character of moral experience and of our dependence upon the moral experience and insights of the communities to which we belong. For the very existence of moral norms or rules means that while each moral experience is truly unique, it also has much in common with other similar experiences. My killing someone is *like* your killing someone, though no two killings are exactly the same. Furthermore, these norms have been formulated and handed on to us by persons and communities who have had experiences with similar moral problems. As such, these norms are a part of our moral heritage, a treasury of moral wisdom tying us to our ancestors and predecessors. Now certainly these norms need to be examined, evaluated and sometimes reformed or—as in the case of Rosa Parks's rejecting the morality of segregation—even discarded; but it would be foolish for any community or person to simply ignore such a rich moral tradition and begin our moral reflections "from scratch" each time. That would be a mistake because it would mean failing to acknowledge either the common features of many moral problems, or the wealth of accumulated moral wisdom that we inherit from those who go before us. We are more communal than that; hopefully, we are smarter than that.

Moral norms are also important because they help us to draw lines around those premoral and moral values which we consider to be important or essential to becoming and being fully human persons and communities. In brief statements they recommend or command that we attend to and protect the goods and values which help make us human. And sometimes they offer specific advice about how to choose or behave when confronted with competing or conflicting goods and/or values. So, for example, while the moral norm forbidding any direct attacks on innocent life commands that we refrain from taking a human life that poses no deadly threat to us, it also acknowledges that we might sometimes be allowed to let a person die, or even to take the life of an unjust aggressor. The norm indicates that life is critically important and must be protected, but not that it must be chosen over every competing value in every setting. Moral norms help us to protect and prioritize values and goods.

Identify—try to write out as carefully as possible—at least two examples of moral norms: one that is a norm of the "secular" community, and one that is a norm of a Christian church. What is the basis of the norm? Where does it come from? How is it helpful? What are its limits? If you were going to make any revisions to the norm, what would they be? Why?

Types of Moral Norms: On Being and Doing

Having a sense of the nature and importance of moral norms, we turn to a description of their basic types, and so in the remainder of this chapter we will distinguish and discuss three distinct types of moral norms. Some, as we shall see, relate primarily to virtues and character traits, to the kinds of persons we are striving to become. Others relate more directly to concrete actions to perform or to avoid. In concert with the insights of other Christian ethicists,[6] we propose that it is helpful to identify *formal, synthetic* and *material* moral norms.

FORMAL NORMS

Formal norms are the simplest, most uncomplicated and noncontroversial type of moral norm. Worded in positive terms, formal norms attempt to point out particular virtues or character traits that we should strive to acquire. They tell us what kinds of persons we are called to be, or the sorts of virtues that we need to become fully human. So very often they begin with the verb "to be." "Be kind," "be patient," "be honest," "be loving" and "be just" are examples of formal norms. In addition, many formal norms relate directly to one's religious tradition; these formal norms point out virtues or character qualities appropriate for one's religious faith. "Be holy, for I the Lord your God, am holy"; "Be ambassadors of Christ"; "Live as temples of the Holy Spirit"; "Be Christlike": these are religiously framed formal norms.

As these examples demonstrate, formal norms are very general in nature. Moreover, they can be taken to be exceptionless. There is no exception to "be loving" or "be just"; there is no exception to "be holy" or "be Christlike." This is true for two reasons: First, it is simply impossible to be moral *and* dishonest, unholy, and/or unloving. Indeed, terms like *honest, holy* and *loving* are simply different ways of speaking about being moral. Also, formal norms are not action-specific. That is, they are not specific or concrete enough to tell us what being loving or just or holy or Christlike might mean in particular settings. Thus, they always apply, though we are not always clear just what they imply about our concrete behavior.

Three further things should be noticed about formal norms. The first concerns application. Among the reasons the application of formal norms to concrete situations is not obvious is that at times one or more formal norm may appear to conflict with one another. How does a parent, for example, discern concretely how to "be loving" and "be just" at the same time when one's particularly sensitive nine-year-old son has "stepped over the line" (again) by speaking sarcastically to his younger sister? He needs to be corrected and perhaps punished. Does "being loving" conflict with "being just"? Does one formal norm take precedence over another in concrete situations? Are there exceptions to formal norms after all? We propose that the answer to these questions is "no." Rather than conclude that sometimes one need not "be loving," it is better to conclude that at times "being loving" must take the form of "tough love." Admittedly, such interpretations and applications might turn out to be tricky business, so perhaps formal norms, at least as we try to connect them to daily life, are not as simple as first meets the eye.

Second, formal norms—at least some of them—can be a little dangerous. They can be overwhelming and can "feed the monster" of the

CHARACTER, CHOICES & COMMUNITY

perfectionism that lurks within too many of us. "Be patient"; "be generous and self-sacrificing"; "be compassionate as your heavenly Father is compassionate"; "be Christlike": for many of us (on some days, at least) this kind of formal norm is not good news at all. In some moments we may well want to cry out, "I can't! I just can't do it!" And perhaps at other moments, in a grin-and-bear-it burst of self-perfectionism, we may dig in with all our moral muscle and try "to do it all."

If that is the effect of formal norms upon us, then we have missed the point. The call, the "tug," to "be loving" and to "be Christlike" is a lifelong call, one that is never fully accomplished and certainly never fully finished. In a very real sense such formal norms point out the moral *ideals* worth striving for. It is important to keep in mind that at any given time one must simply try to do the best one can. Let's not take ourselves too seriously!

Finally, with all these caveats about formal norms—their very general nature, the difficulty in applying them, the danger of perfectionism—are they really helpful? Do they serve any real purpose? We think that they do. In some ways formal norms are "condensed stories" or "mininarratives" that capture some of the most important wisdom of the communities of which we are a part. "Be compassionate as your heavenly Father is compassionate" is a formal norm that in eight words captures a good deal of the core of biblical faith. It reminds us of who God has been for us and how we are to be with one another. No, it doesn't tell us exactly what to do in every circumstance, but in eight words it tells us quite a lot.

Name two of the most important formal norms in your own life—two formal norms that "capture" some of truth about the kind of person you are striving to become.

SYNTHETIC NORMS

Synthetic norms are an elusive type of moral norm. Many scholars, such as theologian Richard Gula,[7] consider them to comprise a particular subset of formal norms. Because they are expressed not in the language of being but of doing, they can also be confused with material norms, which, as we will see, attempt to point out specific actions to perform or avoid. So take note; synthetic norms are a bit slippery.

"Don't lie!" and "Thou shalt not steal!" are examples of synthetic moral norms. They are expressed in negative terms; they seem to tell us things we should not do; and they have an absolute or exceptionless quality about them: lying and stealing are always wrong.

But—and here is why they are slippery—notice that synthetic norms, even though they *seem* to point out specific actions to avoid, fall short of actually doing so. Why? Because the terms that are used in the norm include an "already made up" moral evaluation. "Lying" and "stealing" are *by definition* always wrong. But whether or not a particular action of not disclosing or of actually distorting the truth (such as a prisoner under interrogation might do in a wartime situation) constitutes an action of lying—that is quite another question. "Lying" is a synthetic term in that it refers to an action of **unjustified** nondisclosure or distortion of the truth. Hence the norm "don't lie" does not really provide us with new information about specific actions to avoid, but rather it tells us to avoid something that presumably we already know to be wrong.

"Thou shalt not murder" is another example of a synthetic norm. That is quite a different sort of imperative than "Thou shalt not kill." Whether or not a particular type or instance of killing constitutes murder is really the more difficult question. Someone might be killed in a hunting accident without being murdered; someone may be put to death through capital punishment, and many people would not call such an action murder. There are no exceptions to the synthetic norm "Thou shalt not murder"; however, Western civilization has made plenty of exceptions to the material norm "Thou shalt not kill."

Three other things are important to note about synthetic norms: First, notice that among the things that synthetic norms have in common with the formal norms we saw above is that they both point to *moral values and disvalues,* though they do so in different ways. The formal norm "be honest" lifts up honesty as a moral value, indeed a virtue, for which we should strive. The synthetic norm "don't lie" points to a *moral disvalue* that should always be avoided: dishonesty. Norms point to values; they try to protect and promote values. Formal norms, such as "be honest," point to *moral values* and tell us always to strive to be a certain kind of person—in this case, honest. Synthetic norms, such as "don't lie," point to *moral disvalues* and tell us always to strive to avoid being a certain kind of person—in this case, dishonest. The emphasis here on the moral values and disvalues that formal norms and synthetic norms address is important because, as we will see, material norms address yet another reality: ***premoral values and disvalues.***

A second (and probably simpler) point concerning synthetic norms is that, like other types of norms, they have a narrative quality about them. Like formal norms, synthetic norms are also "condensed stories," "mininarratives," the full meanings of which make sense in the contexts of the larger communal narratives from which they originate. Not surprisingly, both the Hebrew Scriptures and the New Testament are filled with synthetic norms. An example may help:

> Do you not know that your bodies are members of Christ?…Shun fornication.…Or, do you not know that your body is a temple of the Holy Spirit within you, which you have from God, and that you are not your own? For you were bought with a price; therefore glorify God in your body." (1 Corinthians 6:15, 18a, 19–20)

"Glorify God in your body!"—a powerful and profound formal norm that flows from the Christian narrative. In the Christian dispensation, because of God's coming among us in the flesh of Jesus Christ, we who claim to live "in Christ" are called to make our embodied existence a way of giving praise and glory to God! "Shun fornication!"—a strong synthetic norm which, in the context of the New Testament story about the holiness of our very bodies, calls us to avoid anything that would disfigure the holiness of our embodied selves. To be sure, synthetic norms like this do not tell us exactly which behaviors would constitute such fornication (that is the work of material norms), but they do point to the radical incompatibility of immoral behavior with who we are as followers of Christ.

Third, it is important to note the place that synthetic norms have— more precisely, the place they do not have—in moral argument. Imagine a group of demonstrators keeping vigil outside a federal prison where, in a few hours, another inmate will be put to death through capital punishment. The demonstrators carry a number of signs, and among them is one that reads simply "Thou shalt not murder." Who could possibly disagree with that statement? Carrying the sign in that setting, however, the demonstrator probably wants to say something more. Probably the demonstrator wants all to know that in his or her view what is going to take place in that prison in a few hours is nothing less than murder. There is great value in expressing one's convictions, in making such assertions, especially when done peacefully and publicly. Even so, the sign should be recognized for what it is and what it is not: it is an assertion, not an argument. If the demonstrator wants to make an argument *why* capital punishment is murder, if he or she wants to convince others of its moral wrongness, then something more than a synthetic norm will be necessary.

Consider the following: "How selfish." That's what she felt. Lisa is understandably pretty upset at her friend Teresa. They had arranged to go to a movie together and then to go out for something to eat. Frankly, Lisa had had other plans, but she cancelled them in order to spend some time with Teresa, who is in the middle of a rather difficult divorce. It seemed important for Lisa to try to spend some extra time these days with Teresa. What happened, however, is that Teresa just didn't show up. Lisa waited and called and waited some more, to no avail. Much later in the evening—after it was far too late to do anything else—Lisa heard from a mutual friend over the phone that Teresa had gone out with some of her friends from work. "How selfish." That's what it seemed to Lisa, so that's what she said (to herself).

Lisa is now having a kind of mental conversation with herself in preparation for the next time she talks to Teresa. She's tempted to tell Teresa just what she thinks: that what she did was pretty selfish. Maybe it would be good for Teresa to hear it, and maybe it would be good for her to say it. Maybe not.

"Don't be selfish"—a perfectly good synthetic norm. Did Teresa violate it? What does this little scenario suggest about the usefulness of and/or danger of synthetic terms and synthetic norms?

MATERIAL NORMS

If, as we have seen, formal norms and synthetic norms relate to *being* by pointing out specific character qualities—virtues or vices—which we would do well to strive for or to avoid, material norms relate to *doing* by pointing out specific actions we would do well to perform or to avoid. Material norms help us answer the question "What is the right thing to do in a particular setting?"

The phrase "help us answer the question" in the previous sentence is important. Material norms are not a substitute for personal and social moral responsibility. More specifically, as we saw in our consideration of the third sense of conscience, or conscience as judgment, moral agents—be they individuals, families or communities—retain the responsibility for discerning concretely how they might make a fitting response or "do the right thing" in specific situations. At their best, material norms help us make such concrete moral judgments by getting us in touch with the wisdom and guidance of others. If, as James Hanigan has suggested, conscience is "...the ultimate, subjective norm of morality,"[8] then material norms provide the objective norms of morality.

Some examples of material moral norms are the following:

1. Obtain the informed consent of the patient before doing invasive procedures.[9]

2. "...the direct and voluntary killing of an innocent human being is always gravely immoral."[10]

3. Medical treatments that offer the patient a reasonable hope of benefit and that can be used without excessive burden are morally appropriate.[11]

4. "All members of society have a special obligation to the poor and vulnerable. Society as a whole, acting through public and private institutions, has the moral responsibility to enhance human dignity and protect human rights."[12]

5. "Thou shalt not kill" (Exodus 20:13; Deuteronomy 5:17).

6. "When you reap the harvest of your land, you shall not reap to the very edges of your field, or gather the gleanings of your harvest. You shall not strip your vineyard bare, or gather the fallen grapes of your vineyard; you shall leave them for the poor and the alien" (Leviticus 19:9–10).

"How far can we go?" That was the question put to Dr. Williams. He is the principal of a local high school and he was part of a panel of "experts" involved in a program on sexuality formation for junior high school students in his community. The question, asked by an eighth-grader, was an honest one; it did not take Dr. Williams (the father of four children, two teenagers) off guard. Without any real hesitation he offered the following guidelines: "Certainly hugs and some

kisses for those who have become good friends are OK; but at this stage of your life, if those embraces and touches pretty directly get you 'turned on,' or if they start to lead to genital contact in any way, or if you find yourself starting to remove clothing, then you have gone too far." Most of the parents in the audience liked Dr. Williams's guidelines; many of the students did not. What do you think of his attempt to formulate a material moral norm about teen sex? What rule(s) would you offer?

As these examples illustrate, material norms are marked by complexity, diversity and, often enough, controversy. We ought not be surprised; these norms concern themselves with very specific human activity. In some ways they address "the bottom line" of moral experience. Volumes have been written about this type of moral norm. We will limit ourselves to three reflections.

The first point will serve to contrast material norms from formal and synthetic norms. All three types of moral norms seek to protect or promote basic human goods and values. That is their reason for existing. But it is worth noting that formal and synthetic norms do this differently from material norms. As we have seen, formal and synthetic norms are directed toward **moral values and moral disvalues** by telling us the kinds of character traits—virtues and vices—to strive for or avoid (honesty, love, etc.). Material norms, in contrast, are directed toward **premoral values and premoral disvalues.** And what are these? These are not character traits/virtues and vices, but other kinds of human goods and values that are important for being moral persons (and as such are goods and values that should be protected and promoted), but which are not in themselves **moral** qualities in the way that honesty and love are **moral** qualities, **moral** values. Life, health, wealth, liberty, pleasure and knowledge are examples of **premoral values.** Obviously, these are very important for human living and flourishing; we value them as goods and values to be protected and promoted, and that is why we have norms concerning them: material norms.

But *premoral* values are not essential ingredients of the moral life in the way that *moral* values are. Honesty and love are character traits that define moral goodness; moral goodness depends absolutely upon the existence of such traits of character. Formal and synthetic norms, which are directed to these moral values, are accordingly absolute in nature: there are no exceptions to "be honest" or "be loving." In contrast, premoral values, though very important, do not define moral goodness in the same way. It is possible for one to be a very good person without having a great deal of wealth and pleasure, and perhaps even without having a great deal of liberty. In fact, in the Catholic tradition at least, even life itself is not an absolute good or value, but a "relative value," which means that at times one may be called upon to give up one's life for an even greater good or value.[13] This is the what the phrase "premoral values" attempts to convey.

A second point that is important to note concerning material norms flows from what has been said about this concept of premoral values. As the above paragraph has explained, premoral values are important, but they are not absolute. Accordingly, the material norms which attempt to protect and promote premoral values are not absolute. Put differently, while there are no exceptions to "be honest" and "avoid immorality," there are plenty of exceptions to material norms like "obtain the informed consent of the patient before doing invasive procedures"; and there are even exceptions to "Thou shalt not kill." That biblical imperative names an extremely important value; human life commands respect and protection, particularly when it is most vulnerable. Even so, life itself is a premoral value, not a moral value. If that were not the case, then killing in war, in self-defense, and in capital punishment would be unthinkable for those of biblical faith. Thus, while material norms like "Thou shalt not kill" should be taken very seriously (there should be a presumption against killing), and while there may well be material norms which *for all practical purposes* are without exception (Richard Gula calls these "virtually exceptionless"), material norms are at least theoretically open to exception. Many Catholic scholars, espousing this view with us, would probably agree that a material norm like "the direct and voluntary killing of an innocent human being is always gravely immoral" is an example of a material norm that should be taken to be "virtually exceptionless."[14]

What is being suggested here regarding the nature of material norms—the fact that, theoretically at least, they are all open to exception—relates to the nature of moral experience itself. As we suggested in chapter 1's discussion of moral experience, as well as chapter 7's explanation of "Conscience as Process," concrete moral experience (about which material norms are concerned) has both a commonality and a particularity about it. One person's or one community's moral experience invariably has enough in common with the moral experience of other persons or other communities to make it unreasonable **not** to attend to the wisdom of others in discerning how to "do the right thing." That, in fact, is the ground of all moral norms. At the same time, however, moral experience is also characterized by particularity; every moral situation has unique dimensions to it, sometimes morally relevant ones. And this is the reason that it is both unrealistic and unwise to expect concrete material norms to provide ready-made answers for all of life's moral questions. Guidance and direction, yes; prepackaged solutions, no. Material moral norms are meant to serve conscience formation, not replace it.

A final observation about material norms concerns their genesis and their revisability. Material moral norms do not fall from the sky. They are the work of communal human intelligence. And, to be sure, this is true of the material norms that emerge from within the context of the Christian community. The unique sources of wisdom that the church has at its disposal—Scripture and tradition—may well provide valuable perspectives on the moral issues of the day, but they do not provide in-advance answers to contemporary moral questions. Reflecting on its own ongoing moral experience, the Christian community must use all the resources of human intelligence and creativity to connect the enduring commitments of Christian faith to ever-new moral issues and challenges. To be a genuine moral community, therefore, the Christian community must strive to be a community of moral discourse, a community that is ready and willing—anxious, in fact—to receive moral insight and reflection from whoever voices it, whether from within the Christian community or beyond its borders.

As the history of Christianity attests, sometimes it becomes clear (usually only gradually, and most often not without controversy) that the community's existing material norms are in need of revision. The Christian communities' attitudes and stances in regard to slavery serve as an example. Over the centuries the churches have moved from a posture of acceptance to a call for equality and freedom. The concrete moral teachings of the church—its material norms—evolve, change and develop as successive communities of believers seek to understand what the Spirit of God is calling them to become and to do in changing situations and contexts.

Theologian Josef Fuchs, among others, has reflected with insight on the fact that material norms are conditioned by the particular cultures of which they are a part. This means that they reflect the strengths and weaknesses, insights and blind spots, commitments and biases of particular communities. Very often, Fuchs suggests, material norms are stated in "too generalized a manner," unaware of, or at least giving insufficient attention to, important morally relevant circumstances and particularities.[15] Such norms fall short of genuinely enlightening the moral situation, and when enough members of the community notice this, there is invariably a call for revision. And this, in fact, is what it means for the Christian community to be a community of moral discourse: to be humble enough to acknowledge that its own moral wisdom is never a finished project, that it is in need of ongoing revision; and to be confident enough to truly hear the voices that call for such revision; and to hear them not as threat, but as gift.[16]

Name at least two material moral norms that seem to you to be "virtually exceptionless." Why do they seem to be "virtually exceptionless" to you? Do they appear so to others?

Name a least two material norms that, in your view, seem to be in need of revision. Why is revision called for? How do you suggest the revision be made?

Moral Norms — Some Conclusions

1. Moral norms are the general or specific instructions directing persons and communities toward virtue and/or right action.

2. Because we are not "moral islands," because we live in communities, because we can and do learn from one another, because we can and must strive to contribute to the "moral quality of life" of one another, moral norms and rules are important for morality.

3. The life story of Jesus Christ is the central and fundamental norm for Christian living.

4. Formal norms are the simplest, most uncomplicated and noncontroversial type of moral norm. Worded in positive terms, formal norms

attempt to point out particular virtues or character traits that we should strive to acquire.

5. Synthetic norms are expressed not in the language of being but of doing. "Don't lie!" and "Thou shalt not steal!" are examples of synthetic moral norms. They are expressed in negative terms; they *seem* to tell us things we should not do; and they have an absolute or exceptionless quality about them: lying and stealing are always wrong.

6. Material norms relate to *doing* by pointing out specific actions we would do well to perform or to avoid. Material norms help us answer the question "What is the right thing to do in a particular setting?"

7. Formal and synthetic norms are directed toward ***moral values and moral disvalues*** by telling us the kind of character traits—virtues and vices—to strive for or avoid (honesty, love, etc.). Material norms, in contrast, are directed toward ***premoral values and premoral disvalues.*** These are human goods and values which are important for being moral persons, but which are not in themselves *moral* qualities the way that honesty and love are *moral* qualities, *moral* values. Life, health, wealth, liberty, pleasure and knowledge are examples of ***premoral values.***

Chapter Ten.
Moral Reasoning: Our Whole Selves

Introduction: "...with all your heart, soul, mind and strength" (Mark 12:30)

1. Scene one: "Well, it's hard to say," replied Uncle Tony (by everyone's standard, the creator of the best spaghetti sauce in the Angelotti family). "I guess it has a lot to do with experience; usually I can just tell how much garlic and pepper to put into the sauce. It depends on a lot of things. Years ago I followed a recipe, but now I just know."

Scene two: "Well, it's hard to say," replied Aunt Martha (by everyone's standard, one of the most respected members of the Johnson family). Over the years people have come to recognize Aunt Martha as a woman of great integrity and good judgment. Her husband died many years ago, leaving her with two small boys to raise in a pretty tough part of the city. She struggled to "keep the ship afloat," as she says, and indeed she did. "There is no simple handbook for raising sons in this day and age. I have relied on my guts and on my God. When I wasn't sure how to deal with my boys, God helped me to see: to see which battles were worth fighting and which ones were better to let pass. On balance," she says, "God and I have done all right."

2. "And during supper Jesus...got up from the table, took off his outer robe, and tied a towel around himself. Then he poured water into a basin and began to wash the disciples' feet....After he had washed their feet, had put on his robe, and had returned to the table, he said to them, 'Do you know what I have done to you? You call me Teacher and Lord—and you are right, for that is what I am. So if I, your Lord and Teacher, have washed your feet, you also ought to wash one another's

feet. For I have set you an example, that you also should do as I have done to you.'" (John 13:2–4; 12–15)

3. "I have a dream that one day right down in Georgia and Mississippi and Alabama the sons of former slaves and the sons of former slave owners will be able to live together as brothers....I have a dream this afternoon that one day little white children and little Negro children will be able to join hands as brothers and sisters....I have a dream this afternoon that one day my four little children will be judged on the basis of the content of their character and not the color of their skin....With this faith I will go out to carve a tunnel of hope through the mountain of despair; with this faith I will go out with you and transform dark yesterdays into bright tomorrows; with this faith we will be able to achieve this new day when all of God's children—Black men and White men, Jews and Gentiles, Protestants and Catholics—will be able to join hands and sing with the Negroes in the spiritual of old, 'Free at last, free at last, thank God Almighty we're free at last.'" (Dr. Martin Luther King, Jr.)

This book has been about moral experience. We have said that moral experience concerns the "tug" or drive that calls us to strive to be good persons, to search for the way to do the right thing, and to seek to contribute to the building of just communities. Ethics, we suggested, is simply the study of moral experience; more specifically, it is the systematic and communal reflection on and analysis of moral experience. Christian ethics is ethics done in the light of Christian faith.

This present chapter is an investigation of two sets of words in the definitions just recalled. We wish to probe what is entailed in "reflecting on" and "analyzing" moral experience. And so this chapter is about moral reasoning. Christian ethics, like any other sort of ethics, of course, calls for moral reasoning; it is a work of human intelligence. But Christian ethics does *not* entail moral reasoning done in some "cool," dispassionate or antiseptic manner. It is not (or should not be) ivory-tower theorizing about esoteric questions that have little if any impact on human experience.

This is why the second set of words—"strive," "search" and "seek"—are important in the description of moral experience and important for the kind of moral reasoning that Christian ethics requires. Those words suggest passion, dedication and zeal. At its best, the moral reasoning of Christian ethics is aroused with *passion for*

175

goodness, because nothing short of the moral quality of our lives is at stake; it is done with *dedication to rightness,* because what we do has profound impact on other people and on the world around us; and it is pursued *zeal for justice,* because building just communities has everything to do with nothing less than God's reign on this earth.

To invoke the words of the Gospel, if we are driven to love God with all our heart, soul, mind and strength, we think it is also the case that the search for goodness in being, rightness in action and justice in community must also be done with all our energies of heart, soul, mind and strength. And if that is true, then analysis of what goodness, rightness and justice really require of us ought not be "cool," but should be marked with passion, dedication and zeal. Are not discussions of moral questions and issues often lively and heated? Are they not marked often by a high degree of energy and emotion? That is the way it should be. To be sure, the moral reasoning that Christian ethics calls for ought not be characterized by quick-tempered, raw or unreasoned emotional responses. But neither should it be marked by some sort of head-only, disembodied and dispassionate form of logic. The pursuit of goodness, rightness and justice calls for all of our energies. So too, the work of Christian ethics is the work of the whole person and the whole of the Christian community.

This chapter will proceed as follows. First, we will look at a centuries-old approach to moral reasoning by discussing briefly what philosophers and theologians have called "the natural moral law." Second, we will examine several different but related efforts by recent scholars to expand the horizon on what moral reasoning entails. Specifically, we will discuss the moral imagination, the place of emotion in moral reasoning, and, drawing on the insights of liberation theologians, the particular kind of moral reasoning and moral knowing that comes "from the underside," from the margins of the human community.

The Natural Moral Law:
"And All We've Got to Do Is Act Naturally"

One of the most ancient and influential modes of moral reasoning in Western civilization has been through the use of the concept of the natural moral law. With origins in Greek (and especially Stoic) philosophy, as well as in the Roman law tradition, natural-law thinking found its way into Christian philosophy and theology in the early centuries of the church. Many would argue that this mode of moral reasoning reached a high point in the writing of Thomas Aquinas (d. 1274) in the high Middle Ages. Without question, the use of natural-law concepts by influential thinkers like Aquinas accounts for the centrality of this way of thinking about the moral life within Catholicism, as well as its influence even beyond. It remains an important and influential expression of moral reasoning even today.[1]

What is the fundamental presupposition and what are some of the most general concepts of the natural moral law? What is the significance of the distinction between general principles and specific applications as far as the natural law is concerned? What are the two most important ways of interpreting what the word *natural* really means? And what is the worth of this type of moral reasoning? Let us proceed to answer these questions.

THE FUNDAMENTAL PRESUPPOSITION

The most fundamental presupposition of natural law theology[2] is really quite a positive one, indeed an optimistic one. It proceeds as follows. The universe is a good and orderly place; it bears the mark of the good and loving God who created it! Further, God's creation is intelligible: we human beings are capable (potentially at least) of recognizing the goodness and the orderliness of the universe and of all things within it.

To say this slightly differently, the universe itself and all things in it "work" or act according to their natures, that is, according to intelligible, established patterns or ways of being. A dog has a certain nature, which is different from the nature of the oak tree, which is different still from the nature of a human being. Each creature acts—must act— in accord with its proper nature.

We human beings are part of this divine plan, this divine law. We too have a certain nature and the key, the secret perhaps, to human flourishing is that we too must first recognize what our nature actually is, and then we must strive to act in accord with it. In a sense we must "go with the flow" of how we have been created. To live and act in accord

177

with our nature is, in this way of thinking, to live and act morally. To live and act contrary to our natures is to live and act immorally.

And just how shall we describe our human nature? What does it mean for human beings to live and act according to their natures? Historically perhaps the most influential answer to these questions has been Aristotle's answer. Ours is a *rational nature,* pinpointed the Philosopher; that is the distinguishing characteristic of what it means to be human. We share much with the rest of our fellow creatures (bodiliness, for example—an important aspect of who we are), but what makes us distinctively human is our ability to think, to reason. And so the most fundamental and central norm of the natural moral law is that we must act in accord with reason; and to do the reasonable thing is, of course, to do the right thing.

What seems appealing about the idea of the natural law so far? In what way is the most fundamental presupposition of the natural law optimistic? How does it "square" with floods and hurricanes? With the existence of cancer? With genetic "abnormalities"? With human selfishness and greed?

GENERAL PRINCIPLES AND SPECIFIC APPLICATIONS

So the natural law suggests that we should act in accord with our nature; we should act in accord with reason. Who could disagree with this? The key, of course, lies in determining what we think our nature actually is, and in discerning concretely whether or not something is "natural" or not. For example, is forgiving one's enemy natural? And what about sacrificing one's time or even one's life for another, or paying taxes to support the more vulnerable members of society, or performing or undergoing cardiac bypass surgery or in vitro fertilization? Are such things compatible with or contrary to our nature?

Enter a distinction. In his extended discussion of the natural law, Thomas Aquinas asked the seemingly odd question of whether or not the natural law is the same for all people, and, if it is, whether all people know equally what the natural law demands of us. He began his response by distinguishing two aspects of human reason: speculative reason and practical reason. To paraphrase, Aquinas argued that the most general or abstract natural-law principles (the kinds of principles

178

our "speculative reason" is able to determine) are indeed the same for all and are able to be known by all. Very general principles like "act in accord with reason" and "do good and avoid evil" are examples. But when it comes to much more detailed questions (questions which engage our "practical reason"), the natural law may not be the same for all, and on such specific questions it may not be able to be recognized or known by all. Hence, the concrete, material norms that human beings formulate and claim to be founded upon or reflective of the natural law will prevail, at the most, "in the majority of cases."[3]

So let us return to some specifics: Is it natural to forgive one's enemy? What would be natural and what would be "right" for Arabs and Israelis in the Middle East, or for Protestants and Catholics in Northern Ireland? Is it natural to pay taxes to support the more vulnerable members of society? And, if so, does this mean the current welfare system in the United States is natural? Is cardiac bypass surgery natural? In vitro fertilization?[4] Would it ever be natural to remove a feeding tube from a comatose patient?[5] Could homosexual relations ever be considered "natural" for persons who seem to have a "given" and permanent homosexual orientation?[6]

Aquinas, of course, does not answer these questions, most of which emerge from our culture. We will not attempt to answer them here either. The point is simply to illustrate what natural-law thinking yields and what it does not. What it yields is a way of looking at moral questions and issues: Is a proposed human action in accord with or not in accord with human nature? Is it in accord with or not in accord with human reason? Those are worthwhile questions. Living and acting in keeping with what it means to be human seems very reasonable indeed. But Aquinas's insight remains important: the more general the formulation of a norm of the natural law, the more likely will be its absoluteness and the more likely that all will concur with its truth. Thus, there is little argument about the statement "do good and avoid evil." "But as to certain matters of detail" (the way Aquinas puts it) such as whether or not removing a feeding tube could "square" with the natural law, the path to the truth is much more painstaking. These norms of the natural law are likely to be arrived at with much greater difficulty, and will not likely be grasped equally or agreed upon by all. Therefore, at the most, they are likely to prevail only in the majority of cases. Perhaps what Aquinas was really saying is that the natural law is an invitation to think, and not a quick and easy set of instructions for the moral life.

Two "Strains of Interpretation"

Drawing on the insights of other scholars, Richard Gula has noted that it is possible to identify two rather different ways of interpreting what the natural moral law is.[7] Historically, these "strains of interpretations" seem to reflect different perspectives, or at least different emphases, on what it means to be human.

The two strains of interpretation may be called "nature as physical" and "nature as rational." The first perspective takes the physical order to be the primary clue for what is natural. For human beings, to act in accord with our nature is to pay great attention to our bodily "givenness." Our physical nature, after all, is an aspect of who we are that we share in common with the rest of creation. To act in accord with nature, in this way of thinking, is to pay careful attention to the structures and functions of our bodies.

Gula suggests that in Catholicism this interpretation of the natural law has been most influential on moral issues related to sexuality and reproduction. Thus, Pope Paul VI's encyclical letter on birth regulation (1968) maintained that the use of artificial means of contraception is wrong because such practices interfere with or "impede the development of natural processes." What might at times be right about a couple's use of "natural methods of birth regulation" (timing one's sexual activity in relation to the woman's monthly cycle of fertility and infertility) is that in this instance "the married couple make legitimate use of a natural disposition" (par. 16). In both cases, the meaning of the word "natural" seems to be based heavily (if not exclusively) upon the word "physical": *to respect the physical order is to respect the natural order, which is to do the right thing*. Put simply, that is the first strain of interpretation of the natural law: the clue to what it means to act in accord with our nature is to attend carefully to the physical dimension of who we are.

The second interpretation of the natural law emphasizes, instead, "nature as rational." This perspective starts with the conviction that what distinguishes human nature from that of other creatures is our rationality, our ability to think. This view emphasizes that rationality, creativity and ingenuity are the distinguishing marks of human nature. And so, to act in accord with our nature is to search for the reasonable and sometimes creative thing to do in concrete situations. This interpretation of the natural law puts greater emphasis on the human person's and human community's ability to be open to insight and wisdom from many diverse sources, rather than simply attending to what seems in keeping with the physical or biological order. Norms of the natural law that reflect this interpretation of what is natural for human beings tend to be more open-ended and flexible than the norms that seem to have "biological givenness" as their origin.

In Gula's view, this second interpretation of the natural law has been most influential in Catholicism on issues related to social justice. In their 1986 pastoral letter, *Economic Justice for All: Catholic Teaching and the U.S. Economy,* the U.S. Catholic bishops seem to display this interpretation of moral reasoning and of what it means to be human when they discuss the movement from general principles to concrete policy choices regarding economic justice. They wrote:

> We are aware that…the movement from principle to policy is complex and difficult and that although moral values are essential in determining public policies, they do not dictate specific solutions. They must interact with empirical data, with historical, social, and political realities, and with competing demands on limited resources. The soundness of our prudential judgments depends not only on the moral force of our principles, but also on the accuracy of our information and the validity of our assumptions.[8]

This passage reflects well the second "strain of interpretation" of the natural law. The clue to acting in accord with our nature is not likely to be found by examining carefully the physical, biological order, but by attending to human wisdom and human reason wherever it can be found. To act naturally and rightly, this view suggests, is to act in accord with right reason, with all the nuance and complexity that may result. In concert with what the bishops note in their letter on economic justice, norms that reflect this view of the natural law are likely to have a certain flexibility about them, consistent with Aquinas's insight that such concrete material norms of the natural law will, at the most, prevail in the "majority of cases."

181

Consider in vitro fertilization. Is it natural? Is it morally appropriate? How do the answers to those questions relate to the two "strains of interpretation" of the natural law we have just analyzed?

Does it make a difference who is involved with such procedures—a married couple? A single woman? Does it make a difference whether or not the use of donor sperm or a donor egg is involved? Why? Does it make a difference whether or not some fertilized eggs are "screened out," discarded, as part of the procedure? Why? Does the expense involved "factor in" to its moral appropriateness? Its "naturalness"? Should there be any moral norms and guidelines for these reproductive technologies? If so, what might some of them be? If not, why not?

THE WORTH OF IT ALL

Included in his analysis of the natural law is Richard Gula's suggestion that the value of this tradition is that it provides a helpful mode of moral reasoning. Its helpfulness, he says, lies in the fact that it offers, "an approach to discovering moral value" more than yielding "a body of established content."[9] Further, he suggests that the natural law tradition "yields three basic convictions which are hallmarks of Catholic morality":

1. Natural law claims the existence of an objective moral order.
2. Natural law morality is accessible to anyone independently of one's religious commitment.
3. The knowledge of moral value can be universalized.[10]

We think Gula is right. Those three sentences capture much of what has been beneficial about the natural law tradition as a way of moral reasoning. Even so, without attempting a lengthy analysis of these three points, it seems important to acknowledge what "the other side of the coin" is in relation to each of them.

First, the natural-law tradition's presupposition that there is something objective about our moral obligations seems right; goodness and badness, rightness and wrongness, justice and injustice are not simply a matter of individual whim or opinion. Nevertheless, natural-law thinkers have often erred in the opposite direction by not attending enough to the subjective nature of knowledge, including moral knowledge. Truth is not "out there" like some sort of intellectual tree stump, waiting for human beings to stumble upon it. Rather, if thinkers like Bernard Lonergan are right—and we think they are—then truth is a judgment, a conclusion, that we human knowers make after having been attentive to all that we need to be attentive to and critical in analyzing what we have attended to before we conclude that something is true.[11] In other words, knowledge, including moral knowledge, inevitably has a subjective dimension to it.

The natural-law tradition's insistence that there is an objective moral order is not wrong, but as that tradition has been understood by many, it may be incomplete. If there is still a place for the natural-law tradition it needs to account for the fact that, in Lonergan's words, "... objectivity is simply the consequence of authentic subjectivity, of genuine attention, genuine intelligence, genuine reasonableness, genuine responsibility."[12]

In concert with this, many recent scholars suggest that too much of natural-law reasoning in the past has presumed a view of nature that was static, individualistic and overly concerned with the biological order. Increasingly, the personal and communal nature of persons and of moral experience has been emphasized. Seen in this light, moral experience and human nature itself are seen as dynamic, historical and social.[13] That is why in chapter 2 we emphasized that human persons are free, intelligent, responsible, social, unfolding and spiritual. There may indeed still be a place for natural law as a mode of moral reasoning, but it will need to take emphases such as these into account.

A second strength of natural law morality is that it is accessible to anyone independently of one's religious commitment. Catholic tradition reflects this thoroughly by mounting its moral arguments on its view of what is and is not in keeping with human nature, with human reason. In this way, Catholic moral teachings on everything from the appropriateness or inappropriateness of hi-tech reproductive procedures to issues of contraception and sterilization to issues of economic justice have been based, predominately at least, not on the teachings of the New Testament, but on the natural moral law.

Sometimes strengths, from a different angle, are revealed as weaknesses. Accordingly, much recent scholarship—including from within Catholicism—have pointed out the "down side" of this dimension of natural-law reasoning. By emphasizing that our fundamental moral obligation is to be reasonable, to be human, does natural-law thinking tend to "factor out" Christian faith? Does it trivialize the Gospel message? What about being Christlike and being a disciple? Does emphasis on the natural law marginalize the powerful scriptural stories and narratives that are so much at the heart of what it means to be a follower of Christ?[14] The point is that without necessarily rejecting the entire natural-law tradition, many contemporary theologians are issuing a call for Christian ethics—for Christian moral reasoning—to be much more *directly and explicitly* Christian.

A final strength of natural-law thinking has been its conviction that knowledge of moral value can be universalized. There is much that is true and important here. Based upon this kind of conviction, the United Nations not only asks but attempts to respond to moral questions that impact humankind across cultures. Concern for our common natural resources (indeed for the planet itself!), solidarity with our fellow human beings who suffer oppression or hunger, and commitment to take action when the human rights of others are violated all seem to point to the fact that at least some moral and premoral values and disvalues are universal in nature.

At the same time, however, another question lingers (not unlike the one Aquinas asked centuries ago): is what is "natural" the same for all people? And if so, is it able to be known in the same way by all people? Just what role does history and culture play in determining how we understand the "nature" of institutions like marriage or economic justice in different times and places? Is democracy more "natural" than other political orders? And concerning the physical and biological orders, consider questions like these: could it be that in vitro fertilization could be "natural" for one culture/one couple, but not for another? How shall we understand the phenomenon of "homosexual orientation"? *If* such an orientation is found to be an aspect of one's biological "givenness," does that make it natural for such a person, and if so, would that mean that homosexual genital activity could be morally appropriate in some instances?

There is something very attractive—indeed important—about the "universal" aspects of the natural-law tradition. Our need for moral dialogue across cultures may well require such a mode of moral reasoning. Even so, as some of the questions in the previous paragraph may suggest, if there is still room for natural-law reasoning, it will need not only to attend to what is common to all, but will need to make room for what is unique about each.

Moral Reasoning: Expanding the Horizon

The natural-law tradition has been an important part of the history of Christian ethics, and that is why we have given it prominence here. In recent decades, however, many scholars have been expanding the horizon on human reasoning, including moral reasoning. We human beings are capable of many ways of learning, as these scholars have stressed. There are many routes to the discernment of goodness, rightness and justice; attention to them all is important in order to do justice to moral reasoning. And so, to mention just a few contributions to this expanding notion of human reasoning, Howard Gardner has proposed a theory about "multiple intelligences"; Mary Field Belenky and colleagues have called attention to "women's ways of knowing"; William Spohn has written about "the reasoning heart"; Springer and Deutsch (and others) have noted human "left-brain and right-brain" capacities; Philip Keane has highlighted the place of "the moral imagination"; and Sidney Callahan has discussed "reason and emotion in moral decision making."[15]

Combined with some points from the critique of the natural-law tradition we have seen — the need to "own up to" the subjective nature of moral knowing; the search for a way to make the Christian story more central for the Christian moral life; and the need to attend more fully to the particularities of moral experience — one might well conclude that the natural law, as a way of moral reasoning, may simply be too small. At the very least, moral reasoning is much "bigger" (and more elusive) than mere logical deduction from general principles to concrete conclusions, which is how much of natural-law reasoning has proceeded over the centuries. The search for goodness in being, rightness in action and justice in community must be conducted, not simply with logic, not simply with our "right brain," but with all of our energies of heart, soul, mind and strength.

It is not possible to comment here on the insights of all the scholars just mentioned. Grouping several of them together, let us look at the expanding horizon on moral reasoning by discussing briefly "the moral

185

imagination," the place of emotion in the moral life and the particular kind of reasoning and truth that emerges "from the margins," that is, from the experience of those who suffer, from those who are oppressed.

Moral Reasoning: Room to Imagine

Philip S. Keane, SS, is not the first moral theologian to call attention to the place of the imagination in the moral life and in Christian ethics. In fact, in his 1984 book, *Christian Ethics and Imagination,* he stressed that for centuries scholars have acknowledged the role of the imagination in morality, even though the significance of that role has been underplayed.

As Keane stresses, to argue for the importance of imagination in morality is not to call for chaos or for irrationality. In chapter 1 he makes this point well:

> ...the word *rational* can and should be used to describe all of our human thought processes, not simply our logical processes. With this deeper sense in mind, it is not accurate to describe imagination as antirational or as critiquing rationality. Instead, the book will argue that imagination is indeed a rational process even though it involves a different kind of rationality from what we find in logical thought.[16]

What, then, does "moral imagination" entail? What kind of moral reasoning is engaged by the imagination? Imagination involves a host of things, of course, many of which we cannot do justice to here, but the following passage from Keane's book displays a particularly important contribution that the imagination makes to moral reasoning:

> ...imagination can be described as the basic process by which we draw together the concrete and the universal elements of our human experience. With imagination we let go of any preconceived notions of how the abstract and the concrete relate to one another. We suspend judgment about how to unite the concrete and the abstract. We let the two sides of our knowing play with one another. By allowing the interplay between the two aspects of our knowing, we get a much deeper chance to look at what we

know, to form a vision of it. With this deeper, imagining vision of reality we are able to make a more appropriate connection between conversion and abstraction.[17]

Later on Keane stresses that by drawing on our intuition and emotion, and by bringing the concrete and universal aspects of moral experience into dialogue with one another, our imagination "helps us find objective or human moral truth."[18]

Three brief comments on this may be helpful. First, Keane's description of the way in which our imagination helps bring together the concrete and the abstract aspects of moral experience connects magnificently with what we have said takes place in "Conscience as Process" and "Conscience as Judgment." Previously we have called attention to two distinct but related aspects of moral experience: "particularity" and "commonality." When it is engaged in well, "Conscience as Process" enables moral agents—individuals or communities—to attend to both of those aspects of a moral situation. It is the imagination that helps us "suspend judgment" (to hold off on "Conscience as Judgment") until those two dimensions of experience, those two "sides of our knowing" have really listened to one another. The imagination, in other words, helps us to be creative, because when these two dimensions of moral experience are brought into dialogue, new and possibly liberating—but also potentially challenging—moral possibilities may emerge, possibilities that might not have been seen with the simple logical deduction of moral conclusions from general principles.

Second, as Keane and others[19] have noted, our rational ability to imagine is related to the human capacity to reason by way of analogy. Over the centuries, many scholars have noted that when we affirm something to be true about God, we do so by way of analogy. Put differently, our truth statements about God "point to" God; though they may affirm something real, they do not exhaust the mystery of God—neither singly nor even in concert with one another. They all limp. And so we might say that just as a rock is strong and provides a firm foundation on which to build, so too God is like a rock; God's love for us is strong and provides a firm foundation upon which to build our lives. And as we might say (as did the prophet Isaiah, 66:11–13) that just as a mother, with love and tenderness, nurses her children, so too God is like a loving and tender mother who nurses and nurtures us.[20]

187

Our ability to make analogies draws on our ability to imagine, to make rational connections and to "jump" from one affirmation to another.

Something similar to this is at work in the moral imagination. At the heart of what is involved in making moral judgments is our ability to make rational comparisons, connections and analogies between one moral situation and another. Over the centuries, ethicists have called this activity *casuistry:* the practice of making moral judgments not by deducing conclusions from major premises, but by analyzing "paradigm cases" and noting how one moral situation or case is similar to or different from others.[21] Out of such comparing and contrasting a reasonable, practical moral judgment may emerge, one that has attended to commonality by analyzing the judgments of others in similar situations, and one that has attended to particularity by noting carefully the unique features of the moral situation at hand.

By way of example, scholars have argued back and forth in recent years over whether or not it might ever be appropriate to remove a feeding tube from a comatose patient. The practice of casuistry led ethicists to ask whether such an action would be like removing other forms of life-sustaining medical treatment (something almost all would agree to be justified when the treatment has become more burdensome than beneficial), or whether removing a feeding tube is more like depriving someone of a simple and basic form of nursing care. The point is to note the kind of reasoning involved: comparing, contrasting and analogizing. It is close to the heart of practical moral decision making.

A final comment on imagination concerns experience. Can the moral imagination be trusted? What is to prevent it from missing the mark, from comparing, contrasting and analogizing in ways that distort rather than reflect reality? Our response is that there are no guarantees! Of course we can miss the mark; of course we can get it wrong. But so too can rational deduction, logic and discursive reasoning. At times those modes of reasoning may fail to attend sufficiently to important details in the moral situation, and at times moral principles and norms may themselves bear the marks of the prejudices and biases of the culture from which they come (one thinks of laws and norms that reflect "isms" like racism and sexism).

Moral imagination can be skewed just as well. Even so, two "checks and balances" for moral imagination are *experience* and *community.* The vignette that opened this chapter described Aunt Martha: a woman of great integrity and good judgment. She seems to know just when to speak and how to act morally. We suspect that her moral imagination is well developed, and that it became so by way of experience. She has many years worth of experience in making good, practical moral judgments; she has become good at letting the two sides of moral experience, the concrete and the abstract, "play with one another," suspending judgment until a creative and fitting response in the situation emerges.

A second help for the moral imagination is community. The activity of comparing, contrasting and analogizing is usually not best done alone, but in dialogue with the wisdom of trusted others, that is, in the context of community. Back to the opening vignette: if Uncle Tony is good at making the sauce and if Aunt Martha is good at making moral judgments, they didn't get there by themselves. Recipes and rules, consultation and dialogue, and, yes, plenty of sauce that was too spicy and quite a few judgments that were "unfitting" were undoubtedly made along the way. Like most worthwhile things in life, a well-developed moral imagination is not fashioned without flaws; it is not formed without seeking the advice of others, starting over and trying again.

Consider the second vignette at the opening of this chapter: the story of Jesus washing the feet of the disciples. Note the conclusion: "I have given you a model to follow, so that as I have done for you, you should also do."

How does one follow a moral model? How do we move from seeing what another has done to what we should do? In what way does such a movement call for moral imagination?

Give two examples of how this story about Jesus might serve as a moral model: a model for an individual person and a model for a community.

How might we "miss the mark" in moving from this moral model to our own situation? How might **experience** *and* **community** *serve as "checks and balances" that might help us make the movement well?*

Moral Reasoning: The Place of Emotion

In recent years, as more and more philosophers and theologians have come to argue for the important and positive role that emotions can play in the moral life, they have often begun their reflections by noting that in too much of Western civilization's approach to morality, emotions have been seen as more harmful than helpful for good moral living, more of a threat than a gift to moral reasoning. William C. Spohn, for example, begins a very fine summary article on "Passions and Principles" by noting that, "(s)ince religious morality fears emotional excess, many a preacher echoes Charles Chauncy, the foremost critic of the Great Awakening in 1740: 'There is such a thing as real religion...and 'tis in its nature a sober, calm, reasonable thing.'"[22] The idea is an ancient one: the more that emotion can be eliminated from moral reasoning, or at the least the more it can be *ruled* by sober and calm reason, the better.

Is there truth here? Can the emotions, the passions, interfere with moral reasoning? Of course they can. How many of us have ever let our anger — to take one example — "get the better of us"? How many of us have ever had to say, "I'm sorry; I wish I hadn't said that; I wish I hadn't acted to impulsively"? So be assured, what follows is not an argument that emotion alone is the key to moral living.

What, then, shall we say about the emotions in moral reasoning and in the moral life? We will highlight just three things: the way emotions relate to values, the way they energize us for action and the way they are "schooled" by the stories we have learned in the interpersonal relationships and communities of which we are a part.

The first thing to note about the emotions in moral reasoning is that they have a certain location. Their best "place," we believe, is at the beginning of moral reasoning. The way theologian Bernard Lonergan put it, what is morally important about our feelings is that they help us to recognize values — perhaps that a *moral value* like honesty or integrity is in danger of being compromised, or that a *premoral value* like life or liberty is being threatened.[23] Our emotional responses in such situations are healthy and important signals that something morally significant is at stake. So if a situation stirs us to anger, to rage, that may be the critically important beginning of moral reasoning.

In a recent book, theologians Daniel C. Maguire and A. Nicholas Fargnoli have elaborated on this initiating role of emotion in moral reasoning. Their insights are worth quoting at some length, particularly because of the way they argue that our "affective responses" are a part of moral reasoning itself.

An affective response is part of the evaluative process of ethics and qualifies as a kind of moral knowledge. We should listen to our feelings. They may, at times, be smarter than our abstract reasonings. It is possible that some persons might not be able to explain or defend their affective responses, yet they have them. It is also possible that some people might go on to think about their first feelings on a moral matter and reverse their position. A negative response might, upon further reflection, yield to a positive judgment or vice versa. Any change should occur within a process that is morally informed. The change should be one from knowing to knowing better. Something happens in the affective response that must be called knowledge, and that knowledge leads us on to subsequent rational analysis that may confirm or deny the original feeling.[24]

Maguire and Fargnoli have it right: our affections, our passions and emotions, are not the end-point of moral knowledge, but a critically important doorway to it. This is what led Sidney Callahan to suggest that we should "...be especially aware that graver moral danger arises from a deficit of moral emotion than from emotional excess."[25] And so, for example, when a moral agent—a person or a community—is no longer angered and outraged by injustice, when passion for justice has been so deadened that the atrocities connected with violence, racism or sexism are no longer felt or perhaps even seen, then the problem is not too much emotion, but too little.

A second role the emotions play in the moral life and in moral reasoning is that they energize us for action. Morality, after all, is not simply about good thoughts. It is about striving to become good persons; it is about the drive for doing the right thing; and it is about our effort to build just communities. None of those things happen without energy, because most often goodness, rightness and justice are accomplished only after a long and difficult uphill battle. Our passions, our emotions, are what provide us with the moral energy needed for such quests.

Martin Luther King, Jr. knew this well. His "I Have a Dream" speech was directed not only to the heads of his listeners, but to their imaginations, their hearts, their "guts." He was not interested simply in sober and calm reasoning, but in stirring the moral energy of the country for change, for justice. For that he needed to move hearts. He did.

Something of the same thing is seen in the stories of Jesus in the New Testament. So often there are scenes of Jesus being "moved with compassion" at the sight of a hungry crowd, a suffering woman, a despised sinner or a grieving loved one. But note that these stories are not simply portraits of Jesus' emotional life. Predominately they are stories of action, tales of controversial deeds like healing on the Sabbath or taking liberties with some of the laws and customs of his religious community. Jesus of Nazareth, like anyone worthy of being held up as a moral model, was not without emotion and passion. Those energies fueled his moral life. And as it was with Jesus, so it must be with all of us: deeds of compassion and healing, courage and justice do not get accomplished from the neck up. They begin with emotion stirring in our hearts, and they are brought to completion by the passion that is the fuel in our guts.

A third important way the emotions function in the moral life is that they are fashioned in the context of our relationships with persons and communities, and they are "schooled" by the stories that provide the meaning of those relationships. In other words, for good or for ill, our emotions are fashioned by *relationships* and *stories*.

In a book entitled *Virtuous Passions: The Formation of Christian Character,* G. Simon Harak, provides a helpful analysis of the passions in the thought of Thomas Aquinas. Harak suggests that for Aquinas the passions are essentially interrelational:

> [Aquinas]...takes seriously the fact that we are created by God, that we need God, and that we come toward God better through being drawn, being loved, *being moved,* than by our own direct efforts. Our passions, then, can be understood as receiving empowerment from an other....For Thomas, then, the human being is a "moved mover."[26]

If Aquinas (via Harak) is right, then what is true in a preeminent and unambiguously good way of our relationship with God (the Other) is true in a less perfect way of our relationships with persons: these relationships move us; they shape and frame our "way-of-seeing-and-being-in-the-world." Put differently, the way we are "moved" in our relationship with *the Other* (God) and in our relationships with all others influences profoundly the formation of our character. Anyone who has ever fallen in love knows this. The movement of heart of such an experience can shape and reshape one's way of seeing oneself and one's world, and it can refashion one's way of living: "Doesn't Tom seem to be just a different sort of person these days? Isn't it remarkable what falling in love has done for him? Would that Melissa had come along years ago!"

There is, of course, a very important implication to this: the persons and communities we associate with are critically important for our moral lives. This is acted out in an obvious way in the anxiety of parents who become aware that their son or daughter has started to "hang out" with a local gang. It is acted out much less obviously every time we "breath in" a community's subtle, nearly invisible, but pervasively influential attitudes, like racism or sexism. We are *moved* affectively by the relationships and communities of which we are a part, and our character is shaped by such movement—that is the point. Sometimes the movement is positive, sometimes not.

There is a narrative dimension to all of this. And here we only need to recall chapter 5's discussion of how stories "work on us." As William C. Spohn puts it, what stories do for us morally is that they "school our affections."[27] And what is crucial in this respect, as we have seen, is that our affections, our emotions, are critically important because they help us to recognize moral and premoral values in the first place, and because they energize us for the sustained striving toward goodness, rightness and justice.

The implication of this last point also deserves further attention. What kind of stories are we taking in—in our relationships, in our families or through the media? And what kind of stories are we sharing with others, particularly our children? The stories we take to be true, and the stories that we tell as a way of providing meaning for our lives have profound impact on our affective ability to recognize what is valuable and to respond to it in a genuinely human manner. And so it may be worth taking stock of the stories we are told and the stories we tell about everything from what it means to be successful, to what the relationship of the sexes is "supposed to" be like, to the rightful or not-so-rightful place of violence in human life, to what the relationship might be between self-sacrifice and happiness, to the meaning of death. We are bombarded with images, symbols and stories about all of those realities; our affections and dispositions are "schooled" by them. Our affections, in turn, impact our recognition of and response to values. Thus, if it is true that moral reasoning does not take place simply with the use of logic, it is equally true that it does not take place in isolation from others. Our capacity for moral reasoning is shaped by the relationships and stories of which we are a part.

Tell two stories—one about an individual's moral experience, the other about a community's—that illustrate the way in which emotion can been helpful in moral reasoning. Tell two more stories that illustrate how emotion can interfere with moral reasoning.

Consider a contemporary and controversial moral issue—physician-assisted suicide, capital punishment, welfare/"workfare," etcetera—and discuss the role that emotion plays in moral reasoning about that issue.

Moral Reasoning: Truth from the Margin

From start to finish, this book attempts not to move too far away from concrete moral **experience.** We have said throughout that Christian ethics is the systematic and communal reflection on and analysis of moral experience in the light of Christian faith.

At this point it is worth asking, "Whose experience?" "Whose experience is to count as important for, indeed worthy of, reflection and analysis?" That may seem to be an odd question. Ought not the answer be, "Well, everyone's, of course!" If life were played on a level playing field, that answer might be sufficient. But the field is not level, and so the answer will not do.

This is a world into which the power of sin has been unleashed. And as we discussed in chapter 4 on community and will examine further in the final chapters on sin and conversion, human sinfulness is imbedded in the very structures of human relationships, into the social structures that make human communities "tick." So there exists not only the injustices of individual persons, but the patterns and practices of injustice in the social structures of human communities. Conversion from sin, therefore, must be not only an individual enterprise, but a social one.

If this is not daunting enough, the same reality must be named concerning the processes of human reasoning itself, including moral reasoning. Our capacity for moral reasoning is itself marked and marred (not destroyed) by human sinfulness. The primary way in which this manifests itself in Christian ethics is by the marginalization of the moral experience of the powerless by the powerful. Whose experience counts? Whose moral experience is worthy of reflection and analysis? To whom shall we listen in our effort to discern moral wisdom, moral truth? Too often the experience of the powerful has made the experience of the powerless invisible; the reflections and analyses of slave owners have negated the insights of the slaves; the voices of men have drowned out the voices of women; the practices of the oppressor have muted the contributions of the oppressed. Sadly, the answer to the question, "Whose experience should count?" is not the same as the answer to the question, "Whose experience has counted?"

In recent decades, however, increasing numbers of philosophers and theologians have been issuing a call for a much more *inclusive* approach to moral reasoning. Put differently, reflection on what goodness, rightness and justice really entail requires that the moral experience of all be brought to the table. Moreover, to take it a step further, liberation theologians have suggested that if we are really interested in moving forward, if we really want new insights into goodness, rightness and especially justice, then the voice of the previously voiceless needs to be given a special hearing. "Preferential option for the poor"—a frequently invoked theme in contemporary social-justice teaching in the Catholic Church[28]—does *not* mean greater acts of charity trickling down from the rich to the poor, but, much more profoundly, the *liberation of both the oppressed and the oppressor* from the patterns and practices (the social structures) that are the mark of such humanity-dividing injustices in the first place.

Enter Paulo Freire's *Pedagogy of the Oppressed*. Published in the early 1970s, the insights of this Brazilian educator have left their mark far beyond the borders of his country. He has proposed that what is needed is an approach to education—indeed, an approach to moral reasoning—that has as its aim nothing less than the liberation of the oppressed from unjust and dehumanizing social structures.

At the beginning of his book, Freire states the central question or problem that drives his work:

> How can the oppressed, as divided, unauthentic beings, participate
> in developing the pedagogy of their liberation? Only as they dis-
> cover themselves to be "hosts" of the oppressor can they contribute

195

to the midwifery of their liberating pedagogy. As long as they live in the duality in which *to be* is *to be like,* and *to be like* is *to be like the oppressor,* this contribution is impossible. The pedagogy of the oppressed is an instrument for their critical discovery that both they and their oppressors are manifestations of dehumanization.[29]

Why is it important that the moral experience of the oppressed—named and voiced in the first person, that is, by oppressed persons themselves—be given a prominent and even preferential place in moral reflection? Because their own liberation from oppression cannot happen otherwise *AND* because the liberation of the perpetrators of oppression cannot happen otherwise either! In order for the full humanization (and indeed Christianization) of both the oppressed and the oppressors to move forward, "moral truth from the margin" must be given a voice. The "gift" of the oppressed to the oppressor is the naming of oppression and the insistence that it need not/must not be so.

Freire goes on to name two distinct but related stages of this human-ist and libertarian pedagogy:

> In the first, the oppressed unveil the world of oppression and through the praxis commit themselves to its transformation. In the second stage, in which the reality of oppression has already been transformed, this pedagogy ceases to belong to the oppressed and becomes a pedagogy of all people in the process of permanent lib-eration....In the first stage this confrontation occurs through the change in the way the oppressed perceive the world of oppres-sion; in the second stage, through the expulsion of the myths cre-ated and developed in the old order....[30]

Freire's insights drive home the message that the answer to the question, "Whose experience is to count as important for and worthy of moral reflection and analysis?" matters a great deal. Because oppression and injustices are not simply the conscious and intentional choices of individual persons, but, more insidiously, part of the air we breathe, part of the commonly accepted social patterns and practices of the day, they tend to be nearly invisible. And of course those least like-ly to recognize them are those whose lives are made comfortable by those unjust and oppressive social structures. Hence, if moral truth—in all its wholeness and liberating challenge—is to emerge, it needs to be voiced from the margins, from those whose lives are made burdensome and at times unbearable by oppression and injustice. The liberation of all—oppressed and oppressor—hangs in the balance.

Freire's pedagogy was articulated with the economic and political oppression of his Brazilian sisters and brothers in mind. Even so, the general lines of his thought shed light on the processes of oppression and liberation as they are played out in other places and cultures. Perhaps this is most clear in feminist theology, which is so often thought of and explicitly named as *feminist liberation theology.* To take just one example from the vast contributions of contemporary feminist theologians, the title of a recent collection of articles on different aspects of feminist theology edited by Catherine Mowry LaCugna is instructive: *Freeing Theology: The Essentials of Theology in Feminist Perspective.*[31] Freeing theology, freeing theology of its one-sidedness, of its predominately male-centered ways of thinking, of its tendency to image God and most other sacred realities in male categories, freeing moral theology of the way it has too often been blind to the injustices and oppression experienced by women—all of these comprise the agenda of feminist liberation theology. It is cut from the same cloth as Freire's pedagogy of the oppressed; both are strategies for a much more inclusive approach to moral reasoning; both are vehicles that allow moral wisdom and moral truth to emerge from the margin. The liberation of all—oppressed and oppressor, poor and wealthy, women and men—is at stake.

To conclude this chapter on moral reasoning, it seems clear that any cohesive group striving to be a community that promotes the full human development and flourishing of all—and without question the Christian community is called to such a task—must not only be open, but ready to listen to the voices of moral wisdom wherever and from whomever they are spoken. That would be sufficient if everyone had access to the conversation. But not everyone does, so we must do better than openness. If Freire is right—and the wager here is that he is—the voice of moral wisdom is not easily heard from the margins. The voice of the powerful tends to mute what is spoken from the periphery. Accordingly, there must be a special and preferential place at the table for "the other," particularly the oppressed. Room must be made at the table. No, the presence of "the other" in the conversation is usually not comfortable; their utterings are likely to be unfamiliar, uncomfortable and unsettling. But the full human development and flourishing *of all*

197

requires that their place at table be reserved. To return to another of Freire's images, when "the other" shows up at table, it may well happen that "the other" turns out to be "host" to those who naively and mistakenly thought it was their table. Moral truth from the margin yields such surprises.

"Moral Truth from the Margins": Give two examples of this kind of moral truth—one from your own experience, and one that reflects social moral experience.

"Preferential Option for the Poor": what seems right about this phrase? What seems uncomfortable, even dangerous, about it? Try to name an individual person and then a social structure that seems to reflect a "preferential option for the poor."

Moral Reasoning—Some Conclusions

1. The most fundamental presupposition of natural-law theology is that the universe is a good and orderly place; it bears the mark of the good and loving God who created it! Further, God's creation is intelligible: we human beings are capable (potentially at least) of recognizing the goodness and the orderliness of the universe and of all things within it.

2. The most general natural-law principles (which our "speculative reason" is able to determine) are the same for all and are able to be known by all. Very general principles like "act in accord with reason" and "do good and avoid evil" are examples. But regarding more detailed questions (those which engage our "practical reason"), the natural law may not be the same for all or recognized by all. Hence, the concrete, material norms human beings formulate with the claim that they are based on or reflective of the natural law will prevail, at the most, "in the majority of cases."

3. Two strains of interpretation of the natural law may be called "nature as physical" and "nature as rational." The first perspective takes the physical order to be the primary clue for what is natural. For human beings, to act in accord with our nature is to pay great attention to our bodily "givenness." The second interpretation of the natural law emphasizes, instead, "nature as rational." This perspective starts with

the conviction that what distinguishes human nature from that of other creatures is our rationality, our ability to think. This view emphasizes that rationality, creativity and ingenuity are the distinguishing marks of human nature.

4. Natural law "yields three basic convictions which are hallmarks of Catholic morality":
   a. Natural law claims the existence of an objective moral order.
   b. Natural-law morality is accessible to all, regardless of religious commitment.
   c. The knowledge of moral value can be universalized.

5. "It is not accurate to describe imagination as antirational or as critiquing rationality; imagination is indeed a rational process, even though it involves a different kind of rationality from what we find in logical thought. Imagination can be described as the basic process by which we draw together the concrete and the universal elements of our human experience. With imagination we let go of any preconceived notions of how the abstract and the concrete relate to one another. We suspend judgment about how to unite the concrete and the abstract." (Philip S. Keane, SS, in *Christian Ethics and Imagination,* pp. 16, 81)

6. The place of the emotions in the moral life is "at the beginning": they help us to recognize value. The emotions also energize us for sustained and often difficult moral action. Our emotions are "schooled" by the stories we have learned in the interpersonal relationships and communities of which we are a part.

7. Because oppression and injustices are not simply the conscious and intentional choices of individual persons, but, more insidiously, part of the air we breathe, part of the commonly accepted social patterns and practices of the day, they tend to be nearly invisible. Those least likely to recognize them are those whose lives are made comfortable by such structures. Hence, if moral truth—in all its wholeness and liberating challenge—is to emerge, it needs to be voiced from the margins, from those whose lives are made burdensome and at times unbearable by oppression and injustice.

Chapter Eleven.
Sin and Morality

1. Have mercy on me, O God, according to your steadfast love;
according to your abundant mercy blot out my transgressions.
Wash me thoroughly from my iniquity, and cleanse me from my sin.

For I know my transgressions, and my sin is ever before me.
Against you, you alone, have I sinned,
   and done what is evil in your sight,
so that you are justified in your sentence
   and blameless when you pass judgment.
Indeed, I was born guilty,
   a sinner when my mother conceived me. (Psalm 51:1–5)

What does the psalmist mean by "transgressions"? Are these different from the "sin" committed against God, or the guilt we are all born into? Why are these faults, this sin, and that guilt confessed to God? What does the psalmist seek from God?

2. Lisa remembers how she used to answer people's simple questions: "How are you doing?" "How's your family?" "Fine, just fine," she'd say. She believed it was true. It wasn't until she got older that Lisa began to get a better insight into her own life and into her own family. Things have not been fine, and, as she has learned, things have not been "normal."

Lisa doesn't like to place all the "blame" on one person, but it is true that a lot of what has not been fine in her family starts with her father, Bill. On one hand, Bill is a "nice guy": outgoing, jovial, friendly. All that is true, at least when Bill has not been drinking. Unfortunately, that has too seldom been the case. Lisa grew up thinking about her dad as a social drinker: a few drinks after work to relax, some drinks in the course of the evening until he "got tired and went to bed," and, of course, his "weekend-relax-time," when he would drink even more "seriously." Those were some of the hardest times. Often when her dad drank he just got sleepy and "messy." (Lisa remembers how she didn't like to have her friends come over to her house.) Sometimes it was a lot worse than "messy." Lisa knows now that she was blind to it earlier in her life, but she has gradually become aware that all along the way—especially on these weekend binges—her dad would be a bit violent and abusive, especially of her mother. Lisa always thought of her mother as "a saint" because of the patience with which she dealt with her dad, but she wasn't aware of the whole picture. Now she's not sure if "saint" is the right word.

The turning point for Lisa—the "cold-water-in-the-face" eye-opener —came when she stumbled into a conversation a couple of years ago between Alison, her oldest sister, and her mom. They were talking about the sexual "encounters" between her dad and Alison. Apparently this went on for some time. Alison was pretty young, and didn't know how to respond to her dad's drunken advances. She has learned. But it was devastating to Alison in the long run, and it has left quite a mark on Lisa, too.

All this was a while back. Since then Dad got into treatment—treatment that he's still struggling with. Mom and Dad are separated now, and who knows where the marriage is headed. But for the first time ever, over these last couple of years, things have gradually come out in the open. It's not pretty, but at least it's real.

How would you describe the kinds of things happening in this story? Does the word "sin" seem appropriate? Inappropriate? Explain?

3. "To be sure the disturbances which so frequently occur in the social order result in part from the natural tensions of economic, political and social forms. But at a deeper level they flow from human pride and selfishness, which contaminate even the social sphere. When the structures of affairs are flawed by the consequences of sin, human persons, already born with a bent toward evil, find there new inducements to sin, which cannot be overcome without strenuous efforts and the assistance of grace." (Vatican II, The Pastoral Constitution on the Church in the Modern World, par. 25)

What does this passage say about the relationship between our per-sonal choices and the unjust social structures in our world? How do these two dimensions of our lives shape and influence one another? What is the role of grace in dealing with this situation, and where does this grace come from?

Introduction: The Experience of Moral Evil and the Notion of Sin

More than twenty years ago the title of Karl Menninger's best-selling book asked its readers *Whatever Became of Sin?* That is a question that continues to haunt many contemporary Christians.[1] On the one hand, members of our parents' and grandparents' generations remember a time when the clergy regularly railed against the power of sin, and when Saturday evening confessional lines wrapped around both sides of the church. Whatever happened to all those sermons and confession-al lines? Where did sin go? On the other hand, many in our own gen-eration find ourselves confused by theologians and bishops who cry out against so-called social sins like racism, sexism and militarism, and urge us to go into our voting booths and reform sinful political, eco-nomic and social structures. How can structures or systems commit sins, or repent of their sinfulness? Does a city, country or church feel guilt or remorse, or face eternal damnation?

Of course many Christians are quite happy with these changes, relieved that we have moved away from some of the fire and brimstone of old-time religion, that we are giving sin a smaller place in our the-ology and preaching, spending more time and energy proclaiming the good news of God's mercy and grace, and that we are finally address-ing some of the social injustices that tear at the fabric of our commu-nities and oppress the poor. Others, however, are deeply concerned that we may be losing our sense of sin, that we may be in denial about our brokenness, malice or need for salvation. Still, whatever confusion or disagreement we may be experiencing on this topic, there is little rea-son to fear that sin itself has gone away. Even a cursory reading of the daily newspaper or a glance at the evening news make it clear that as persons and communities we continue to have a nearly unlimited capacity for inhumanity to one another. Stories about religious, racial and ethnic violence in Ireland, Bosnia and Rwanda; political corruption and cover-ups in Washington; financial scandals and deceptions in our banks and corporations; and sexual abuse and domestic violence in our homes make it clear that sin has certainly not gone on vacation.

So then, what is this thing called sin? How are we to understand the mystery of human sinfulness, a question that biblical and religious authors down through the ages have seen as one of the central themes of our faith? What is this seemingly ineradicable and pervasive moral evil that continues to show up in our hearts, our deeds and our structures? Is sin a crime we commit against God's laws, a tragic flaw we inherit as part of our human condition or an evil power that seduces and enslaves us? Do we freely choose to sin, or are we led into sin by some trait inherited from our ancestors, or by the influence and example of unjust social structures?

Whatever the answers to these questions are, we need first to acknowledge that sin is a religious concept. Unlike purely ethical notions like *good* and *bad, right* and *wrong, just* and *unjust,* or legal terms like *crime, felony* and *misdemeanor,* the idea of sin situates our conversation in a religious context. For sin is ultimately about a rift in our relationship with God. Thus, all sin-talk is ultimately linked to God-talk and makes no sense outside this setting. This does not mean that sin is not also a moral issue, for sin is clearly about the moral evil we feel ourselves drawn to, and all too often choose to commit. Still, sin is not just about doing evil; it's about saying no to God.

Given the religious nature of sin, then, it makes sense to turn to Scripture and church teaching to get a better understanding of what we are talking about here. Thus, in this chapter we will first take a look at what the Bible has to say about the experience and meaning of human sinfulness. Then, from an historical perspective, we will examine briefly some important Catholic teachings relative to sin. Finally, and more extensively, we will investigate several contemporary theological analyses of human sinfulness.

Where does sin show up in our lives? Can we see it in our choices, our relationships, our communities? Does sin have any lingering effects on us, our families or our world? Take some time with yesterday's newspaper and see if you can find any signs or results of human sinfulness.

Examining the Biblical Data:
Some Key Terms and Ideas

It would be impossible to identify one single scriptural understanding of sin. Biblical language and theology is far too rich and complex to allow us to isolate a univocal meaning for the mystery of human sinfulness. In the Hebrew Scriptures alone it is possible to identify more than fifty words for sin, and differing literary genres and theological voices throughout the Bible offer the reader a variety of understandings of this concept.[2] Nonetheless, it is possible to pick out a few key biblical terms and ideas associated with human sinfulness, and in this way to get a general sense of how biblical authors understood the reality of sin.

The three most important Hebrew terms for sin found in the Bible are *hattah, pesha* and *awon,* while *hamartia* is the Greek word used most often for sin in the Christian Scriptures. Both *hattah* and *hamartia* were originally secular terms which meant "to miss," as in "missing the mark," and so to make a mistake. Within the context of Israel's covenant with Yahweh, these terms took on the religious and ethical meaning of failing to meet one's obligations to other persons, thereby breaching one's relationship with God. *Pesha,* a political and legal term signifying a violation of some norm or a revolt against authority, came to mean an intentional transgression of God's law or a willful rebellion against Yahweh's reign. Finally, *awon* is a term often used to describe both the sense of iniquity and the crushing guilt experienced by the sinner, indeed, the profound sense of alienation from God brought about by one's sinfulness.

In general, these terms indicate that biblical authors understood sin as a rift or tear in the covenantal relationship with God, a state of being *sundered* from God. In some earlier writings this rift might be caused by an innocent mistake, an unintended violation of cultic law, the violating of a ritual or dietary taboo. Thus, the law sometimes demanded atonement for actions we would tend to describe as mere accidents. But as the moral consciousness of Israel unfolded and developed, biblical authors—in particular, the classical prophets—came to describe sin as a free and conscious violation of the covenant, a rupture brought about by a failure to meet one's obligations or by some intentional transgression of God's law. Still, even here it is not the violation of the law in itself that constitutes sin, but the decision to reject one's relationship to Yahweh, to say no to God. Sin is a choice in the heart of the sinner, which is expressed and achieved through our actions. Thus, violating the law is a sign of one's deeper rejection of God.

Normally, biblical authors see this rejection of God as being achieved through the sinners unjust behavior toward others. As Robin Cover points out, "the sinner...is one who falls under divine disapproval *primarily* for immoral or unethical conduct toward other humans...thus, while 'sin' as a relational concept usually sets the unethical, immoral or irreligious person against God, the specific 'sins' which inform the categorization 'sinner' are often violations of the dignity and rights of other persons."[3] In other words, sin involves a twofold rift, alienating sinners from both God and neighbor. And, indeed, as the power of sin grows, it eats away at the very fabric of human society, tearing communities apart and creating alienation and hostility between all sorts of persons and groups.

Nor are sinners themselves left unharmed by this rift, for in rejecting God's love and grace sinners become alienated from themselves. Instead of setting persons and communities free, sin distorts and crushes the lives of sinners, enslaves their wills, hardens their hearts, and darkens their intellects. Not just an act of defiance against God or even a rejection of the call to love one another, sin is fundamentally an act of self-annihilation, a rejection of the vocation to become fully human persons, resulting in the ultimate crippling of the sinners.

As a rule, then, we could say that Scripture tends to portray sin as a threefold alienation: alienation from the God who creates and loves us; alienation from our neighbors and from the rest of creation that we are called to love and care for; and alienation even from ourselves. Sin is a rift tearing at every fabric of our lives.

If sin is a rift, are there any ways in which you experience the alienating power of sin? What are some of the ways in which you experience yourself as divided from God, from others (near or far), even from creation itself? Are there any ways in which you experience yourself as alienated or divided, as separated from your best self? What is that about?

At the same time, we are able to identify in the biblical literature three distinct dimensions of this sinful rift. In scripture the term *sin* is

205

used to speak about: (1) a universal condition of being flawed or broken, (2) the wrongful deeds we freely commit against God and neighbor and (3) the resulting wickedness in the human heart. As Timothy O'Connell indicates, sin is described as a *fact* of life, an *act* of persons or communities, and a fundamental *orientation* towards evil.[4]

Various biblical authors speak about sin as a universal human condition, a pervasive and tragic fact of our creaturely existence. In Genesis 8:21, after having witnessed the rebellious disobedience of Adam and Eve, Cain's murder of Abel and all the human iniquity and wickedness that led up to the flood, God complains that the human heart is evil from infancy. Then in Psalm 51, as we read at the beginning of this chapter, the psalmist confesses not merely to having sinned against God, but also—like all humans—to having been conceived in sin. Again and again in Scripture sin is understood as part and parcel of the human condition, and, as we are told in Psalm 143:2, Proverbs 20:9 and Job 4:17, no living person can claim to be righteous or innocent before God. As Paul notes in Romans 3:23, "all have sinned and fall short of the glory of God." All are sinners. All are flawed, broken and incapable of living up to the demands of the covenant.

This biblical insight into the universal sinfulness of humanity is at the heart of the Christian doctrine of "original sin," and echoes our own experience that there is something profoundly wrong with the human condition. It is not just that something is rotten in the state of Denmark. Something is rotten in the state of human affairs. For some reason, human beings and communities do not behave nearly as well as we might, not even as well as we claim we would like to behave. Deep within our hearts and structures there seems to be something broken, flawed, perhaps even malignant. And both the biblical literature and our experience tell us that this condition is both pervasive and tragic. It is, we are somehow certain, not the way things were meant to be.

In some ways, however, it is not enough to describe this experience of being born into sin as a mere fact, as if it were only some sort of disability, some handicap that kept us from achieving our full potential. For in Scripture sin is often a noxious and decidedly malevolent force, and its presence is not experienced simply as a fact, but as a hostile and rebellious power, setting itself up in opposition to God and wreaking havoc on humanity. This is clearly the understanding in John's Gospel when the author describes the world's sinful hostility to Jesus, or when

Paul speaks about the flesh rebelling against God. For these and other biblical authors, sin is more than a fact; it is a malevolent power, a malignancy coursing through the veins and arteries of the human community, binding us together in what Bernard Haring has described as "sin-solidarity." Using Piet Schoonenberg's phrase, "Sin of the World," Kevin O'Shea describes this malignancy in stark terms.

> Biblical thought about sin is dominated by the theme of Sin of the World. We should write it with a capital: the Sin, the Sinfulness of the world. Modern thought is dominated by the idea of the "human act" in which sin happens. St. Paul would have called that a "transgression," he would not have called it "Sin." Sin is a deeper thing, a powerful virus of evil which has a history of its own, on the cosmic plane.

> The Sin of the world is a virus of evil which entered the world as a personal force through original sin and dynamically unfolds itself and tightens its grip on humanity and on the world in an escalating fashion down the ages of history. It is the hidden power which multiplies transgressions in the history of mankind. They are merely its symptoms; it is greater and deeper than all of them. It forms human history into what we might call "perdition history" (to coin the opposite of "salvation history.")"[15]

What also seems clear from this is that the biblical authors were deeply conscious of the social character of human sinfulness. Sin wasn't just a condition that affected isolated individuals, but a malaise eating away at the fabric of human communities everywhere. The sin into which the descendants of Adam and Eve were born was much more than the mere accumulation of individual deeds or actions. It was, as O'Shea indicates, a contagious virus spreading through whole communities and being passed from generation to generation. In Scripture sin has a distinctly social dimension.

Indeed, throughout much of the Hebrew Scriptures sin was primarily understood not as the rebellion or malice of individual persons, but as the infidelity of a people.[6] Again and again the prophets complained that Israel had sinned as a community, and needed to be chastised, punished and called to repentance as a community. For it was the people of Israel who had been called into a sacred covenant with Yahweh, and sin threatened to rupture that covenant and thereby destroy that community.

Still, whether we describe the universal experience of sin as a fact or a malevolent force, it is clear that both the biblical authors and the doctrine of original sin place the responsibility for this moral brokenness not with God, or indeed with some outside demonic force, but within ourselves. In some way human beings, and not their Creator, are to be held accountable for sin, so that although we as individuals or communities may find ourselves born into situations already contaminated by the power and influence of sin, although we may experience ourselves as hampered, distracted or oppressed by the lingering effects of original sin, in the end sin is of human making.

And how are we responsible for sin? Clearly we cannot be held accountable for some action of our ancestors, or even for a sinful state we are born into. No, but we are responsible for the ways in which we strengthen sin's power through our own sinful deeds and actions, and it is this second dimension of sin, sin as act, which biblical authors are referring to when they speak of sins, faults, debts or transgressions. For Scripture doesn't just portray sin as a fact or power, but also as a free choice we make to reject God, a choice that is embodied and expressed in harmful or wrongful acts, usually against our neighbors. When King David confesses in 2 Samuel 12:13 that he has sinned against God, he is referring both to his rebellion against Yahweh and to the specific acts of adultery and murder he has committed. So too, when the prophets chastised Israel for violating their covenant with God, they did so by leveling very specific charges against the Hebrews, accusing them of mistreating widows, orphans and aliens, of abusing their workers or of oppressing the poor. We sin through our sins.

Can you think of any experiences in which your saying no to God took place primarily through your behavior towards another? What are some ways in which our actions or habits are a rejection both of God and of our relationship to our neighbor?

Thus, in Scripture sins or transgressions refer to the way in which persons participate in and deepen sin's unholy power through free and conscious choices. These sinful deeds are wrong and call for repentance because in and through them sinners have chosen to alienate themselves from God. But they are also wrong because they wreak havoc in the world, producing all sorts of harmful consequences on the personal and social levels. These sinful deeds are the blows with which we simultaneously hammer away at our relationship with God and do evil to our neighbors. This is why, in Luke 11:4, we are directed to ask God to "forgive us our sins."

And just what happens to persons and communities who have freely chosen to identify themselves with sin, who through their sins and transgressions have cut themselves off from God? Biblical authors describe such persons and communities as "wicked," or "hardhearted." For they are not merely flawed or broken in the way that all sinful humans are. Rather, they have consciously welcomed sin into their very hearts, and in so doing have become embodiments of sin, person-ifications of a rebellious hardness against God's love. This is the third and final dimension of sin, a fundamental orientation away from God, an abiding and self-chosen hardheartedness set against the face of God's offer of love.

One final comment needs to be made about any understanding of sin that we draw from Scripture: while the power and consequences of sin are seen as very serious, there is in the Bible a deep, overriding faith in the mercy of God. In both the Hebrew and Christian Scriptures God repeatedly offers forgiveness to the repentant sinner, and this divine mercy is seen as more than capable of reversing and overcoming the power of sin. As Paul notes in Romans 5:20, "however great the num-ber of sins committed, grace was even greater," which helps to explain why the author of Psalm 51, someone profoundly aware of sin's terri-fying power, has the courage and confidence to offer this prayer.

> Create a clean heart in me, O God,
> and put a new and right spirit within me.
> Do not cast me away from your presence,
> and do not take your holy spirit from me.
> Restore me to the joy of your salvation,
> and sustain in me a willing spirit.
> Then I will teach transgressors our ways,
> and sinners will return to you. (Psalm 51:10–13)

And, indeed, this is the central message of the Christ story: that the long reign of sin has been broken and that in the death and resurrection of Christ God's mercy has overcome sin's power and redeemed humanity from its brokenness and iniquity. As Paul points out in Romans 5:17–18:

> If, because of the one man's trespass, death exercised dominion through that one, much more surely will those who receive the abundance of grace and the free gift of righteousness exercise dominion in life through the one man, Jesus Christ. Therefore just as one man's trespass led to condemnation for all, so one man's act of righteousness leads to justification and life for all.

Church Teaching: The Story of Penance

To a large degree the history of Christian reflections on sin (and indeed on morality itself) has been shaped by the story of the sacrament of penance. For although 1 John 3:6 notes that "anyone who lives in God does not sin," the early Christian church soon discovered that even after conversion and baptism its very human members continued to have faults and commit transgressions. So it was necessary for the early church to develop a way of thinking about and dealing with these various sins.

When the offenses in question were the minor faults and failings of daily life, Christians were urged to seek forgiveness and make amends by coming to the Eucharist, praying the Lord's Prayer, engaging in a fast or performing works of charity for the poor. But when the transgressions were more serious and constituted not merely a little backsliding but a significant rejection of God's grace, then a stronger medicine was required. So in the early centuries of the church Christians who had committed grievous sins like apostasy, adultery or homicide were commanded to seek the one-time remedy of public penance. After confessing their sins to a bishop or priest, sinners were to enter the order of penitents, setting themselves off from the rest of the community in much the same way that their sins had alienated them from God and their faith community, and engaging in some very public form of penance. Then, at the end of their time of penance (usually at Easter), they would be welcomed back into communion with the church.

One result of this practice was a growing awareness that not all sinful actions were of equal weight, that there was a difference between the ordinary slips or failings of daily life and those more serious and grievous transgressions or habits that did serious harm and represented a significant rejection of God. As time passed this distinction between light and serious offenses resulted in the development of the categories of "venial" and "mortal" sins, which achieved some formal definition at the Council of Carthage in 418.[7]

Although sometimes mistakenly identified with any one of a number of seriously harmful actions, the term *mortal sin* has generally referred to actions in which persons freely and consciously choose to turn away from God in some significant way. Thus, for an action to be mortally sinful it was not enough that the matter or harm involved be serious; it was also required that the person committing this action fully understand what he or she was doing and make this decision with a good deal of personal freedom. For what makes an act mortally sinful is that this choice or deed represents some fundamental rejection of God's love, some sundering of one's relationship with God. Indeed, to build on a biblical insight we could argue that mortal sins are those sorts of choices that render one "hardhearted" or "wicked." This explains why Aquinas argued in his *Summa of Theology* (I-II, q.88, 1) that it was only mortal sins that ought to be called sins at all, and that so-called venial sins were really only sinful in an analogous sense.

What, in your opinion, would be some examples of actions that could constitute serious or mortal sins? Are some sinful acts really more important or dangerous than others? Why, or why not? What do you think happens to us when we commit such important sins?

By the early Middle Ages, however, the practice of public penance had fallen out of use and was being replaced by a private confession of sins, one that could be repeated many times in the life of the penitent and which did not involve the performance of public penance. Over the course of the next several centuries the church produced different books to help train the clergy who were to hear these confessions. These texts—the penitentials, the "Summas of Confessors," and later the manuals of moral theology—sought to offer practical and pastoral guides to priests, helping them to act as judges in the confessional, ascertaining the culpability or guilt of the penitent and assigning an appropriate penance.[8]

Unfortunately, over time the juridical focus of private confession and the approach of the penitentials and other moral theology texts resulted in a certain amount of legalism and individualism in Christian morality. For instead of paying attention to the way in which sin alienates persons and communities from God, neighbor and self, or to the power of God's merciful forgiveness, the practice of the sacrament and the texts used to train the clergy tended to focus on lists of individual transgressions, cataloguing them by species, number and degree of gravity.

All this attention to the weighing and measuring of individual offenses meant that while most Catholics developed a strong sense of sin as a transgression against God's law, there was little if any understanding of: (1) the biblical concept of sin as a threefold alienation, (2) the communal or social dimension of sin, or (3) the overwhelming power of God's redemptive mercy. Instead, the rich biblical theology of sin was replaced by narrow, juridical categories in which sin was envisioned primarily as a crime committed by isolated individuals, a crime which cried out for punishment or atonement. In this way our relationship to God and neighbor was, to a large degree, reduced to a legal bond in which God was understood primarily as a punishing judge, and we saw ourselves as obliged simply to avoid the breaking of any laws or to make amends for the violations we had already committed. Clearly, there were significant disadvantages in such a legalistic and individualistic grasp of sin.[9]

Some Contemporary Reflections on Sin

Fortunately, contemporary Catholic morality has not only recovered some important biblical insights about human sinfulness, but has also been enriched by contributions from depth psychology, virtue ethics and social analysis. As a result, we have a much richer sense of the mystery of human sinfulness, of the way in which sin represents a fundamental break in our relationship with God and of the ways in which sin operates on both the personal and social levels. Finally, by situating sin in the context of the story of God's covenantal and redemptive love for humanity, we are reminded of the divine mercy and forgiveness offered to all sinners.

Persons and Sin: Transgressions, Vices, and "Sin unto Death"

As we saw in our discussion of the subjective dimension of human actions in chapter 3, if we want to get a fully adequate picture of the acting person, we need to pay attention to three levels of human action: individual deeds, habits and fundamental option. So too with sin. If we hope to fully understand the mystery of personal sin, we need to look at the ways in which we sin in our individual transgressions, in the vices we develop and maintain, and in the very core of our being.

SINFUL ACTS

Sinful actions, or what the church has traditionally called "actual sins," are generally understood to be words, thoughts or deeds that express and embody a decision to say no to God. In an earlier era we would have argued that these sins were a violation of Gods "law," but, as we saw in our discussion of mortal sin, what makes such actions wrong is not so much that they break a norm or rule, but that they represent a choice to ignore the moral tug from God, to respond with a "no" to the invitation or vocation to become fully human persons and disciples of Christ.

And just *how* do we say no to God in our actions? Mostly we do this by failing to recognize, respect and respond to our neighbors, for the moral tug we receive from God specifically calls us to love others. In Isaiah 58 the prophet reminds Israel that the love or worship which God demands of the Hebrews is not so much a matter of sacrifices or holocausts, but of showing justice and mercy to the weak, sick and poor. And when Jesus is asked to name the greatest of the commandments, he responds that we are to love God with our whole heart, soul and mind, *and* to love our neighbor as ourselves (Mt 22:34–40). These are the two most important commandments because the primary way in which we love God is by loving our neighbor. For, as the author of 1 John 4:20–21 notes: "Anyone who says 'I love God,' and hates their brother or sister is a liar, since anyone who does not love the brother or sister that they can see cannot love God, whom they have never seen. So this is the commandment that Christ has given us, that anyone who loves God must also love their brother or sister."

213

Thus, generally speaking, in sinful actions we say no to God by behaving badly towards other persons or groups of persons. This is why sin is both a religious and an ethical concept, for it is about our failure to love God and our failure to be good to our neighbor. Does this mean that we need to be fully conscious of rejecting God's love in order for an act to be sinful? Do we need to know in the moment that we choose to harm another that we are also choosing in this act to cut ourselves off from God? Not necessarily. It is normally enough to know that we are doing wrong, that our act is unjust, or that we are failing in our moral obligations to others. As Jesus tells the condemned sinners in Matthew 25:41–46, whenever they failed to offer food to the hungry, shelter to the homeless or clothing to the naked, they failed to do these things for God. This was their sin.

We noted above that traditional Catholic morality has recognized that some sinful actions are much more important than others, primarily because they represent a real decision to turn away from God. Mortal sins were seen as deadly to the soul of the sinner, not simply because they violate an important rule or norm, but because they constitute a fundamental repudiation of God's grace and a rupture of our relationship to the divine. Venial sins were seen as those daily failings or transgressions which, while wrong and harmful, do not represent a significant rejection of God.

Given the fact, however, that a mortal sin constitutes a fundamental breach in our relationship to God, indeed, a reversal of the very direction of our lives, a turning from good to evil, it makes sense to believe that such an act would not only be extremely significant and destructive, but also relatively rare. This is not to say that there are no mortally sinful acts, that no single human act could ever rupture our relation to God or set us on a course to destruction. It is certainly possible, in a critical moment in our lives, to make a choice of such import and malice that it could shape the rest of our lives. Cain may have made such a choice when he took his brother for a walk in the woods, or perhaps Judas committed such an act when he leaned over and kissed his friend lightly on the cheek. Still, acts like these are not common. Deeds that set the die of our character are rare indeed, and we do not commit a dozen of them a year.

Given this understanding of a mortally sinful action, just what kind of deed might represent a mortal sin? Try to describe what you think would need to be going on in someone committing such a sin?

214

So what should we call those deeds which are much more than venial sins, more than occasional foul or angry words, little white lies or minor indiscretions? How are we to describe sinful acts that may not be mortally sinful but are genuinely wrong and harmful, that do significant damage to ourselves and others, that may not rupture our relation with God but clearly undermine and weaken it? We could call them "serious," for that is what they are. Betraying a spouse, striking a child, stealing a significant amount of money, refusing to stand up for an innocent victim; these may not constitute a fundamental rupture of our relationship with God, but they are very serious actions, with very serious consequences. Telling slanderous lies about another, refusing to hire somebody because of race, gender or sexual orientation, turning a deaf ear to the cries of the poor; these are not small, light or venial things. They are acts in which we tear away at the fabric of our relationships to God, neighbor and self. They are deeds that contribute to the malice and chaos in our world. They are things we need to confess, repent and make amends for.

And just what makes a sinful act serious? Again, traditional Catholic morality employed three criteria to determine whether someone had committed a mortal sin: (1) grave matter, (2) sufficient reflection and (3) full consent of the will; and although that tradition was often ready to call too many things mortal sins, these criteria are not a bad place to start our examination of serious sins.

"Grave matter" is present when a wrong choice is capable of producing significant harm, which would mean that for a sinful act to be serious it is usually required that it generate some real damage, or at least that this be the sinner's intent. This damage might be personal, social or ecological. It could be to oneself, but would normally be to others. It might be a violation of someone's body, rights, dignity, freedom, property or good name, or could involve some harm to the common good or the environment. What is critical, however, is that the injury is not slight.

Still, the criterion of grave matter alone doesn't guarantee that a serious sin has been committed. Just as we argued in the chapter on moral actions that freedom, understanding and a certain degree of commitment were necessary for a genuinely *human* act, so too, freedom, understanding and commitment are required for the commission of a truly sinful or *inhuman* act. Since what makes an act sinful is a

215

person's choice to turn from God, it is essential that this act be *personal,* namely, that it involve a certain amount of freedom, understanding and commitment. For this reason, there needs to be "sufficient reflection" about what is being chosen in this deed, and the act in question has to be done with "full consent of the will." Thus, a sinful act is serious, which means that it does real damage to our relation to God, neighbor and self when the decision we are making involves significant harm and when we freely and knowingly choose to commit such an act.

SINFUL HABITS

The truth is, however, that for most of us it is usually the sinful deeds that we repeat over and over again which are more important and more deadly than our isolated, individual acts. It is the sins we've gotten used to committing, that we've grown comfortable with, like an old pair of slippers, that are really dangerous. Like millions of snowflakes slowly but ever so steadily accumulating into a massive and impenetrable glacier, these sinful habits are the things that harden our hearts against the moral tug and deafen our consciences to the sound of God's voice. Like well-worn forest trails carved out by a thousand trips, these vices are the paths that lead us slowly but irreversibly away from God.

For can any of us really point to a single moment and identify the most deadly choices we've ever made? Can we say, this is the moment in which I chose to be an unfaithful friend, a poor parent, a selfish person? Can any of us really find the one act in which we chose to abandon the poor, adopt a bias against minorities or take care of number one? Aren't these, instead, sins that we have committed in a thousand acts, over a dozen or dozens of years? And even when we can identify a seriously sinful act, a dramatic moment when we clearly chose to turn from God in some significant way, wasn't there usually a trail of smaller decisions leading up to this act, a set of deepening habits that prepared the way for this betrayal? Don't we find it incredible when someone tells us about an awful deed that seemed to have no prelude, no warning signs?

Aristotle argued that we are what we do regularly, and for most of us our sin is to be found not so much in those dramatic and profound

216

moments when we make radically important choices, but in the things we do all the time, in the things we do over and over again. In our hearts we know that the greatest predictor of how we will behave in the crucial moments of our lives is to be found in how we behave every day, because these are the things that shape character. So we don't expect the coward to suddenly do a brave deed, or the miser to break into a fit of generosity. We know that if we want to be able to make the correct or virtuous choice in a hard situation we will need to develop the habit of doing the right thing in smaller affairs.

This is why traditional Catholic morality described vices like sloth, avarice, envy, lust, wrath, gluttony and pride as *deadly* sins, because habits like these slowly but steadily eat away at our character and turn us away from God and others. It is also why Aquinas begins his discussion of sin in his *Summa* not with an analysis of actual sins, but of vices and their effect on persons (I-II, 71). For it is through our habits that we are choosing much more than what we will do in this moment; rather, we are choosing the direction we are setting for ourselves.

What would be an example of a sinful habit which might represent a very serious sin for someone? How would such a habit develop and grow in a person, and what effects might such a habit have over the long run?

SINFUL CHARACTER

As we have seen, both biblical literature and traditional Catholic morality end up arguing that *real* sin, the heart of human sinfulness, is more than mere transgressions. It is a choice to become wicked, to become hardhearted, to turn one's face and soul away from God. In Scripture transgressions are ultimately important because they reflect and help to shape an abiding state of hostility to God, a rupture in the relation to the divine. And in traditional Catholic morality mortal sin was not merely a grievously wrongful act; it was also, and more truly, a state or condition brought about by that act. To be in the state of mortal sin was to be severed from God, to be alienated from our neighbor and ourselves, to be dead.

All of this suggests that in its fullest sense, wickedness and mortal sin actually refer to a fundamental option against God, a decision to

217

reject God, not just in this act or moment, not merely in this habit or area of our lives, but with our whole being. Indeed, wickedness and mortal sin are better understood as decisions that become ways of being. True mortal sin is an abiding choice to set and hold the course of our lives *away* from God, a decision to become and remain someone who is dead to God, neighbor and self. Wickedness is a way of being that permeates every part of our lives: our deeds, affections, attitudes, beliefs and desires.

The decision to sin mortally, then, to reject God in the core of our being and with the whole course of our lives, is a choice so large and so deep that it reaches beyond all our individual actions and habits. This is why moralists refer to it as a "transcendental" act. And yet, this very decision to become wicked is also so real that it cannot be made in the abstract. Instead, we can only choose to become mortal sinners by committing sinful transgressions and developing vices. We can only say no to God by failing to meet our moral obligations in the concrete. In the end, then, although the full malice of sin may be much more than we can see in any one individual action, we can only commit mortal sin and become mortally sinful *in* and *through* the decisions to commit actual and habitual sins; which means that these transgressions and vices are ultimately important to the degree that they express, shape and confirm the choice to become mortal sinners.

Communities of Sin

As we noted above, biblical literature provides us with a strong sense of the social character of sin, pointing both to the ways in which entire communities are implicated in sin and to the fact that even before committing any transgressions, we find ourselves situated in and poisoned by larger sinful contexts. The classical prophets chastise all of Israel for having violated the covenant with Yahweh, while Paul speaks about the way the whole human race shares in the burdens of Adam's sin. In Scripture sin is more than something we do as individual persons, it is something that ties us together, and ties us down. Two terms Christian moralists have used to speak about this social character of sin are "original sin," and "social sin."

ORIGINAL SIN

Richard Gula argues that the Christian doctrine of original sin "is the theological code word for the human condition of living in a world where we are influenced by more evil than we do ourselves."[10] What this means is not that we are guilty of the sin of our first parents, or indeed of anyone else who went before us, but that in some way both we and our world have been marked and wounded by this sin. The chaos and destruction let loose by sin has somehow become embedded in the human community and in each of its members.

Long before any of us ever decide to actually *do* anything wrong, we find ourselves born into a world that has already been fractured by the power of sin and situated in all sorts of settings and relationships already wounded by human sinfulness. Indeed, we experience our very selves as hampered, our hearts and minds somehow flawed and damaged, and our will to do good sluggish and burdened by the effects of choices we never made. As traditional moral theology has put it, we suffer from a concupiscence which has made us a house divided against ourselves, so that, as Paul notes in Romans 7:19, we do not do the good we intend, but are drawn instead to the very evil we wish to avoid. Thus, the concept of original sin refers both to the ways in which our world and its structures have been contaminated and disordered by sin, and to the impact this sin has had on each of us. Unlike our personal transgressions, we are not guilty of this sin, but we must still deal with it.

We often hear people say that we will never eradicate things like war or inequality because it's part of human nature to want things that aren't ours, or to want to be in charge. Looking around at our world, can you see any signs of original sin? Can you detect any signs of this sin in yourself? What are these signs?

SOCIAL SIN

And yet we do bear some responsibility for the continuing power of sin in our world, for the ways in which our present social structures and institutions are disfigured by greed, malice and bias, for the ways in which our political, economic and cultural systems oppress and

219

marginalize the poor and weak, contribute to increasingly intolerable levels of violence and wreak irreparable damage on our planet. Even if we are not the persons or generation who created and developed these unjust policies and structures, we are certainly the ones who maintain and cooperate with them. And while it is certainly true that we have been born into a world already governed and influenced by unjust social systems, and that such systems have shaped, anesthetized and distorted our own consciences long before we ever did anything to add to their malice, it is also true that these injustices, embedded as they are in our world and our hearts, could not continue to exist without some help from us.

And indeed it is the recognition of this interdependent connection between our personal actions and social structures which has led to the development of the concept of "social sin," a notion referring both to the ways in which our personal sins become embodied in unjust social structures, and to the ways in which these same structures, having taken on a life of their own, make it harder and harder to resist the temptation to sin.[11]

As we noted in the chapter on moral communities, groups and structures are formed and sustained by persons making free choices. Indeed, it seems fair to argue that social structures and systems are the ways we act *as* communities. They are our communal deeds. For, by collaborating with others we establish and maintain these larger social systems, and in this way our individual patterns of thinking, communicating and behaving get expressed and embedded in the fabric of our societies. Thus, it makes sense to say that unjust, oppressive and alienating social systems are not simply accidents of nature or mere facts of life. Instead, they are the social embodiment of lots of sinful choices made by all sorts of persons. This is the point of the citation from The Pastoral Constitution on the Church in the Modern World at the beginning of this chapter, and it is what John Paul II is arguing in the following passage from his 1988 social encyclical, On Social Concern:

> "Sin" and "structures of sin" are categories which are seldom applied to the situation of the contemporary world. However, one cannot easily gain a profound understanding of the reality that confronts us unless we give a name to the roots of the evils which afflict us...it is not out of place to speak of "structures of sin" which...are rooted in personal sin, and thus always linked to the

concrete acts of individuals who introduce these structures, consolidate them and make them difficult to remove. And thus they grow stronger, spread, and become the source of other sins, and so influence people's behavior. (No. 36)

And the reason that these structures of sin "grow stronger, spread, and become the source of other sins" is that, as we also previously noted, once formed, groups and structures tend to take on lives of their own, with their resulting momentum shaping and influencing the hearts, minds and deeds of successive generations of individual members.[12] And so, in a vicious cycle where sinful acts beget sinful structures and sinful structures beget more sinful acts, we encounter sin on both the personal and social levels. Indeed, for a fully adequate account of our experience of the real power and mystery of human sinfulness, it is never enough to speak only, or even primarily, of our individual deeds. We must also address the reality of social systems which oppress and alienate the poor, blind us to our complicity in injustices and make it harder and harder to resist the temptation to sin more and more.

What are some ways in which the political, economic and cultural structures in our society harm and oppress people? How is it that we usually manage to overlook or ignore these injustices? What are some ways in which these very systems tempt us to commit our own sins?

On the Nature of Sin

At its core sin represents a rupture of our relationship to God, neighbor and self, a rupture caused by our turning away from God in some fundamental way. But just what is the nature of this rupture? How are we to describe the core process or processes by which we sin? How are we to name exactly what it is we are doing when we sin?

In an earlier era, when a more juridical understanding of sin and our relation to God dominated Catholic morality, "disobedience" was the controlling metaphor we used to describe human sinfulness, and, as we noted above, we tended to think of sin primarily as a crime or infraction of one of the laws of God, nature or the church.[13] This is clearly the understanding operative in the definitions of actual and mortal sin offered in the 1943 edition of *The New Baltimore Catechism*.[14]

221

Q. 158 "What is actual sin?"
A. 158 "Actual sin is any willful thought, desire, word, action, or
omission forbidden by the law of God."
Q. 161 "What is mortal sin?"
A. 161 "Mortal sin is a grievous offense against the law of God."

Recently, however, contemporary moralists, influenced by biblical
and theological insights into the way in which sin violates our
covenantal relationship with God, have turned to other metaphors or
understandings of sin. O'Connell argues that for the biblical authors,
sin is ultimately a matter of idolatry, of putting ourselves or some part
of creation in God's place. And at the heart of this idolatry, O'Connell
argues, is not just the worship of golden calves or other graven images.

> Rather, idolatry at its worst is idolatry of self. Self-sufficiency is
> the greatest sin. From the story of Adam and Eve in Genesis to the
> era of the prophets, the people are most forcefully condemned and
> most forcefully rebuked for daring to "go it alone."...It is their
> pride that Yahweh finds most offensive. They fail to love God, to
> serve God. They seek to make themselves God and to take divine
> prerogatives to themselves.[15]

Gula says something similar when he describes sin as a form of selfishness. "In sin, we cease to pay attention to, or care about, anyone outside ourselves. Selfishness is self-absorption. It is the failure to love
and accept love. All sin springs from a love turned in on itself." Indeed,
Gula goes on to note that the heart of this sinful selfishness can be
found in a certain "arrogance of power," a desire of what he describes
as the imperial "I" to elevate and impose itself on others.[16]

And yet a number of feminist theologians and moralists have argued
that while *selfishness* and *pride* may well describe the ways in which
some men and oppressive groups have been tempted to sin in our cultures, they are not helpful metaphors for naming the experience or
temptations of women and other oppressed communities. For instead
of experiencing their sinfulness through arrogance of power, calloused
indifference to the sufferings of their neighbors or excessive dominion
over the weak and powerless, a number of feminist authors and liberation theologians argue that most women and oppressed minorities

around the planet have been socialized to love and attend to themselves too *little*.

In a world shaped and contaminated by patriarchal, colonial and racist structures, the temptation which many struggle with is not too much pride, arrogance or selfishness, but learned helplessness and a passive participation in one's own victimization. As a result of sinful social structures disordering political, economic, cultural and ecclesial relationships, women and oppressed people everywhere have often been encouraged to tolerate far too much injustice, oppression and violence, to offer too little resistance to assaults on their rights and dignity and to forgive their abusers and oppressors before any genuine repentance or restitution was offered.[17]

Given these insights into the two-sided face of sin in human relationships and social systems, it might be better to suggest that the rupture of sin is only partially described by terms like selfishness and the arrogance of power, and that this rupture is experienced by many as a lack of care or love for the self. Christine Gudorf has suggested that sin is ultimately about the misuse of power, whether overt or covert, and Mary Stewart Van Leeuwen argues that while men have traditionally been tempted to sin by exercising too much dominion, women's involvement in sin has been about avoiding responsibility or manipulating relationships.[18] This would seem to suggest that the heart of human sinfulness is to be found in our failure to create and sustain "right relationships" between persons and communities, to behave individually and socially in ways that distort the mutual respect and love which should tie us to all other persons and groups in genuine peace and justice. Perhaps that is why the biblical authors thought sin was a threefold alienation, distorting our relation to God, neighbor and self.

Sin—Some Conclusions

1. Sin is a religious and ethical concept referring to a threefold alienation from God, neighbor and self. This rupture in our transcendental relation to God, whom we do not see, is brought about by our wrongful behavior in the world that we do see.

2. Human sinfulness is experienced both as something we choose to engage in, as well as a noxious condition in which we find ourselves.

Notions like personal and actual sin tend to focus on the ways in which we "commit" sin, while concepts like original and social sin point to the fact that sin influences and shapes our experience before we have made any choices about good and evil.

3. Persons sin in their actions, habits, and—most fully—in the core of their being, for in and through our sinful deeds and habits we express and shape a deeper choice to turn away from God. Thus, these acts and vices are important to the degree that in them we freely and knowingly choose to embrace evil.

4. At the same time, we also sin through the creation and maintenance of unjust social structures which oppress and alienate the weak while deadening our consciences to the presence of evil in the world. As a result, these sinful structures are both the fruit and the seeds of our personal sins.

5. As powerful and deadly as sin is, the redemptive power and liberating grace of God is far greater, and, as we will see in the next chapter on conversion, the ultimate response of God to the sinner is an offer of forgiveness, reconciliation and salvation.

Chapter Twelve.
Christian Moral Conversion

Introduction: "Come, let us return to the Lord." (Hosea 6:1)

1. "Meanwhile Saul, still breathing threats and murder against the disciples of the Lord, went to the high priest and asked him for letters to the synagogues at Damascus, so that if he found any who belonged to the Way, men or women, he might bring them bound to Jerusalem. Now as he was going along and approaching Damascus, suddenly a light from heaven flashed around him. He fell to the ground and heard a voice saying to him, 'Saul, Saul, why do you persecute me?' He asked, 'Who are you, Lord?' The reply came, 'I am Jesus, whom you are persecuting. But get up and enter the city and you will be told what you are to do.'" (Acts 9:1–6)

How does this event change the life of Saul? How did it affect the story of the church? What is there about Saul that is different after this event? Who, exactly, brings this change about in Saul? Does he participate in this change? Are there other examples of this sort of transformation in Scripture? Can you think of the stories of other biblical characters or saints who underwent this sort of transformation?

2. In Charles Dickens' classic tale, *A Christmas Carol,* Ebenezer Scrooge is an embittered and lonely old miser, a hard and mean-spirited employer who indignantly rebuffs all requests for charity and complains at having to give his clerk Bob Cratchit the day off for Christmas. But on Christmas Eve the miserly Scrooge is visited first by the ghost of his old partner, Jacob Marley, who warns him of the punishment that awaits him for his greed and selfishness, and then by the

spirits of Christmas past, present and future, who hold up mirrors to Scrooge's life. Awakening on Christmas morning to find that he still has a chance to reform that life, Scrooge is both elated and grateful, and rushes out to try and undo as much of the damage he has inflicted as possible. Overnight the bitter miser has become the joyous benefactor, and as Dickens's story closes, the reborn Scrooge is described by all who know him as a man who truly understands the meaning of Christmas.

What, exactly, has happened to Scrooge in this story? Who, in your opinion, do the ghosts of Marley and Christmas past, present and future represent? Does Scrooge have any role in this change? Why does this story happen around Christmas? Which of Scrooge's attitudes and relationships are affected by this change? Is such a change really possible in a person?

3. "The word of the Lord came to Jonah a second time, saying, 'Get up, go to Nineveh, that great city, and proclaim to it the message that I tell you.' So Jonah set out and went to Nineveh, according to the word of the Lord. Now Nineveh was an exceedingly large city, a three days' walk across. Jonah began to go into the city, going a day's walk. And he cried out, 'Forty days more, and Nineveh shall be overthrown!' And the people of Nineveh believed God; they proclaimed a fast, and everyone, great and small, put on sackcloth. When the news reached the king of Nineveh, he rose from his throne, removed his robe, covered himself with sackcloth, and sat in ashes. Then he had a proclamation made in Nineveh: 'By the decree of the king and his nobles: No human being or animal, no herd or flock, shall taste anything. They shall not feed, nor shall they drink water. Human beings and animals shall be covered with sackcloth, and they shall cry mightily to God. All shall turn from their evil ways and from the violence that is in their hands.'" (Jonah 3: 1–8)

What happens to Nineveh in this story? Why do people put on sackcloth and cover themselves with ashes? Why does the author suggest that the king, the nobles, the people and even the animals do this? Is the transformation of a metropolis like Nineveh different from the conversion of an individual? How? Can you think of other transformations of societies that might be comparable to this?

Conversion:
The Central Moral Message
of Christian Ethics

As we saw in the preceding chapter, both Scripture and Catholic tradition affirm that while the power and consequences of human sinfulness are quite serious and pervasive, the condition of the sinner is by no means hopeless. Sin is a fundamental part of the human story, but it is not the final chapter. Throughout the Scriptures and the Christian story God intervenes again and again on behalf of persons and communities who have fallen into sin, calling them to repentance and rebirth, offering them merciful grace and loving forgiveness. We hear this call in the cry of the prophets Isaiah, Jeremiah and Hosea, challenging the Israelites to remember and renew their covenant with Yahweh, promising them God's compassionate mercy if they repent. We hear it in the voice of John the Baptist, who "appeared in the wilderness proclaiming a baptism of repentance for the forgiveness of sins" (Mark 1:4). And we hear it in the proclamation of Jesus at the start of his public ministry. "The time is fulfilled, and the kingdom of God has come near; repent and believe in the good news" (Mark 1:14). This is the message of the one who chastises the self-righteous and invites sinners to break bread with him. It is the message of the parables of the good shepherd, the prodigal son, and the woman with the lost coin (Luke 15). And the message is that we have a God who comes out to find lost sinners and invite them home.

As a result of our faith in such a God, Christian theology has always affirmed the possibility of making a return to the Lord and overcoming the threefold alienation of sin (even on the level of character and community). Otherwise, of course, it would make no sense to call sinners to repentance. For if we could not repent or be forgiven of our sins, preaching the good news of the Gospel to sinners would be an act of cruelty, and the message of Jesus would be a lie. This does not mean, however, that sinful persons or communities can make this return on their own, that we can bootstrap our way back into God's graces. The damage done by sin makes that impossible, and, besides, forgiveness is always God's gift, never our due. Nevertheless, Christians do believe that with the power of God's grace all things are

227

possible, even transforming lives and communities crippled by sin. This means that we believe in a call to conversion.

Indeed, not only do we believe in such a call to rebirth and transformation, but a number of contemporary moral theologians argue that this call is at the very heart of Christian ethics. Charles Curran notes that "conversion is the central moral message of Jesus," while James Hanigan contends that "conversion is the foundational experience of Christian life and so of Christian ethics."[1] As Curran goes on to note, the central moral demand of the New Testament is not to obey a specific set of rules or laws, but to be transformed by the word of God.

> Jesus is direct, straightforward, simple; and yet Christian teaching and preaching today is too often legalistic in tone. People are warned to do this, to avoid that. The emphasis falls on a particular action or mode of external conduct. The authentic Christian message, however, calls above all for a change of heart—a radical internal change of the person.[2]

And so Jesus informs Nicodemus that "no one can see the reign of God unless he be born again" (John 3:3). For at the heart of Jesus' moral message is a radical demand to die to all one treasures and "come, follow me." Everyone who encounters Christ or is touched by his message must do this. Some are told to hand over their possessions or birthright. Others are told to get up from their stretchers or leave behind their boats and nets. Still others are called to surrender their moral superiority, religious titles or pseudoinnocence. But all are called to leave behind everything they know and treasure and become his disciples, to die to their present attitudes, attachments and achievements and be born again in the Holy Spirit, to repent of their sins and failings and injustices and turn back to God.

But just what is this conversion that Jesus calls us to? Many of us have grown up thinking of conversion as a process of switching allegiance from one faith or denomination to another. David converted to Catholicism, or Alice is a convert to Judaism. Is that what conversion is—changing churches? And do we make a choice or change like this all by ourselves? Where does God, or the community fit into the notion of conversion? And what if we have been born and raised in a Christian denomination from which we are not inclined to change?

Must we then have one of those peak emotional experiences so often associated with young people's first powerful encounter with God's love? Is this what it means to be "born again"? What if we end up going through our lives without being able to point to the *one single moment* in which our lives were permanently transformed? Does that mean that we have not been—or are not being—converted? Is everyone's experience of conversion the same, or are there different paths of conversion?

Conversion, as it forms the central moral message of Jesus, is certainly more than just joining a new church. It is, as a number of theologians have noted, "a basic transformation of a person's way of seeing, feeling, valuing, understanding and relating."[3] It is a fundamental and joyous change of one's heart, mind and soul, a transformation of one's habits, attitudes, affections and relationships. More specifically, as the biblical language indicates, conversion is a turning away (*metanoia*) from sin and alienation and a turning toward (*epistrophe*) God, and while this turning depends on our free consent, it also depends on the gracious intervention and support of God. We are not ever alone in the experience of conversion. Nor is conversion something that happens only or even primarily to individuals. Instead, whole communities are called to undergo conversion, summoned to a transformation that will affect their members, structures, systems and institutions. Furthermore, while there are certainly peak moments or critical turning points when we hear and respond to the call to conversion with a special clarity, this is a lifelong process. We are, as they might say at an AA meeting, "in conversion." And finally, though all are called to conversion, there are a variety of paths by which one might journey.

In this chapter, then, we will seek to do five things in our reflections on conversion. First, we will explore contemporary reflections on the nature of Christian conversion, trying to unpack the shape and character of this transformative call. Next, we will examine the ways in which God and humans participate in the process of conversion. Then we will take a look at the personal and social dimensions of the call to conversion, followed by a reflection on the critical moments and lifelong process of turning from sin and toward God. Finally, we will sketch out three distinct but interconnected paths of conversion that seem to show up in both Scripture and contemporary thought.

Conversion: What Is It?

In the closing chapter of his work, *Christian Conversion*, Walter Conn offers two reflections that help us to frame a fuller understanding of this notion. First, he notes that "Christian conversion is essentially an *invitation* to a life not only dedicated to the love of neighbor but focused and empowered by the mysterious presence of God at its *vital* center." Then he goes on to suggest that "conversion is the transformation of conscience."[4] These two statements highlight the central elements of conversion: (1) that it involves a transformation of persons at the level of character, reshaping basic habits, attitudes, affections and relationships, leading to the formation of a new fundamental option; and (2) that this radical change is initiated and made possible by, as well as directed to, the love of God.

Conversion involves a transformation of every part of our lives, not just of our deeds, but of our very ways of seeing, thinking, feeling and relating. This is why Conn notes that Christian conversion includes an intellectual, affective, moral and religious transformation.[5] For conversion represents a radical change of our hearts, minds and souls, a change in the basic direction and focus of our lives, and ultimately a change in our very identities. It should be no surprise then that Josef Fuchs sees conversion as the formation of a new fundamental option, one in which we attain our full dignity as human beings precisely by giving ourselves away to God, by transcending the narrow boundaries of our sinful selves.[6]

At the same time, because we are social and spiritual beings, conversion is not merely a change of our interior lives or character. It is also a radical transformation of our relationships; personal, social and religious. We will see later that, as we change, so do our connections to our neighbors, our world and indeed to God. In conversion we are overcoming the threefold alienation of sin, repenting past harms and offenses to God, neighbor and planet, bandaging old wounds and building new bridges. As we change, we are altering the web of relationships in which we are immersed, answering a call to wholeness, holiness and love of neighbor.

And at the heart of all this change is the grace of God, which is both the fuel and focus of conversion. For conversion is not the act of the rugged individual rising unaided from the depths of sin, nor a kind of "self-help" promulgated on all of the talk shows. Instead, God's grace summons, surrounds and supports us through every step of the journey of conversion. This grace is the invitation and challenge which first awakens us to our sinfulness, the courage and compassion which empowers us to confront our sin and reach out to others, and the love and warmth which draws us like the morning light.

Consider some of your favorite films or novels. Try to identify a character who experiences a "tug" to change, to be transformed. Recount that story in your own words, paying close attention to the kind of change that was called for, the factors that made it difficult but possible, and how it happened that the transformation did or did not take place.

God's Grace and Our Freedom: A Dance

If, then, morality is the "tug" through which God summons us to our fullest humanity, conversion is the core or engine of that tug. It is God's "amazing grace" breaking into our lives in a way that proclaims and empowers our forgiveness and liberation from sin. It is that same grace making a radical demand upon us, calling us to repentance and discipleship. But conversion is also our joyous and heartfelt response to that call, to that incredible offer of grace and love. Just as Michelangelo's famous scene on the ceiling of the Sistine Chapel has God and humanity stretching out their hands to each other, so too conversion is an embrace into which God's love summons and sweeps us, but an embrace which we must freely choose to enter. It is a dance, and even though one of the dancers is but a child being held in her mother's arms, they both have a part to play.

It is a central tenet of the Christian faith that God saves us, and that our liberation and conversion from sin is primarily a gift from God, a gift we do nothing to merit, indeed a gift to which we can respond only with the help of God's grace. Still, instead of making us feel small or inadequate, this news should fill us with joy. For it means that God is for us, loves us and has come with outstretched arms to embrace and bring us home. We are not alone, abandoned or unaided. We are the children of a loving and forgiving God.

And how does God initiate the process of conversion? How are we touched, moved and empowered by this gracious love? It can happen, of course, in an endless variety of ways. God may prick our conscience with a story of injustice on the evening news, the reproof of a friend or the face of a poor person. We may feel the tug in the beauty of sunlight dancing on a lake, in the poignancy of a pastor's sermon or at the bedside of a loved one. Some have been called to conversion by a dream that woke them cold and sweaty in the night, by the growing responsibilities of parenthood or by the example of a long dead saint. God has as many ways of inviting us to dance as there are stars in the sky.

Still, as Bernard Haring notes in *Free and Faithful in Christ,* "the focal point of Christian conversion is always Christ...Christ is the original and perfect sign of redemption and the effective call to conversion."[7] Describing Christ as the "original sacrament of conversion," indeed, the very embodiment of God's offer of conversion, Haring goes on to describe the various ways in which God's grace breaks into our lives and summons us through the life and story of Jesus. Christ is *the* prophet in whom the reign of God is proclaimed and introduced. His words and life are a challenge to the consciences of the self-righteous and an offer of mercy to sinners. Christ is the reconciler who has overcome the threefold alienation of sin, the liberator who sets us free from the enslavement of personal and social sin, and the one who sends forth God's Spirit upon us.

One of the primary ways in which Christians encounter Christ, the sacrament of conversion, is in and through the church. For not only is this the community of disciples to whom Christ promised to send the Holy Spirit, but it is also the group that receives this commission at the end of Matthew's Gospel.

> Go therefore and make disciples of all nations, baptizing them in
> the name of the Father and of the Son and of the Holy Spirit, and
> teaching them to obey everything that I have commanded you.
> And remember that I am with you always, to the end of the age.
> (28:19–20)

With all its frailties and brokenness, the Christian community has been blessed by the Holy Spirit and entrusted with the sacred Scriptures. In age after age Christ is present to and through this pilgrim people, a community of saints and sinners who are both a sign of God's love and a needy recipient of that same converting grace. For as Matthew notes elsewhere, "where two or three are gathered in my name, I am there among them" (18:20). And so we encounter Christ not only in the face of the poor and in the wonders of creation, but also in the community of disciples gathered around him. We encounter Christ in the various prayers and liturgies of the church, in its psalms, songs and sacraments; most especially in that central sacrament of the Eucharist, in the breaking of the bread. Furthermore, we are chastised, comforted and challenged by Christ in the proclamation and preaching of Scripture. And we are touched by the courageous and compassionate example of a constellation of saints both living and dead. In all its humanity and holiness, in all its frailty and fullness, the church is a sacrament of *the* sacrament of conversion.

*"Play" with the image of conversion as a **dance** for a while. More concretely, imagine that you are watching a championship dance contest. All of the couples are amazing. They move not as two, but as one. What goes into a couple becoming a championship dance team? What are some of the things they need to overcome to become such a team? What does this suggest about conversion? About moral conversion?*

Our Free Response: Personal and Social

And just how are we to respond to this call to conversion? What is our role in this process? For even though conversion is primarily the work of God's love, it remains an *invitation,* a "tug" which awaits our acceptance or refusal. Our freedom is engaged, not overcome or violated by this loving offer. We can say yes or no. And we say this yes or no not just with a word or a deed, but with our very lives. For the freedom which this invitation engages is our most basic, fundamental freedom, the freedom to become our most authentic selves—or to hand ourselves over to sin. It is the freedom to say yes to the summons God has placed in the core of our being, or to destroy that self with a resounding no. Our part in the process of conversion is to say "amen" to the grace of conversion by opening our hearts and minds and lives to God's call. As John the Baptizer says, our part is to "prepare a way for the Lord, make straight his paths" (Mt. 3:3).

In essence, then, the convert's part in the process of conversion is to open our hearts, minds and lives to the grace of God, to say yes to the invitation from Christ and to cooperate in the process of overcoming sin's threefold alienation. At different times we may experience the demands of conversion as an invitation to *repentance* from sins, as a call to *discipleship* or as a challenge to take a *prophetic* stance against injustice; but at the center of this summons is a demand that we hand over our lives to the grace of God, that we enter into the mystery of the death and resurrection of Christ. We are to die to ourselves and be born anew in Christ.

And how are we to know that we are cooperating with God's grace? How do we know when we are involved in a process of authentic conversion? The clearest sign is to be found in our relationships to others. Are we loving, just, compassionate towards others? And does our love for them "do" anything? Does it put bread in the mouths of the hungry or clothes on the backs of the naked? How do we actually treat our neighbors, especially those without voices or power? How do we treat strangers or our enemies? Do we show the mercy and compassion that was first shown to us? Or do we claim to love the God we cannot see while despising or disregarding the neighbor who is right before us? As we read in John's Gospel (15:12–17), we will know that we are accepting the invitation to be Christ's friends if we keep his commandment to love one another. The converted heart is a loving heart.

As we have noted a number of times already, we are both unique and social beings. Thus we experience the call to conversion just as we experience the moral tug—as persons *and* communities. It is not just individuals, but whole communities that are challenged by Christ's proclamation of God's reign, whole communities that are trapped in sin and in need of reform, and thus whole communities that are called to conversion. The prophets call *all* of Israel to repentance and conversion—its people, its kings, and its priests. Similarly, St. Paul reminds us that in Christ *all* of creation is reconciled to God (Col 1:20). Thus, our response to the invitation of God's grace must be both personal and communal.

Indeed, as we noted in the chapter on moral communities, authentic personal conversion is impossible and incomplete without the simultaneous transformation and reform of unjust structures, systems and institutions. For as Gustavo Gutierrez argues in *A Theology of Liberation,* the "conversion process is affected by the socioeconomic, political, cultural and human environment in which it occurs. Without a change in these structures, there is no authentic conversion."[8] Or, as Conn notes, "personal conversion does demand the transformation of social structures. But the transformation of social structures is also required for personal conversion. The Gospel calls us to work for both simultaneously....Private conversion is really no conversion."[9]

Therefore, genuine conversion demands not only that we repent of our personal sins and open our hearts, minds and lives to the grace of God and the love of our neighbors. It also demands that we awaken to the sinful social structures which oppress and marginalize much of the world's population, and that we join with others in a sustained struggle for political, economic and social justice. This is why the 1971 Synod of Bishops document, Justice in the World, notes that "action on behalf of justice and participation in the transformation of the world fully appear to us as a constitutive dimension of the preaching of the Gospel, or, in other words, of the Church's mission for the redemption of the human race and its liberation from every oppressive situation."[10] The transformation of unjust systems is part and parcel of the conversion called for by the proclamation of the Gospel. We must be converted from personal and social sin.

And how are we to go about this two-pronged conversion? As we saw in our discussion of the reform of communities, Peter Henriot has suggested that the church needs to become involved in an ongoing three-step process that includes: (1) proclaiming a prophetic word that unmasks injustice, (2) giving a symbolic witness by standing in solidarity with the victims of injustice and (3) taking political actions to reform the structures in question.[11] In other words, we must continually seek to see and speak the truth about unjust structures and their harmful effects; we must be willing to move into a place where we are standing *with* those who are struggling for justice; and we must be willing to work for real changes in the ways power, wealth and authority are structured in our societies.

Consider some of the stories that are most important to you—stories from films, literature and history, as well as stories from your own life.

235

Try to identify some stories that involve the conversions not only of individual persons, but of whole communities. Tell one of these stories in your own words. What are some of the ways in which personal conversion is related to social conversion?

Conversion: A Lifelong Journey

For many Christians, Paul's experience on the road to Damascus is *the* conversion story. Short, dramatic and memorable, this tale—which is recounted three times in the book of Acts (9:1–9; 22:5–16; 26:10–18)—seems to capture the very essence of conversion. God intervenes suddenly, a life is changed forever, and the person sets off in a new direction. Nor is this the only biblical account we have of such a sudden conversion. Abraham, Jacob, Moses and Isaiah each encounter the power of God in a stunning and miraculous fashion, and the course of their lives is forever changed. And indeed the New Testament is filled with the stories of people who, in one definitive moment, seem transformed by their encounters with Christ. James, John and Peter leave everything behind and follow after Jesus (Luke 5:1–11), as do Mary Magdalen, Susanna and Joanna (Luke 8:1–3). Both the tax collector Zacchaeus (Luke 19:1–10) and the man born blind (John 9:1–42) are changed forever by their meetings with Christ, and in the account of the Samaritan woman at the well (John 4:5–42), not only she, but an entire town is converted when Jesus stops there for an afternoon. Furthermore, on the feast of Pentecost we are told that a crowd of about three thousand were converted by Peter's preaching of the good news (Acts 2:37–41).

And there is a way in which these stories capture some basic truths about the experience of conversion: for they point to the fact that nearly all of us have experienced critical turning points in our lives, profoundly important moments in which the very direction of our lives are somehow changed. And they remind us that in such moments we are confronted with choices about our very identities as persons, about who we are and who we will become. Sometimes we recognize those moments for what they are even as they are happening. Sometimes it feels as if a bolt of lightning has struck us down, or as if God is roaring in our ears like thunder. At other times, however, these turning points are more subtle, and we only come to see their real importance when we have traveled quite a while in the new paths they set us upon. Years later we might look back and see that the decision to go on a weekend retreat, visit a shut-in or attend our first AA meeting was such a turning point for us. We are different people today because of what happened to us and because of how we behaved on that day.

But there is also a way in which these short parables of conversion are incomplete. There is another truth which they imply, but which we can tend to overlook in reading them: conversion is the process of a lifetime, a process that is not fully captured or exhausted in any single moment. For although we certainly experience critical moments in which our lives are being turned around, moments which may well lead to our seeing, thinking and relating differently, these moments are but a part—an important part, admittedly—of the larger process of conversion.

For the truth is that many of us experience *more* than one critical turning point in our lives.[12] There may be a moment in which we are so touched by the beauty of creation or the birth of a child that we come to believe in the transcendent, the holy. Or there could be a time when we are deeply moved by God's mercy, when we come to experience the full power of God's compassion for us, and so we find ourselves repenting of our past sins and vowing to reform our lives. We might also have a moment later on when we come to recognize the face of God in the poor, sick and suffering, or suddenly realize our own responsibility for perpetuating sinful social structures. As Conn notes, in each of our lives we may experience numerous critical but distinct moments of moral, affective, cognitive and religious conversion, moments in which our ways of thinking, feeling, caring or relating are being changed. Indeed, we may have moments later on that deepen these experiences of conversion, that take them to a whole new level.[13]

And what does it mean that we experience more than one moment or dimension of conversion? What does it mean when we associate the moral, affective, cognitive or religious dimensions of conversion with different moments in our lives, or that we can have subsequent experiences that seem to take our conversion to a whole new place? It means that conversion is a transformation of the *whole* person, and of our *whole* life, and so it takes us a *whole* life to be converted. It means that we are never done being converted because conversion involves a rad-

237

ical openness to the call of God, and this call is always inviting us to draw closer. The call to conversion asks everything of us, and it takes a whole life to give that gift. It takes us a *whole* life to answer the call to give ourselves completely to God, to achieve our full dignity as loving human persons, to live out our vocations as disciples.

Furthermore, in order for them to be real, these moments of conversion need to be integrated into our lives and character. One visit to a poor person doesn't turn somebody into a St. Vincent de Paul or a Mother Teresa. One AA meeting doesn't mean recovery from alcoholism. One Sunday mass doesn't make us women and men of prayer. The changes effected in these turning points must be woven into the fabric of our lives, which means that we need to develop new habits, attitudes, affections, beliefs and relationships. We need to make amends for the past and build new bridges to the future. We need to lose old habits and incorporate new ways of thinking, behaving and feeling. And all of that takes time, prayer, work and practice. Many people have had moments of blinding insight and a heartfelt desire to change, but have failed to walk the walk. Conversion is not just what we do in the peak moments of our lives; it is what we do as we travel through the foothills and valleys.

It should also be noted that everything we have said about this process of conversion applies equally to the conversion of communities. For although there may be critical turning points in the story of a society (the end of slavery in the United States or the dismantling of apartheid in South Africa, for example), the work of reform and transformation must go on. Sinful social structures are continuously being erected or discovered, new situations of injustice need to be addressed, progress in the protection of human dignity and the common good is always needed. As the theologians of Vatican II noted in their description of the church, we are a pilgrim people, a community "on the way" that is called "to make straight the path of the Lord." For persons and communities, conversion is a work in progress.

*This section has argued that conversion (both personal and social) is an ongoing process. It's not **finishing**, but **staying with it** that is the task. Is this good news or bad news? Explain your answer.*

Conversion: Three Interlocking Paths of Repentance, Discipleship and Prophecy

Traditionally, Christian reflections on conversion have largely focused on the notion of *repentance,* the process by which we turn away from sin and are welcomed home to God's grace. Since Vatican II, however, there has been more attention given to the experience of conversion as a call to *discipleship,* a summons to leave behind all that we treasure and follow after God, even when this leads us into the unknown. And finally, a number of theologians and ethicists have recently focused on the ways in which conversion is experienced as a challenge to become *prophetic* witnesses in the struggle against social sin. This does not mean that there are three radically different kinds of conversion, but that each of these three models—which might be described as coming home, leaving home and cleaning house—points to a different facet of the one mystery of conversion. For surely we cannot accept the call to discipleship without acknowledging and repenting of our sinfulness, nor can we repent of our sins unless we turn away from them to turn toward God. At the same time, the call to struggle against social sin must certainly mean that we are also to repent of our personal sins, and it would be impossible to sustain this struggle without seeking to follow after Christ.

Nonetheless, it may prove helpful to explore the call to *repentance, discipleship* and *prophecy* as distinct moments in the rich mystery of conversion. For each seems to contribute to a fuller understanding of what it means to be converted. Thus, in this final section we will examine the three interlocking paths of repentance, discipleship and prophecy, heeding what is involved in each and how each is related to the others.

Repentance: Coming Home to God from Sin's Alienating Power

Luke's parable of the prodigal son (15:11–32) is certainly one of the most famous biblical narratives of God's mercy. It is also one of the best descriptions of conversion as repentance. For in this parable the call to conversion begins when the young man realizes the devastating and alienating effects of his sinfulness. Cut off from funds, friends and family, he comes at last to his senses, acknowledges his sin against God and neighbor and decides to return home, where he will beg for forgiveness. As in the story of the Samaritan woman at the well (John 4:5–42), the sinful woman who washes Jesus' feet with her tears (Luke 7:36–50) and the good thief's confession on the cross (Luke 23:39–43), this parable portrays conversion as an unfathomably generous offer of grace and an invitation to repentance. Here conversion is an experience of turning away from the threefold alienation of sin and making our way home to the Lord. It is an experience of liberation from the enslavement and exile of personal and social sin, and of a safe and joyous return to the welcoming and loving arms of God.

In these biblical narratives conversion makes certain demands upon the repentant sinner. It calls for an acknowledgment of our sinfulness, a sense of genuine sorrow for what we have done and become, a confession both of our guilt *and* our faith in God's mercy and a commitment to sin no more. We see a number of these same elements in Bernard Haring's discussion of the convert's role in the process of conversion.[14] Envisioning conversion primarily as a repentance from sin, Haring notes the four basic steps required of the penitent sinner: (1) a genuine contrition for our sins, including a sorrow for what we have done, how we have harmed others and who we have become; (2) a firm purpose of amendment, meaning a real commitment to behave differently in the future; (3) a confession of our sin (and sins) to both God and those we have harmed and (4) atonement for our sins, making what amends we can for all the harms we have done.

Still, if we really want to understand repentance we need to remember that conversion is much more than contrition, confession and a firm purpose of amendment. It is a glorious process of falling in love with God, of being liberated from sin. Far more than just sorrow and self-accusation, genuine repentance is a wondrous rebirth of our fractured hearts and lives, and its focus is not upon the sins we have committed or the sinners we have become, but on the God whose mercy has broken into our lives and who is calling us home.

240

We get a sense of that joy in the American folk spiritual *Amazing Grace*.

Amazing grace! How sweet the sound,
That saved a wretch like me!
I once was lost, but now am found,
Was blind, but now I see.

'Twas grace that taught my heart to fear,
And grace my fears relieved;
How precious did that grace appear
The hour I first believed!

Through many dangers, toils, and snares,
I have already come;
'Tis grace has brought me safe thus far,
And grace will lead me home.

Discipleship:
Leaving Home to Follow the Lord

Still, conversion does not always feel like coming home; sometimes it feels like leaving home. Again and again in Scripture God calls people to leave behind all the comforts of home, to go out into the wilderness or journey to a strange and unknown place. This is the challenge given to Abraham and Sarah, to Moses and to Ruth. And in the New Testament Jesus is continually making this sort of demand upon those he encounters. They are to walk away from their homes, leaving behind their jobs and families. They are to get up off their stretchers and sick beds, giving up their crutches and cots. They are to surrender all the advantages of their wealth, power and prestige, and to break bread with the poor, the weak, and, yes, even with sinners. They are to follow after him, through the narrow gate, through the eye of the needle, to the cross.

This is the call of discipleship, the demand for a radical break with all that is safe and secure, a challenge to follow after Christ, whatever the cost, wherever it may lead. This is conversion as an invitation to make a leap of faith, indeed as an invitation to live at risk. Conversion

241

as discipleship is a call to die to self and enter into the mystery of Christ's death and resurrection. It is the challenge to take up the cross. Nowhere is this more starkly put than in this passage from Luke:

> Now large crowds were traveling with him; and he turned and said to them, 'Whoever comes to me and does not hate father and mother, wife and children, brothers and sisters, yes, even life itself, cannot be my disciple. Whoever does not carry the cross and follow me cannot be my disciple.' (14:25–27)

In her essay, "Conversion: Life on the Edge of the Raft," Sallie McFague captures this notion of discipleship as a radical call to take up one's cross and follow after Christ when she speaks about the conversion of some of the church's great saints.

> Conversion has sometimes been understood as bringing comfort, as being a change from a lost and godless state to a god-filled peaceful condition whereby one's life is "put in order," where the "before" and "after" pictures are of a life of disarray and sin on the one hand and a life of peace and stability on the other.

> I would like to suggest that the great conversions—those of such saints of the church as Paul, Augustine, John Woolman, and Dorothy Day—bring not comfort, at least not in any superficial sense, but demand a courage, a willingness to risk and suffer, to live lives of dis-ease and spiritual adventure that is unsettling if not terrifying to contemplate."[15]

Thus, to become a disciple is to live at risk, to live as if God and God alone can truly be counted upon. To accept the call to discipleship is to acknowledge that we cannot rely upon our wealth, power or prestige to keep us safe. That we cannot hope to find ultimate security by obeying the law, keeping ourselves separate from sinners or celebrating rituals. It means acknowledging that there are no armies, ideologies or possessions that can bring us true salvation or happiness. In the end discipleship means surrendering whatever objects or illusions we rely upon to provide us with a sense of security, to hand over our lives ultimately and finally to God, to be willing, as McFague puts it, to live over an earthquake fault.

Prophecy: Confronting and Wrestling with Unjust Systems

Finally, conversion sometimes feels not only like leaving home, but like going to war. In the parable of the man born blind (John 9:1–41), Jesus heals a beggar of his blindness. But instead of throwing a party to celebrate this miraculous cure, the man's family and neighbors—and especially the leaders of the community—turn against him and attack him, eventually picking him up and throwing him bodily out of the synagogue. Hardly an auspicious beginning for his first day as a disciple of Christ.

Still, this is hardly an uncommon experience. When Moses answered his call to conversion, it brought him into mortal combat with all the might of Egypt. And when Israel's prophets dared to speak the word God had put in their hearts, they were often enough attacked, not thanked, for their troubles. This was certainly the experience of Jeremiah, Hosea and Amos. Later Jesus would warn his own disciples again and again that anyone who follows after him should expect to be hated and persecuted (Mt 10:17–25; Mark 13:9–13; Luke 21:12–19). The world, he tells them, will not react well to the proclamation of the reign of God, but will instead despise and seek to destroy those who bring this good news. And the greatest resistance to the Gospel will come from those in the world with power and authority. Indeed, it is a fairly constant theme in the New Testament that the disciples of Christ can expect the "principalities and powers" of this world to rage the loudest against them.

This has certainly been the experience of many modern Christians who have taken the social implications of the Gospel seriously. Women and men who have tried to live in solidarity with the suffering and oppressed, sought to uncover the sources of poverty, violence and oppression, or called for the reform of political, social and economic structures have usually found themselves on the receiving end of a great deal of hostility, vilification and violence. That is the story of Dorothy Day, of Martin Luther King, of Oscar Romero.

And it is the story of Jesus of Nazareth, whose proclamation of the reign of God met with such violent opposition because it threatened to undermine the absolute authority of every human structure and institution, because it put them all on notice that they would need to make room for this reign. For if the call to conversion awakens us to our radical dependence upon the living God, it also unmasks all of our contemporary idols—wealth, power, success and pleasure—*as well as* the structures and institutions we have built to deliver these goods.[16] In this way the call to conversion unmasks and threatens the "principalities and powers" in much the same way that the small child pointed out that the emperor had no clothes. For it reveals the limits of these institutions—that they cannot supply us with the ultimate happiness, fulfillment or salvation which they promise. Even more, it calls for their reform because they are often unjust, oppressive and alienating. Indeed, just as the call of Jesus to "repent and believe in the good news" summons persons to reform their lives, so too it puts our institutions, structures and systems on notice. They are *not* of the reign of God. Instead, they must be reformed to make way for that reign. No wonder the violent response!

And just what is that reform to look like? As the bishops argue in "Justice in the World," it must involve "the redemption of the human race and its liberation from every oppressive situation." This means that the call to conversion not only demands a change of heart and a willingness to leave everything for Christ, but it also challenges us to awaken to the presence of injustice and oppression in all our social structures and systems and to join in a sustained struggle for the reform of those structures. This is the call of conversion as a summons to *prophecy*.

Conversion is like coming home, leaving home and cleaning house. Try to find an example of each kind of conversion. Is all of this just wishful thinking, or can we—personally and socially—really be transformed?

Some Final Reflections on Conversion and Christian Morality

We began this book by addressing our experience of a moral "tug" from God and have, over the course of twelve chapters, examined: (1) the ways in which we are called to respond to this "tug" (in the actions we do, the kinds of persons we become and the sorts of communities we fashion); (2) some of the resources we have for discerning the exact shape and direction of this "tug" (Scripture, reason, experience, tradition, norms and conscience); and (3) the sorts of persons and communities we are (sinful and engraced) who receive this moral "tug."

It seems fitting that we should bring this conversation on Christian morality to a close while on the subject of conversion. This is true for three reasons. First, Christian morality is, like conversion, fundamentally a "tug" in the direction of Christ. For Christians Christ is "the alpha and the omega," the beginning and the end, and our ethics is focused on our attempts to respond to the call of discipleship, the call to "come follow me." Second, Christian morality is, like conversion, suffused with the grace of God. In Christian morality we do not do the good alone. Instead, we are drawn and empowered to do the good by the grace of God. Indeed, in Christian morality we recognize that by far and away *most* of the work being done is God's labor, not ours. Finally, Christian morality, like conversion, is fundamentally an act of thanksgiving, of joyful worship to the gracious one who has first loved us. It is not a morality based on a fear of punishment or a desire for self-improvement, but on grateful love. It is an ethic of a community of persons who have encountered the good news of the Gospel and are trying to make straight the paths of the Lord.

Christian Moral Conversion —
Some Conclusions

1. Conversion, the central moral message of Jesus, is a fundamental and joyous change of one's heart, mind and soul in response to the proclamation of the reign of God. It involves a turning away (*metanoia*) from sin and alienation and a turning toward (*epistrophe*) God.

2. While the call to conversion invites our consent and engages our fundamental freedom as persons, it is a process which depends on the gracious intervention and support of God. Indeed, God's grace summons, surrounds and supports us through every step of the journey of conversion.

3. Since we are both unique and social beings, we experience the call to conversion as persons *and* communities. It is not just individu-

als, but whole communities that are challenged by Christ's proclamation of God's reign, whole communities that are trapped in sin and in need of reform, and thus whole communities that are called to conversion.

4. Conversion is a lifelong process, and although we certainly experience critical moments in which our lives are turned around, moments which may well lead to our seeing, thinking and relating differently, these moments are but a part of the larger process of conversion.

5. Christian reflections on conversion have focused on three interlocking moments or paths: (1) *repentance,* our turning away from sin's threefold alienation and being welcomed home into God's grace; (2) *discipleship,* a summons to leave behind everything and follow after Christ; and (3) *prophecy,* a challenge to enter into the struggle against social sin. All three of these moments or models of conversion point to an important dimension of this call and help to fill out our understanding of Jesus' command to "Repent and believe in the good news."

Notes.

Chapter One.

1. Enda McDonagh, "The Structure and Basis of Moral Experience," *Introduction to Christian Ethics: A Reader,* Ronald P. Hamel and Kenneth R. Himes, eds., (Mahwah, NJ: Paulist Press, 1989), pp. 106–19.

2. The contributions of feminist authors on the importance of attending to experience in an inclusive way has been powerful in recent years. See, for example, *Women's Conscience: A Reader in Feminist Ethics,* Barbara Hilkert Andolsen, Christine E. Gudorf and Mary D. Pellauer, eds., (San Francisco, CA: Harper and Row, 1985); Anne E. Carr, *Transforming Grace: Christian Tradition and Women's Experience* (San Francisco, CA: Harper and Row, 1988); and Georgia Masters Keightly, "The Challenge of Feminist Theology," *Horizons* 14, no. 2 (Fall, 1987): pp. 262–82.

3. Daniel Maguire, "Ethics: How To Do It," *Introduction to Christian Ethics: A Reader,* Ronald P. Hamel and Kenneth R. Himes, eds., pp. 533–50.

4. Mary Catherine Bateson, *Composing A Life: Life as a Work in Progress* (NY: A Plume Book, The Penguin Group, 1990).

5. For an in depth analysis of the "goodness/rightness distinction," especially as it emerges from the thought of Thomas Aquinas, see James F. Keenan, SJ, *Goodness and Rightness in Thomas Aquinas's "Summa Theologiae"* (Washington, DC: Georgetown University Press, 1992).

6. An excellent treatment of the importance of understanding the nature of social experience and of social structures for Christian ethics is found in Paul Steidl-Meier's *Social Justice Ministry: Foundations and Concerns* (NY: LeJacq Publications, 1984).

Chapter Two.

1. Stanley Hauerwas, "Toward an Ethics of Character," *Introduction to Christian Ethics: A Reader,* Ronald P. Hamel and Kenneth R. Himes, eds., (Mahwah, NJ: Paulist Press, 1989), p. 152.

2. For a classic account of the "responsive" nature of moral experience see H. Richard Niebuhr's *The Responsible Self* (NY: Harper and Row, Publishers, 1963). In a similar vein, and very creatively, Mary Catherine Bateson uses the image of the improvisation of jazz musicians to suggest how we "compose our lives": *Composing A Life: Life as a Work-in-Progress* (NY: A Plume Book, The Penguin Group, 1990).

3. Richard M. Gula, SS. *Reason Informed By Faith: Foundations of Catholic Morality* (Mahwah, NJ: Paulist Press, 1989), pp. 6–8: "The Ethics of Being," "The Ethics of Doing."

4. Hauerwas, "Toward an Ethics of Character," p. 154.

5. Avery Dulles, SJ, "Religion and the Transformation of Politics," *America,* 24 October 1992, pp. 300–301.

6. See Walter E. Conn, *Conscience: Development and Self-Transcendence* (Birmingham, AL: Religious Education Press, 1981) and *Christian Conversion: A Developmental Interpretation of Autonomy and Surrender* (Mahwah, NJ: Paulist Press, 1986). For feminist perspectives on this, see Carol Gilligan, *In A Different Voice* (Cambridge, MA: Harvard University Press, 1982).

7. James F. Keenan, SJ, discusses the four cardinal virtues and proposes a new set of them: "Proposing Cardinal Virtues," *Theological Studies,* 56, no. 4 (December 1995): pp. 709–29.

8. *Nicomachean Ethics*, II, 6 (1106a, 15).

9. Thomas Aquinas, *Treatise on the Virtues,* trans. John A. Oesterle (Englewood Cliffs, NJ: Prentice-Hall, 1966), p. 123. See also Paul J. Wadell, *The Primacy of Love: An Introduction to the Ethics of Thomas Aquinas* (Mahwah, NJ: Paulist Press, 1992).

10. Kenneth Overberg, SJ, *Conscience in Conflict: How To Make Moral Choices* (Cincinnati, OH: St. Anthony Messenger Press, 1991), pp. 20–25; and Willard Gaylin, *On Being and Becoming Human* (NY: Penguin Books, 1990), pp. 16–19.

11. For two fine discussions of these concepts, see Richard M. Gula, SS, *Reason Informed by Faith,* chap. 6, "Freedom and Knowledge," pp. 75–88; and Timothy E. O'Connell, *Principles for a Catholic Morality,* revised edition (San Francisco, CA: Harper & Row, 1990), chap. 6, "The Human Person," pp. 65–76 and chap. 8, "Sin: Mortal and Venial," pp. 89–102.

Chapter Three.

1. John A. Gallagher, *Time Past, Time Future: An Historical Study of Catholic Moral Theology* (Mahwah, NJ: Paulist Press, 1990). See also "The Influence of Auricular Confession," Chapter 1 in John Mahoney's *The Making of Moral Theology: A Study of the Roman Catholic Tradition* (NY: Oxford University Press, 1987), pp. 1–36.

2. Bernard Haring's *The Law of Christ* (Paramus, NJ: Newman Press, 1961; translation of *Das Gesetz Christi,* 1959) essentially brought the age of the manuals to a close, ushering in a new approach to moral theology. Subsequent to Vatican II he wrote another three-volume overview of moral theology, *Free and Faithful in Christ* (NY: Seabury/Crossroads, 1978).

3. Jean Porter, *The Recovery of Virtue: The Relevance of Aquinas for Christian Ethics* (Louisville, KY: Westminster/John Knox Press, 1990); see Stanley Hauerwas, *A Community of Character: Toward a Constructive Social Ethic* (Notre Dame, IN: University of Notre Dame

Press, 1981). A very helpful overview is William C. Spohn's "The Return of Virtue Ethics," *Theological Studies*, 53, no. 1 (March, 1992): pp. 60–75.

4. Walter E. Conn, *Conscience: Development and Self-Transcendence* (Birmingham, AL: Religious Education Press, 1981).

5. Timothy E. O'Connell, *Principles for a Catholic Morality,* revised edition (San Francisco, CA: Harper & Row, 1990), pp. 53ff.; James P. Hanigan, *As I Have Loved You* (Mahwah, NJ: Paulist Press, 1986), pp. 502ff.

6. Timothy E. O'Connell, *Principles for a Catholic Morality,* revised edition, chaps. 5 and 6, "Human Action" and "The Human Person," pp. 51–64 and 65–76 respectively. Richard M. Gula, *Reason Informed by Faith: Foundations of Catholic Morality* (Mahwah, NJ: Paulist Press, 1989), chaps. 5 and 6, "The Human Person" and "Freedom and Knowledge," pp. 63–74 and 75–88 respectively.

7. See Anne Wilson Schaef, *Co-Dependence: Misunderstood-Mistreated* (San Francisco: Harper and Row, 1986); *When Society Becomes an Addict* (San Francisco: Harper and Row, 1987).

8. Daniel Maguire, "Ethics: How To Do It," in *Introduction to Christian Ethics: A Reader,* Ronald P. Hamel and Kenneth R. Himes, eds. (Mahwah, NJ: Paulist Press, 1989), pp. 533–50.

9. H. R. Niebuhr's *The Responsible Self* (NY: Harper and Row, 1963); Louis Janssens, "Ontic Evil and Moral Evil," in *Readings in Moral Theology No. 1: Moral Norms and the Catholic Tradition* (Mahwah, NJ: Paulist Press, 1979), pp. 40–93.

10. See Gula's discussion of "synthetic" terms: *Reason Informed by Faith,* pp. 288–89.

Chapter Four.

1. Karl Rahner, "Der Einzelne in der Kirch," *Stimmen der Zeit* 39 (1946–1947): p. 261.

2. Peter Henriot, Edward DeBerri, and Michael Schultheis, *Catholic Social Teaching: Our Best Kept Secret* (Maryknoll, NY: Orbis Books, 1989).

3. Lisa Sowle Cahill, "Feminist Ethics," *Theological Studies* 51, no. 1 (March 1990): pp. 49–64, Thomas L. Schubeck, SJ, "Ethics and Liberation Theology," *Theological Studies* 56, no. 1 (March 1995): pp. 107–22.

4. Virginia Satir, *The New Peoplemaking* (Mountain View, CA: Science and Behavior Books, 1988); Raphael and Dorothy Becvar, *Systems Theory of Family Therapy* (NY: University Press of America, 1982).

5. Antonio Moser and Bernardino Leers, *Moral Theology: Dead Ends and Alternatives* (Maryknoll, NY: Orbis Books, 1990), pp. 9–69.

6. Alexis de Tocqueville, *Democracy in America,* trans. George Lawrence (Garden City, NY: Doubleday and Company, Inc., 1969), p. 435; Robert Bellah et al., *Habits of the Heart* (Los Angeles: University of California Press, 1985).

7. Patrick McCormick, *Sin as Addiction* (Mahwah, NJ: Paulist Press, 1989), pp. 61–64; Thomas Schindler, *Ethics: The Social Dimension* (Wilmington, DE: Michael Glazier, 1989), pp. 60–69.

8. Schindler, *Ethics: The Social Dimension,* pp. 8, 46–56.

9. Mark O'Keefe, *What Are They Saying About Social Sin?* (Mahwah, NJ: Paulist Press, 1990), pp. 45–47.

10. O'Keefe, *What Are They Saying About Social Sin?,* pp. 43–56; Peter J. Henriot, "The Concept of Social Sin," *Catholic Mind* 71 (October 1973): pp. 49–50.

11. John Rawls, *A Theory of Justice* (Cambridge, MA: Harvard University Press, 1971), p. 3; Plato, *The Republic,* trans. Desmond Lee (Great Britain: Penguin Classics, 1955), Book IV, p. 433; John R. Donahue, "Biblical Perspectives on Justice," in John C. Haughey, ed., *The Faith That Does Justice* (Mahwah, NJ: Paulist Press, 1977), pp. 68–78.

12. Schindler, *Ethics: The Social Dimension,* pp. 101–9.

13. Gerhard von Rad, *Old Testament Theology,* trans. D. M. G. Stalker (NY: Harper and Row, 1962), I, p. 370.

14. Donahue, "Biblical Perspectives on Justice," p. 69.

15. Joe Holland and Peter Henriot, *Social Analysis* (Maryknoll, NY: Orbis Books, 1983).

16. Fred Kammer, *Doing Faithjustice: An Introduction to Catholic Social Thought* (Mahwah, NJ: Paulist Press, 1991), pp. 146–60.

Chapter Five.

1. Stephen Crites, "The Narrative Quality of Experience," found in *Why Narrative? Readings in Narrative Theology*, Stanley Hauerwas and L. Gregory Jones, editors (Grand Rapids, MI: Eerdmans, 1989), pp. 65–88. This anthology of articles is quite useful. See also Terrence W. Tilley, *Story Theology* (Wilmington, DE: Michael Glazier, Inc., 1985).

2. William J. Bausch, *Storytelling: Imagination and Faith* (Mystic, CT: Twenty-Third Publications, 1984), pp. 58–60.

3. Robert McAfee Brown, *Persuade Us to Rejoice: The Liberating Power of Fiction* (Louisville, KY: Westminster/John Knox Press, 1992), p. 20.

4. H. Richard Niebuhr, *The Responsible Self* (NY: Harper and Row, 1963), p. 97.

5. Stanley Hauerwas, *Truthfulness and Tragedy: Further Investigations into Christian Ethics* (Notre Dame, IN: University of Notre Dame Press, 1977), p. 76.

6. Timothy E. O'Connell, *Principles for a Catholic Morality,* revised edition (San Francisco, CA: Harper & Row, 1990), p. 75.

7. Bernard Brandon Scott, *Hollywood Dreams and Biblical Stories* (Minneapolis, MN: Fortress Press, 1994), p. 48.

8. Three valuable works on the importance of imagination and morality are: Philip S. Keane, *Christian Ethics and Imagination* (Mahwah, NJ: Paulist Press, 1984); Thomas E. McCollough, *The Moral Imagination and Public Life: Raising the Ethical Question* (Chatham, NJ: Chatham House Publishers, Inc., 1991); and Robert Coles, *The Call of Stories: Teaching and the Moral Imagination* (Boston, MA: Houghton Mifflin Company, 1989).

9. John Dominic Crossan, *The Dark Interval: Towards a Theology of Story* (Sonoma, CA: Polebridge Press, 1988), pp. 31–45.

10. William C. Spohn, "Parable and Narrative in Christian Ethics," *Theological Studies* 51, no. 1 (March 1990): pp. 100–14.

11. Hauerwas, *Truthfulness and Tragedy,* p. 78.

12. Hauerwas offers a similar list in *Truthfulness and Tragedy,* p. 35.

Chapter Six.

1. Richard M. Gula, SS, *Reason Informed by Faith: Foundations of Catholic Morality* (Mahwah, NJ: Paulist Press, 1989) pp. 186–87.

2. Lawrence S. Cunningham offers a very helpful treatment of the ways our Christian vision has been shaped by the stories of different saints in *The Catholic Heritage* (NY: Crossroad, 1993).

3. John Dominic Crossan discusses Jesus the storyteller and Jesus

the "story told" using the categories of Jesus the parabler and Jesus the parable in *The Dark Interval: Towards a Theology of Story* (Sonoma, CA: Polebridge Press, 1988).

4. Dogmatic Constitution on Divine Revelation, (1965), no. 21.

5. Stanley Hauerwas, *A Community of Character* (Notre Dame, IN: University of Notre Dame Press, 1981), pp. 63–64.

6. Ibid., pp. 66–67.

7. Gula, *Reason Informed by Faith,* pp. 185–86.

8. William C. Spohn, *What Are They Saying About Scripture and Ethics?* (Mahwah, NJ: Paulist Press, 1984), p. 4.

9. Gula, *Reason Informed by Faith,* p. 165.

10. Allen Verhey, "Biblical Ethics," in *From Christ to the World: Introductory Readings in Christian Ethics,* Wayne G. Boulton, Thomas D. Kennedy and Allen Verhey, eds. (Grand Rapids, MI: Eerdmans, 1994), p. 17.

11. Spohn, *What Are They Saying About Scripture and Ethics?,* p. 4.

12. Ibid., pp. 12–17.

13. Hauerwas, *Community of Character,* pp. 66–67.

14. Kenneth Himes, "Scripture and Ethics: A Review Essay," *Biblical Theology Bulletin* 15 (April 1985): pp. 65–67.

15. James M. Gustafson, *Theology and Christian Ethics* (Philadelphia, PA: Pilgrim Press, 1974), p. 134.

16. O'Connell, *Principles for a Catholic Morality,* pp. 36–48.

17. Gustafson, *Theology and Christian Ethics,* pp. 136–42.

Chapter Seven.

1. Enda McDonagh, *Doing the Truth: The Quest for Moral Theology* (Notre Dame, IN: The University of Notre Dame Press, 1979).

2. Timothy E. O'Connell, "Conscience," chap. 8 in *Principles for a Catholic Morality* (NY: Seabury, 1978), pp. 83–97; "Conscience," chap. 9, revised edition (San Francisco, CA: Harper & Row, 1990), pp. 103–18; James P. Hanigan, "The Reality of Conscience," chap. 6 in *As I Have Loved You: The Challenge of Christian Ethics* (Mahwah, NJ: Paulist Press, 1986), pp. 119–44; Richard M. Gula, SS, "Conscience," "The Formation of Conscience," and "Conscience and Church Authority," chaps. 9, 10 and 11 in *Reason Informed by Faith: Foundations of Catholic Morality* (Mahwah, NJ: Paulist Press, 1989), pp. 123–35, 136–51, and 152–62 respectively.

3. Sidney Callahan, *In Good Conscience: Reason and Emotion in Moral Decision Making* (NY: HarperCollins, 1991) p. 14.

4. For a helpful discussion of "the superego" in relation to conscience, see Richard M. Gula, SS, *Reason Informed by Faith,* pp. 123–30.

5. O'Connell, *Principles for a Catholic Morality,* p. 106.

6. Vatican Council II, Pastoral Constitution on the Church in the Modern World, 1965, par. 16.

7. Daniel Maguire and A. Nicholas Fargnoli, *On Moral Grounds: The Art/Science of Ethics* (NY: Crossroad, 1996), pp. 149–50.

8. See especially "Conscience," chap. 8 of *Reason Informed by Faith,* pp. 123–35.

9. It would be difficult to overemphasize the centrality of the categories of vision, values and virtue in contemporary Christian ethics. Many of the endnotes of chapter 2 are relevant here. In addition these two works are important: Stanley Hauerwas, *Vision & Virtue: Essays*

in Christian Ethical Reflection (Notre Dame, IN: Fides Publishers, Inc., 1974); Philip S. Keane, SS, *Christian Ethics & Imagination* (Mahwah, NJ: Paulist Press, 1984), see especially pp. 64–78.

10. St. Thomas Aquinas, *Summa Theologiae,* (NY: Benziger Brothers, 1947), I-II, q. 106, art. 1.

11. The following works all discuss the relationship between the spiritual life and the moral life: Michael K. Duffey, *Be Blessed in What You Do: The Unity of Christian Ethics and Spirituality* (Mahwah, NJ: Paulist Press, 1988); Mark O'Keefe, OSB, *Becoming Good, Becoming Holy: On the Relationship of Christian Ethics and Spirituality* (Mahwah, NJ: Paulist Press, 1995); *Spirituality and Morality: Integrating Prayer and Action,* edited by Dennis J. Billy, CSSR and Donna Lynn Orsuto (Mahwah, NJ: Paulist Press, 1996).

12. Richard M. Gula, SS, *Reason Informed by Faith,* p. 132.

13. St. Thomas Aquinas, *Summa Theologiae,* (NY: Benziger Brothers, 1947), II-II, q. 47, art. 2.

14. For a previous and more extensive elaboration on the idea of "bipolarity," see Russell B. Connors, Jr., "Conscience and Community: Achieving Moral Wisdom," *CHURCH* (Winter 1987): pp. 3–9.

15. Daniel Maguire, "Ethics: How To Do It," in *Introduction to Christian Ethics: A Reader,* Ronald P. Hamel and Kenneth R. Himes, eds. (Paulist Press: New York, 1989) pp. 533–50.

16. Paul VI, *Humanae Vitae,* 1968, par. 12.

17. Vatican Council II, Declaration on Religious Liberty, 1965, par. 14. See also Francis A. Sullivan, SJ, *Magisterium: Teaching Authority in the Catholic Church,* especially chap. 7, "The Non-Definitive Exercise of Papal and Conciliar Teaching Authority" (Mahwah, NJ: Paulist Press, 1983), pp. 153–73.

18. James P. Hanigan, *As I Have Loved You,* p. 120.

19. *Catechism of the Catholic Church* (Mahwah, NJ: Paulist Press, 1994), nos. 1777–94.

Chapter Eight.

1. Walter Conn, *Christian Conversion: A Developmental Interpretation of Autonomy and Surrender* (Mahwah, NJ: Paulist Press, 1986), p. 94.

2. Cited in Conn, *Christian Conversion,* p. 17, from John Macquarrie, *Three Issues in Ethics* (NY: Harper and Row, 1970), pp. 114–15.

3. Jean Piaget, *The Moral Judgment of the Child* (NY: Harcourt Brace, 1932); Lawrence Kohlberg, *The Philosophy of Moral Development: Moral Stages and the Idea of Justice* (San Francisco: Harper and Row, 1981); Erik Erikson, *The Life Cycle Completed: A Review* (NY: Norton, 1982).

4. Sidney Callahan, *In Good Conscience: Reason and Emotion in Moral Decision Making* (NY: HarperCollins, 1991), pp. 177–83.

5. Callahan, *In Good Conscience,* p. 193.

6. Ronald Duska and Mariellen Whelan, *Moral Development: A Guide to Piaget and Kohlberg* (Mahwah, NJ: Paulist Press, 1975), p. 100.

7. Callahan, *In Good Conscience,* pp. 95–113; 186–90.

8. Conn, *Christian Conversion,* p. 94.

9. Conn, *Christian Conversion,* pp. 43–45; 52–53; 59–62. See also, Kohlberg, *The Philosophy of Moral Development,* pp. 409–12.

10. Callahan, *In Good Conscience* pp. 172–73.

11. For a discussion of the importance of moral or virtuous passions

for the development of character, see G. Simon Harak, *Virtuous Passions: The Formation of Christian Character* (Mahwah, NJ: Paulist Press, 1993).

12. See Stanley Hauerwas, *Character and the Christian Life: A Study in Theological Ethics* (San Antonio, TX: Trinity University Press, 1975). See also Hauerwas's *Vision and Virtue: Essays in Christian Ethical Reflection* (Note Dame, IN: Fides, 1974), pp. 48–67.

13. For a classic example of this sort of writing, see Ignatius Loyola, *The Spiritual Exercises of St. Ignatius,* trans. Louis J. Puhl, SJ (Chicago: Loyola University Press, 1951).

14. Callahan, *In Good Conscience,* p. 173.

15. From an interview with Timothy E. O'Connell regarding his upcoming text on the transmission of moral values.

16. Anne E. Patrick, *Liberating Grace: Feminist Explorations in Catholic Moral Theology* (NY: Continuum, 1996), p. 11.

Chapter Nine.

1. Richard M. Gula, SS., *Reason Informed by Faith: Foundations of Catholic Morality* (Mahwah, NJ: Paulist Press, 1989), p. 283.

2. Bernard Haring, CSSR, *The Law of Christ, vol. I, General Moral Theology* (Paramus, NJ: The Newman Press, 1961), p. vii.

3. William C. Spohn, "Jesus and Ethics," *Proceedings of the Forty-Ninth Annual Convention of the Catholic Theological Society of America,* vol. 49, Paul Crowley, editor (Santa Clara, CA: CTSA, 1994), p. 49. See also chap. 5, "Scripture As Basis for Responding Love," in Spohn's *What Are They Saying About Scripture and Ethics?,* revised edition (Mahwah, NJ: Paulist Press, 1995), pp. 94–126.

4. The suggestion that Christ is the fundamental norm for Christian living presumes a commitment to come to know Christ—to

be known and loved by God in Christ—through prayer and meditation. For references concerning the unity of the spiritual and moral life, see note 8 of chap. 7.

5. This is why, in Roman Catholicism, it is necessary that the "deeply reasonable" nature of its moral teachings be made as evident as possible (Paul VI, On The Regulation of Birth, 1968, par. 12). They ought to be persuasive. If this were not the case "moral teaching" would degenerate into authoritarianism.

6. Timothy E. O'Connell, *Principles for a Catholic Morality,* revised edition (San Francisco, CA: Harper & Row, 1990), chap. 15, "Morality: Values and Norms," pp. 174–86; Richard M. Gula, SS, *Reason Informed by Faith,* chap. 19, "Moral Norms," pp. 283–99.

7. Richard M. Gula, SS, *Reason Informed by Faith,* chap. 19, "Moral Norms," pp. 288–89. We agree that a synthetic norm is a particular kind of formal norm. Even so, because of their often confusing "slipperiness," we think it is best to treat them separately. Gula's category is "Formal Norms in Synthetic Terms."

8. See the discussion of the three dimensions of Conscience in chap. 7 and, in particular, note 17.

9. For a fine discussion of this centerpiece norm in contemporary medical ethics in the United States see, chap. 3, "The Principle of Respect for Autonomy," in *Principles of Biomedical Ethics,* third edition, Tom. L. Beauchamp and James F. Childress (NY: Oxford University Press, 1989), pp. 67–119.

10. John Paul II, *The Gospel of Life* (Vatican City: Libreria Editrice Vaticana, 1995), no. 57, p. 101.

11. Gerald Kelly, SJ, "The Duty to Preserve Life," *Theological Studies* XII (1950): p. 550.

12. US Catholic Bishops, *Economic Justice for All:* Pastoral Letter on Catholic Social Teaching and the US Economy (Washington, DC: US Catholic Conference, 1986), nos. 16 and 18, pp. x–xi.

13. John Paul II, *The Gospel of Life,* nos. 2 and 47, pp. 4 and 83 respectively.

14. Richard M. Gula, SS, *Reason Informed by Faith,* chap. 19, "Moral Norms," pp. 294–95. Gula's clear and helpful discussion incorporates the insights of Josef Fuchs, Richard McCormick, Louis Janssens and others.

15. Josef Fuchs, SJ, "The Absoluteness of Behavioral Moral Norms," in *Personal Responsibility and Christian Morality* (Washington, DC: Georgetown University Press, 1983), pp. 115–52; p. 144 cited here.

16. The "threat"/"gift" categories come from Enda McDonagh's *Gift and Call: Toward a Christian Theology of Morality* (St. Meinrad, IN: Abbey Press, 1975). See especially pp. 34–7.

Chapter Ten.

1. The textbooks of both Timothy E. O'Connell and Richard M. Gula, SS, include chapters on the natural law that are more extensive than we have provided here. They are both valuable: O'Connell, *Principles for a Catholic Morality,* revised edition (San Francisco, CA: Harper & Row, 1990), chap. 13, "The History of Natural Law, pp. 149–60, and chap. 14, "A Vision of Natural Law," pp. 161–73. Gula, *Reason Informed by Faith* (Mahwah, NJ: Paulist Press, 1989), chap. 15, "The Natural Law in Tradition," pp. 220–30, and chap. 16, "Natural Law Today," pp. 231–49.

2. Although one could approach natural law from a strictly philosophical perspective, the option here is to consider this tradition in its theological expression. As we shall see, this includes viewing the universe as **creation,** as well as seeing the "orderliness," the intelligibility and the goodness of the universe as expressions of the Creator's way of being.

3. St. Thomas Aquinas, *Summa of Theology,* (NY: Benziger Brothers, 1947), I-II, q. 94, art. 4.

4. A fine analysis of this question by two Catholic scholars, with the text of current official Catholic teaching on the topic is *Religion and Artificial Reproduction: An Inquiry into The Vatican "Instruction on Respect for Human Life"* by Thomas A. Shannon and Lisa Sowle Cahill (NY: Crossroad, 1988).

5. This remains a controversial issue for many, including scholars. There is an enormous body of literature on the topic. One very helpful review of the issues is that of Lisa Sowle Cahill, "Bioethical Decisions to End Life," *Theological Studies,* 52, no. 1 (March 1991): pp. 107–19.

6. Two works that provide very different answers to this question are James P. Hanigan's *Homosexuality: The Test Case for Christian Sexual Ethics* (Mahwah, NJ: Paulist Press, 1988) and Patricia Beattie Jung and Ralph F. Smith's *Heterosexism: An Ethical Challenge* (NY: SUNY Press, 1993).

7. Richard M. Gula, SS., *Reason Informed by Faith,* chaps. 15 and 16; see especially pp. 239–40. The endnotes to these chapters of Gula's document well the sources for this "two strains of interpretation" approach to the natural law. Although we are indebted to Gula's analysis, our names for the two strains of interpretation differ from Gula's.

8. US Catholic Bishops, *Economic Justice for All: Catholic Teaching and the US Economy* (Washington, DC: US Catholic Conference, 1986), par. 134, p. 68.

9. Richard M. Gula, SS, *Reason Informed by Faith,* p. 241.

10. Ibid. pp. 241–42.

11. Bernard Lonergan, SJ, *Method in Theology* (NY: Seabury Press, 1972), p. 265.

12. Ibid.

13. For a discussion and helpful synthesis of many of these ideas, see Gula's treatment of shifting "worldviews" in *Reason Informed by*

Faith, chap. 3, "The Context of Contemporary Moral Theology," pp. 25–40.

14. These are the kinds of questions raised by both Protestant and Catholic ethicists in recent years. Among Protestants, see Stanley Hauerwas's *The Peaceable Kingdom: A Primer in Christian Ethics* (South Bend, IN: University of Notre Dame Press, 1983), especially chap. 4, "On Beginning in the Middle: Nature, Reason, and the Task of Theological Ethics," pp. 50–71. In this chapter Hauerwas discusses "Nature and Grace: Why Being Christian Is Not Equivalent to Being Human." Among Catholics, the work of William C. Spohn is very valuable. See his "Parable and Narrative in Christian Ethics," *Theological Studies,* 51, no. 1 (March, 1990): pp. 100–14; and also "Jesus and Christian Ethics," *Theological Studies,* 56, no. 1 (March 1995): pp. 92–107.

15. Howard Gardner, *Frames of Mind: The Theory of Multiple Intelligences* (NY: Basic Books, 1985); also *Multiple Intelligences: The Theory in Practice* (NY: Basic Books, 1993); Mary Field Belenky, et. al., *Women's Ways of Knowing: The Development of Self, Voice, and Mind* (NY: Basic Books, HarperCollins, 1986); William C. Spohn, "The Reasoning Heart: An American Approach to Christian Discernment," *Theological Studies* 44, no. 1 (March 1983): pp. 30–52; Sally P. Springer and Georg Deutsch, *Left Brain, Right Brain* (San Francisco, CA: W. H. Freeman and Co., 1981); Philip S. Keane, SS, *Christian Ethics and Imagination: A Theological Inquiry* (Mahwah, NJ: Paulist Press, 1984); Sidney Callahan, *In Good Conscience: Reason and Emotion in Moral Decision Making* (San Francisco, CA: Harper Collins, 1991).

16. Philip S. Keane, SS, *Christian Ethics and Imagination,* p. 16.

17. Ibid., p. 81.

18. Ibid., p. 90.

19. David Tracy, *The Analogical Imagination: Christian Theology and the Culture of Pluralism* (NY: Crossroad, 1981).

20. For an outstanding brief exposition of the place of analogy in theology—very traditional Catholic theology as well as contemporary feminist theology—see Elizabeth A. Johnson, CSJ, *She Who Is: The Mystery of God in Feminist Theological Discourse* (NY: Crossroad, 1993), especially pp. 113–20.

21. Albert R. Jonsen and Stephen Toulmin, *The Abuse of Casuistry: A History of Moral Reasoning* (Berkeley, CA: University of California Press, 1988).

22. William C. Spohn, "Passions and Principles," *Theological Studies* 52, no. 1 (March 1992): p. 69.

23. Bernard Lonergan, SJ, *Method in Theology,* pp. 36–41, 64–69.

24. Daniel C. Maguire and A. Nicholas Fargnoli, *On Moral Grounds: The Art/Science of Ethics* (NY: Crossroad Publishing Co., 1996), chap. 9, "The Wisdom of the Heart," p. 91.

25. Sidney Callahan, "The Role of Emotion in Ethical Decisionmaking," *Hastings Center Report* (June/July, 1988): p. 14.

26. S. Simon Harak, SJ, *Virtuous Passions: The Formation of Christian Character* (Mahwah, NJ: Paulist Press, 1993), p. 96.

27. William C. Spohn, *What Are They Saying About Scripture and Ethics?*, revised edition (Mahwah, NJ: Paulist Press, 1995), pp. 114–16.

28. Donal Dorr, *Option for the Poor: A Hundred Years of Catholic Social Teaching,* revised edition (Maryknoll, NY: Orbis Books, 1992).

29. Paulo Freire, *Pedagogy of the Oppressed,* new revised 20th anniversary edition (NY: Continuum, 1996), p. 30.

30. Ibid., pp. 36–7.

31. Catherine Mowry LaCugna, editor, *Freeing Theology: The Essentials of Theology in Feminist Perspective* (NY: HarperCollins,

1993). See also Anne E. Patrick, *Liberating Conscience: Feminist Explorations in Catholic Moral Theology* (NY: Continuum, 1996).

Chapter Eleven.

1. Karl Menninger, *Whatever Became of Sin?* (NY: Hawthorne Books, 1973).

2. Robin C. Cover, "Sin, Sinners: Old Testament," in *The Anchor Bible Dictionary* (NY: Doubleday, 1992), vol. 6, p. 31.

3. Ibid., p. 37.

4. Timothy E. O'Connell, *Principles for a Catholic Morality,* revised ed. (San Francisco, CA: Harper & Row, 1990), pp. 82–87.

5. Kevin F. O'Shea, CSSR, "The Reality of Sin: A Theological and Pastoral Critique," in *The Mystery of Sin and Forgiveness,* ed. Michael J. Taylor, SJ (NY: Alba House, 1971), pp. 94–95.

6. John Coventry, "Sixteenth and Twentieth Century Concepts of Sin," in *The Way Supplement* 48 (Fall 1983): pp. 51–52.

7. Piet Schoonenberg, *Man and Sin: A Theological View* (Notre Dame, IN: University of Notre Dame Press, 1965), pp. 27–28.

8. For an historical sketch of these differing texts, see John A. Gallagher, *Time Past, Time Future: An Historical Study of Catholic Moral Theology* (Mahwah, NJ: Paulist Press, 1990), pp. 5–45.

9. Patrick McCormick, *Sin as Addiction* (Mahwah, NJ: Paulist Press, 1989), pp. 54–75.

10. Richard Gula, *Reason Informed by Faith* (Mahwah, NJ: Paulist Press, 1989), p. 106.

11. Peter Henriot, "The Concept of Social Sin," *Catholic Mind* 71 (October 1973): pp. 38–53.

12. Mark O'Keefe, OSB, *What Are They Saying About Social Sin?* (Mahwah, NJ: Paulist Press, 1990), pp. 43–56.

13. Henri Rondet, SJ, *The Theology of Sin* (Notre Dame, IN: Fides, 1960), p. 83.

14. The catechism is simply repeating the formulations of Augustine (*Against Faustus* 2.27) and Aquinas (*Summa Theologiae* I-II, q. 71, a. 6), both of whom described sin as "a word, deed, or desire which is against eternal law."

15. O'Connell, *Principles for a Catholic Morality,* p. 78.

16. Gula, *Reason Informed by Faith,* pp. 101–2.

17. Christine M. Smith, "Sin and Evil in Feminist Thought," *Theology Today* 50 (July 1993): pp. 208–19.

18. Christine E. Gudorf, "Men vs. Women: Do They Sin Differently?" *US Catholic* 60 (November 1995): pp. 6–13. Mary Stewart Van Leeuwen, "The Christian Mind and the Challenge of Gender Relations," in *Sexuality and the Sacred: Sources for Theological Reflection,* eds. James Nelson and Sandra Longfellow (Louisville, KY: Westminster/John Knox Press, 1994) pp. 120–30.

Chapter Twelve.

1. Charles E. Curran, "Conversion: The Central Moral Message of Jesus," in *A New Look at Christian Morality* (Notre Dame, IN: Fides, 1970), p. 25; James Hanigan, "Conversion and Christian Ethics," in *Theology Today* 40 (April 1983): p. 25.

2. Curran, "Conversion: The Central Moral Message of Jesus," p. 26.

3. June O'Connor, "Dorothy Day's Christian Conversion," in *The Journal of Religious Ethics* 18, p. 159.

4. Walter Conn, *Christian Conversion: A Developmental Inter-*

pretation of Autonomy and Surrender (Mahwah, NJ: Paulist Press, 1986), pp. 212, 267.

5. Ibid. p. 267.

6. Josef Fuchs, "Sin and Conversion," in *Theology Digest* 14 (Winter 1966): pp. 297–98.

7. Bernard Haring, *Free and Faithful in Christ: Volume One* (London: St. Paul Publications, 1978), pp. 417–26.

8. Gustavo Gutierrez, *A Theology of Liberation: History, Politics, and Salvation,* trans. C. Inda and J. Eagleson (Maryknoll, NY: Orbis, 1973), pp. 204–5.

9. Conn, *Christian Conversion,* p. 204.

10. 1971 Synod of Bishops, "Justice in the World," in David J. O'Brien and Thomas A. Shannon, eds., *Renewing the Earth: Catholic Documents on Peace, Justice, and Liberation* (Garden City, NY: Doubleday Image, 1977), p. 447.

11. Peter J. Henriot, "Social Sin and Conversion: A Theology of the Church's Social Involvement," in *Chicago Studies* 11 (Summer 1972): pp. 115–30.

12. Josef Fuchs, "Sin and Conversion," in *Theology Digest* 14 (Winter 1966): pp. 300–301.

13. Conn, *Christian Conversion,* pp. 26–31.

14. Haring, *Free and Faithful in Christ,* pp. 445–67.

15. Sallie McFague, "Conversion: Life on the Edge of the Raft," in *Interpretation* 32, no. 3 (July 1978): p. 255.

16. Antonio Moser and Bernardino Leers, *Moral Theology: Dead Ends and Alternatives,* trans. Paul Burns (Maryknoll, NY: Orbis, 1990), pp. 175–98.